What Dare
We Hope?

THEOLOGY FOR THE TWENTY-FIRST CENTURY

Theology for the Twenty-first Century is a series sponsored by the Center of Theological Inquiry (CTI) located in Princeton, New Jersey, an institute dedicated to the advanced study of theology. This series is one of its many initiatives and projects.

The goal of the series is to publish inquiries of contemporary scholars into the nature of the Christian faith and its witness and practice in church, society, and culture. The series will bring investigations into the uniqueness of the Christian faith. But it will also offer studies that relate the Christian faith to the major cultural, social, and practical issues of our time.

Monographs and symposia will result from research by scholars in residence at the Center of Theological Inquiry or otherwise associated with it. In some cases, publications will come from group research projects sponsored by CTI. It is our intention that the books selected for this series will constitute a major contribution to renewing theology in its service to church and society.

WALLACE M. ALSTON, JR., ROBERT JENSON,
AND DON S. BROWNING
SERIES EDITORS

What Dare We Hope?

RECONSIDERING ESCHATOLOGY

Gerhard Sauter

TRINITY PRESS INTERNATIONAL
Harrisburg, Pennsylvania

Trinity Press International, P.O. Box 1321, Harrisburg, PA 17105
Trinity Press International is a division of the Morehouse Group.

Cover art: Variierte Rechtecke, Wassily Kandinsky/Christie's Images/SuperStock
Cover design: Trude Brummer

Library of Congress Cataloging-in-Publication Data
Sauter, Gerhard.
    What dare we hope? : reconsidering eschatology / Gerhard Sauter.
        p.   cm.
    Includes bibliographical references and index.
    ISBN 1-56338-271-7 (pbk. : alk. paper)
    1. Eschatology. 2. Hope – Religious aspects – Christianity.
I. Title.
BT821.2.S258
236 – dc21   99-27529

Printed in the United States of America

99   00   01   02   03   04   10   9   8   7   6   5   4   3   2   1

To My Daughter
Hanna Verena

CONTENTS

Preface to the American / English Edition ix

1. The Term "Eschatology" and Its Changing Nature. 1

    1.1. Eschatology — A Word with Many Meanings / 1
    1.2. Typical Applications of the Term "Eschatology" / 2
    1.3. Tensions and Controversies / 21

2. Jesus of Nazareth, "Bearer of Hope"? 27

    2.1. The Kingdom of God: A Distant Prospect? / 27
    2.2. Jesus' Proclamation of the Kingdom of God:
        Summer Lightning? / 32
    2.3. What Remains of the Hope of Christ? / 36
    2.4. Hoping for Christ / 41
    2.5. Jesus Christ: The Final One, the Coming One / 47

3. The Activity of God in Humanity and in Its History. 68

    3.1. Eschatology as Boundary Marker of Theology / 69
    3.2. Eschatological Orientation of Christian Existence / 80
    3.3. In the Darkness of Hope / 90
    3.4. The Shining of the New Being in History / 93
    3.5. Radical Eschatology — Theology with a New Horizon / 97

4. The God of Hope — The Sovereignty of the Future 119

    4.1. Outbreaks and Breakthroughs / 119
    4.2. God in Global History: The Answer to the Foundational
        Crisis of Christianity and the Western Crisis
        of Meaning / 126
    4.3. World-Transforming Hope as an Answer to the Crisis
        of Relevancy within Christianity / 132
    4.4. Eschatology as Religio-Political Theory of Action:
        Hope of Liberation for the Oppressed / 138
    4.5. History as Context of Discovery / 147

5. One in Hope? Ecumenical Perspectives 160

    5.1. The Stunted Dialogue / 160
    5.2. The Certainty of Hope / 169
    5.3. Eschatology as the Yardstick for the Self-Understanding
         of the Church / 179

6. Hope in the Life of the Churches 184

    6.1. Accounting for Hope as Intellectual Pastoral Care / 184
    6.2. Hope beyond Death: "Immortality of the Soul"
         or "Resurrection of the Dead"? / 188
    6.3. The Promise of the Coming One / 197
    6.4. "Purification" as Therapy? / 199
    6.5. The Lord's Supper: Proclamation of the Coming Christ / 202

7. Basic Questions of Eschatology. 209

    7.1. Conceptual Sources of Friction / 209
    7.2. Controlling Questions / 214
    7.3. Where Do We Look When We Answer? / 216

Index of Scriptural References 225

Index of Names 227

Index of Subjects 230

PREFACE TO THE
AMERICAN/ENGLISH EDITION

In the spring of 1994, I received an invitation from the American
Academy of Religion to attend a conference in New York City. To
make the topic "Apocalypticism, Millennialism: The Crisis of the
Environment and the Social Milieu" sound more exciting, the invitation alluded to recent natural catastrophes and to a widespread
apocalyptic mood in religious circles which may have led in turn to
rash actions — such as the self-destructive behavior of the Branch
Davidians, who were followers of David Koresh, in the spring of
1993 at Waco, Texas:

> With the approach of the year 2000, the Waco catastrophe,
> and widespread speculation about the "meaning" of recent
> natural catastrophes such as the Midwest floods, popular
> interest in this topic is high.

Are we heading toward the final times? Might it, therefore, be
time to reconsider the topic of eschatology? We urgently need to
bring these events and the public moods they create down to earth,
without disillusioning ourselves. An attitude that arrogantly ignores these contemporary hopes and fears would deaden our senses
to the signs of the times.

My reconsideration of eschatology will examine the difficult
issue of its logos or rationality.[1] This requires first of all an answer to the question: "What dare we hope?" The emphasis in this
sentence rests on the word "dare" — on what are we *allowed* to
hope — and thereby on the *reasons* for hope. This is why "eschatology" does not refer to a demographic survey of hopeful or

---

1. See Gerhard Sauter, *Eschatological Rationality: Theological Issues in Focus*
(Grand Rapids, Mich.: Baker Book House, 1996).

fearful moods, or to an explanation of unsettling events in an effort to shape public opinion. Questioning how expectations of the future arise and how these expectations are connected to attitudes and patterns of behavior is the task of sociology and psychology, or a combination of both disciplines. Indeed, assumptions about the future and ideas of another world beyond history, especially ideas of religious origin, have for a long time been a favorite research subject of religious sociology and related sciences.

The religious landscape of the United States offers extremely rich and diverse material for this study. Ever since immigration to North America and its settlement by various European peoples, ideas with religious background have shaped immigrants' visions of the new country and its inhabitants; frequently, these ideas had immediate impact on the structuring of society. Biblical images and promises were used to interpret the immigrants' situation, interpretations sometimes based on a very literal reading of the Bible. By means of biblical comparisons one could discern the prospects for the future; sometimes these biblical comparisons included predictions of the date of the end of the world, or at least of some significant break in history.

A term such as "millennialism" — virtually unknown in Europe — took on meaning in the United States as signifying a thousand years of positive change that will affect all aspects of society (see Rev. 20:2–6 about the thousand years preceding the end of the world). In New York an advertising leaflet welcomes people to the "Millennium" and affirms "what the Millennium can do for you"; the name refers to a hotel — close, incidentally, to Wall Street.

The widespread hope for such an ideal period appears in two versions: some people expect this period to result from a radical break from beyond history, from an event not immediately connected to human efforts (premillennialism); others expect the improvement of human and social affairs as a result of progress within history — an expectation that requires and encourages all human effort, and that envisages the future as having long since begun (postmillennialism). However, less enthusiastic and more critical people like Jonathan Edwards (1703–58) have never ceased cautioning themselves and others that history is not unlimited in its possibilities and that it will finally end in catastrophe. The kingdom of God was seen as revealing these shortcomings and putting an end to these possibilities, precisely when they appeared to have fully developed.[2] Yet toward the end of the nineteenth and at the beginning of the twentieth century, leading liberal Protestants in America were convinced that they were living and working within *the* Christian century; this is why they initiated the journal *The Christian Century*. But after all this century has witnessed, there is now a tendency even in the United States to postpone this self-confident view for a later time.

Politically no less fascinating — and often just as influential and dangerous — is the way in which individual biblical images of catastrophes are "taken literally" and related to current events. Thus, many engineers who were Seventh Day Adventists or who belonged to the Pentecostal movement did not have conscientious objections to working on the production of atomic bombs; they thought they were preparing the way for the second coming of Jesus Christ, which according to "biblical information" would be preceded by an enormous global fire.[3]

As fascinating as the observations and analyses of such hopes and fears concerning the future seem, they do not lead to eschatology, but rather away from it. Eschatology involves clarifying what it means "to give an account of hope," and to be "accountable to everyone who raises questions about the hope that is in you" (1 Pet. 3:15).[4]

This is why I will speak in this book of *eschatology as comprehensive theological argumentation*, whose task is to give an account of the "hope that is in you." Theological doctrine unfolds this reason, but it exhausts itself when it loses contact with the elementary expressions of a hope based on faith. Accordingly, theology should beware of getting bogged down in debates in the academy that are now sterile and isolated, directing all energies and efforts fruitlessly into themselves.

---

2. See Robert W. Jenson, *America's Theologian: A Recommendation for Jonathan Edwards* (New York: Oxford University Press, 1988), 134–35, 137.

3. A. G. Mojtabai, *Blessed Assurance: At Home with the Bomb in Amarillo, Texas* (Boston: Houghton Mifflin, 1986).

4. NRSV: "Always be ready to make your defense to anyone who demands from you an accounting for the hope that is in you."

A discussion of eschatology should pay attention to the dead end of an argument, to the points at which the train of thought is broken, and at which aporias arise that very often prove to be more fruitful than smooth answers to polished questions. The edges and fissures of a concept are generally quite revealing; eschatology, at closer look, turns out to be a field of theological argument and debate of a fundamental nature. It provides a "lesson" in theological methodology.

For a while I had hoped to further illuminate the question, "What dare we hope?" by means of answers found in other religions. How difficult it is to discover such answers, however, soon became clear. Studies in religion may inform us about expectations and attitudes concerning the future and another world. Yet these pieces of information are on a different level than what we do when we try to give an account of hope. How little we in fact get to know about the hope of other religions and how difficult it is unequivocally to explain one's own account without appearing aggressive, may be seen, for example, in the story of the Christian-Jewish debate about the hope for God — a story which until now has only rarely reached the level of a real dialogue. Due to this and other complications, I therefore prefer to leave the topic of hope in other religions out of this reconsideration and to turn to it later in a monograph on our reasons for hope, a constructive eschatology on which I am now working. I will also pay more attention there to topics which, in the framework of this book, had to be dealt with only briefly.

Most of this book was written at the Center of Theological Inquiry in Princeton, where I had the opportunity to deal with contributions to eschatology written by North American scholars, and where perspectives on the future in North American theology gave me impulses for my own work. The English-American edition is a revised and enlarged version of the German edition, published in 1995.

In the United States I was frequently asked how my approach relates to the theology of Wolfhart Pannenberg and to Jürgen Moltmann's *Theology of Hope*. Both Moltmann and Pannenberg understand eschatology as a theology of history. For Pannenberg, world history is a unified structure whose interrelations can be discovered through its center, which is the resurrection of Jesus Christ;

at Easter the meaning of the whole history shines out, which is God's power over a world captured by death. This view of a "universal history" derives its name from the philosophy of history of German idealism (particularly Georg Wilhelm Friedrich Hegel), and it makes it possible to integrate everything into global history as a whole and to see it with the eyes of hope. Moltmann is also influenced by an idealistic philosophy of history. However, following the Marxist philosopher Ernst Bloch, he puts a much stronger emphasis on the political struggle by which history is pushed forward. Moltmann understands the kingdom of God as contradicting those historical conditions and powers which insist on the "status quo" and which thereby resist any genuine progress toward justice, peace, and humanity.

One has to ask, however, whether such a theology of history — both in its more integrating and its more protesting version — is really able to grasp the reason for Christian hope, for the expectation of God's coming. One also has to ask whether it deals with the question "What dare we hope?" adequately, in its extended and spiritual depth. This is why I confront in this book the type of eschatology that can be described as a "theology of history," forcefully represented by Pannenberg and Moltmann, with two other important types. My purpose is to initiate a discourse among the three types.

Albert Schweitzer is credited with naming the first type *konsequente Eschatologie*. The term is not easily translated because it is imprecise. American and English speakers use "consistent eschatology," but this does not seem much clearer. Schweitzer's point was that eschatology can only be understood as the expectation of imminent events, i.e., the *Naherwartung* of a global catastrophe through which the kingdom of God breaks into our reality in order thoroughly to transform it. Expectation is consistent only in this sense; anything else, according to Schweitzer, would be a questionable compromise between hope for God's acting and resignation in the face of the world's reality.

The second type of eschatology I call "radical eschatology." "Radical" means "to go to the roots," and an eschatology that is radical in this sense (rather than in a superficial sense, as in the label of a political attitude), asks for the deepest reason and foundation of Christian hope, in which it is grounded on God's acting.

This character of eschatology is radical because it is rooted in the hope of faith, which — as Paul shows by the example of Abraham — is essentially "hoping against hope" (Rom. 4:18). In faith people set their hopes on God, "who gives life to the dead and calls into existence the things that do not exist" (Rom. 4:17). The basic question of radical eschatology, therefore, is: "Why are we allowed to hope?"

We may be full of wishes and expectations of all kinds, but does not the hope for God tear us away from all that we desire? Is it not like an anchor by which we are fixed on God's promise? Is it not a hope to which God gives rise and by which God calls us out of our worries and wishes, a hope by which we may thoroughly change our minds about time and space, past, present, and future?

Because the term "radical eschatology" encompasses all these aspects, a mere translation of the word "radical" is not sufficient to convey the term's meaning unambiguously. In colloquial speech the words *konsequent* and "radical" may even be used with almost the same meaning. In this book, however, they signify very different conceptions of eschatology.

Both conceptions as well as the theology of history type may be confronted with yet another version of doing eschatology, the perception of *God's promise as a pledge by which God points us in the direction where we must set out.* This is how the Reformers, particularly Martin Luther and John Calvin, understood the biblical term "promise." The term was at the center of their theology as well as their preaching and pastoral counseling. Hope is what we receive through *justification*, i.e., through God's pronouncing judgment on who we are, on our doing and letting things go undone, and through God's acting which orients us to God. This is why we must consider the relationship between justification and hope as well as the relationship between God's promise and our future: this is the task of eschatology.

I certainly hope that hearing God's promise and expecting God's judging and saving action will help Christians in the English-speaking world on their way. All Christians are called to give an account of the "hope that is in you." Is this a hope which we carry within us and which we may only use against opposition from within or without? Or is it rather a hope "among you" —

as Jesus Christ is among us with his word, his spirit, and his gifts? To interpret thoroughly the sentence from 1 Peter 3:15 in all its perspectives would, I think, be a big enough assignment for eschatology. To lead readers toward this task, to introduce them to eschatology's basic questions and to the related intellectual experiences of theology, at least as framed in the last century before the beginning of the next millennium, is the intention of this book. I wrote it with a concern for ecumenical communication, to support exchange and conversations across the Atlantic, and to contribute to the dialogue between Protestants and Roman Catholics. I also wrote with a view to the Eastern Orthodox churches and to churches from different cultural backgrounds. The exclamation of the church of Jesus Christ, "Our Lord, come!" (1 Cor. 16:22) unites Christians to a witness of hope. By our shared calling we also received *one* hope, common to all of us (Eph. 4:4).

When I accepted the assignment to write this book I assumed this task would be far less complicated than it turned out to be. After writing my second thesis, *Future and Promise: The Problem of Future in Contemporary Theological and Philosophical Discussion* (Zurich: Zwingli Verlag, 1965), I thought I was sufficiently familiar with the essential questions of eschatology. If the goal had been an overview of theological literature or an encyclopedic outline, it probably would have been rather easily achieved. However, because "eschatology" has become an umbrella term for extremely diverse questions and complex conceptions, I realized that an adequate introduction would require special care. Introducing readers to eschatology means to lead them into a jungle of opinions in which a path can hardly be seen amidst the proliferation of arguments, rhetorical associations, and methods. On the other hand, a number of answers that at first glance seemed to cut through the confusion did not adequately disentangle the problems. "Outlines" were given which seemed to be insensitive to questions of permanent relevance.

The task was both enriched and made more difficult by the fact that the series in which the book was to be published understood itself as ecumenically focused. Especially in eschatology, differences between and among churches have to be taken into consideration — and, therefore, carefully described.

All of this may explain why it took such a long time for me to present this book in its finished form. I tried several different approaches and rejected many of them. To reduce the assignment to an overview of the history of the subject would have been a questionable concession to the following striking developmental stereotype: Eschatology is an area of theology shaped by a continuous development of problems. On the other hand, a wholly constructive approach was not advisable either, for the basic problems of eschatology *did* emerge out of permanent arguments and debates; it would have been deceptive to ignore these various states of discussion.

Classes on special topics of eschatology, joint seminars with my colleague Josef Wohlmuth (faculty of Catholic theology, University of Bonn) and with colleagues at the University of Oxford, and conversations with my doctoral students proved to be helpful for the clarification of didactically useful approaches. Their critical responses and impulses helped me enormously as well as the information and suggestions provided by Professors Diogenes Allen and Daniel Migliore of Princeton Theological Seminary, Professor Mark Reasoner (Bethel College, St. Paul, Minnesota), and Professor Daniel Hardy, former director of the Center of Theological Inquiry at Princeton. I am honored by the decision of the current director of the Center, Dr. Wallace M. Alston, and the director of research, Professor Don S. Browning, to include this book in the new series of the Center. I want to express my special thanks to Dr. Rainer Fischer, Dr. Caroline Schröder, Birgit Sommerfeld (Bonn), Dr. Ernstpeter Maurer (Dortmund), and Dr. Hinrich Stoevesandt (Basel), who helped me significantly by critically reading the manuscript. I am very grateful to Judith Gilliland (Oxford) and to Caroline Schröder, who translated the book, and to my wife, Annegrete, who helped me revise the translation. The biblical references in most cases are taken from the New Revised Standard Version.

GERHARD SAUTER

– *Chapter 1* –

THE TERM "ESCHATOLOGY" AND ITS CHANGING NATURE

1.1. Eschatology — A Word with Many Meanings

In Origen's treatise *De Principiis* (On first principles), the section that deals with the end of the world opens with the comment that discussion might be a better approach to the subject than definition (1.6.1). It seems to me that a similar approach is advisable in an introduction to the present "state" of eschatology. There has long been a lack of consensus concerning the concept of eschatology, which means that it is difficult to give a clear representation of how the field of inquiry should be approached.

It is this lack of certainty that differentiates eschatology from other theological topics such as Christology, in which doctrine was established long ago by intensive debates within the church and by the process of theological clarification, reflection, and explanation. What is required in order to come to grips with eschatology is an introduction to the multiplicity of ideas about what eschatology is and how it can be conceptualized. No single idea should either be favored or swept aside at the outset. Rather, this introduction should attempt to show *why* there is a multiplicity of conceptions, how the various ideas interact, and what the logical consequences of the differences might be.

It should be possible to gather from the different models for understanding eschatology which formulations of the question are common to all. We cannot simply pick and choose among the fundamental questions. On the contrary, the same questions must *always* be asked. These common questions can be considered indispensable; the proposed solutions, however, can become problematic.

1

1.2. Typical Applications
of the Term "Eschatology"

The best way to approach the diversity of meanings of "eschatology" is to begin by clarifying the differences between some of the more typical applications of the term in current theological discourse.

First, eschatology can mean *the doctrine of the eschata, of the last things*. This definition of eschatology ends Christian doctrine by dealing with what happens at the end of time and beyond time: death and the end of the world, resurrection and new creation, God's judgment as deliverance into eternal life or, alternatively, deliverance to eternal damnation. This arrangement proposes a temporal perspective, that future is the horizon of eschatology.

Second, under the presupposition that future is *not* a vacuum, eschatology can connect to concepts of future and to an attitude of expectation for *the prospects for Christian faith in a continually changing world*. When the ultimate questions posed by the expectation of God's intervention in the course of time are added to this vivid expectation of the future, eschatology takes on another form. The concept is no longer a finale, but rather part of the ferment of theology, challenging and forming theology as a whole. Under the second definition, the questions posed by eschatology *stretch to the roots and furthest boundaries of theology* and lead to its "radical" foundation.

These different meanings of "eschatology" are not simply alternative possibilities. In a sense, they follow one another. They are the consequences of differing theological purposes, which generally reflect deep-rooted motives. These issues will be treated later in more detail, since such motives must be considered.

In general, see Gerhard SAUTER, "The Concept and Task of Eschatology," in *Eschatological Rationality: Theological Issues in Focus* (Grand Rapids, Mich.: Baker Book House, 1996), 136–53. For a historical survey, see *Eschatologie*, vol. IV/7 of *Handbuch der Dogmengeschichte*, ed. Michael SCHMAUS et al. (Freiburg: Herder), published in the following six subparts: Brian DALEY with Josef SCHREINER and Horacio E. LONA, *In der Schrift und Patristik*, 1986; Ludwig OTT, *In der Scholastik*, 1990; Erhard KUNZ, *Protestantische Eschatologie: Von der Reformation bis zur Aufklärung*, 1980; Philipp SCHÄFER, *Trient und Gegenreformation*, 1984; Ignacio ESCRIBANO-ALBERCA, *Von der Aufklärung bis zur Gegenwart*, 1987.

1.2.1. The Doctrine of the "Last Things"

In the seventeenth century, Lutheran theologians generally introduced discussion of the doctrine of the last things, under the title "eschatology" or *De Novissimis,* as the end piece of a general presentation of theology.[1] In Reformed theology, the closing theme usually speaks of perfection, of the completion of the saving work of Christ and the Holy Spirit in the glorification of God. In Roman Catholic dogmatics, particularly in its neoscholastic form, it was usual to close with a tract dealing with the last things. Regarding the outline of the "end," such tracts include many thematic aspects which connect with the basic framework of Protestant teaching, although in the details there are, admittedly, many differences. These differences arise from the fact that the Roman Catholic approach was deeply connected to ecclesiology, the preceding "chapter" in the order of doctrines.

The doctrine of the last things deals with what ultimately lies before the human race and the world which humans are part of; or, to put it another way, it deals with the question of our ultimate destination. The concept of the last things is an attempt to express the questions of what, why, and where. As a compilation of the "objects" of hope, eschatology takes on the question, "What dare we hope?" Eschatology outlines a time after death in which God judges each individual according to his or her faith and deeds, and determines their ultimate fate: either eternal life in communion with God, or perdition. Up to this final decision, hope in salvation and everlasting life must always be accompanied by the fear of eternal perdition. But the hope that comes from faith has reason to be confident — even when fear, particularly the fear of death, is overwhelming — because its foundation is hope of God's grace.

The material for this form of eschatology is taken from biblical texts that deal with death and dying, resurrection and judgment, heaven and hell, and the end of this world and the beginning of the new world. What these texts address is depicted as a closely related whole. What emerges is an overall prospect of the last things,

---

1. Also on the doctrine of the last things, see Sigurd Hjelde, *Das Eschaton und die Eschata: Eine Studie über Sprachgebrauch und Sprachverwirrung in protestantischer Theologie von der Orthodoxie bis zur Gegenwart* (Munich: Chr. Kaiser, 1987).

constructed from a sequence of "states" culminating in a "final state."

In more recent theological history, this doctrine has been increasingly isolated from central theological themes and has been in danger of being reduced to the status of an appendix. Protestant "compendia" of the nineteenth century content themselves with putting together proofs and examples from earlier dogmaticians and explaining them in summary terms.[2] Catholic materials show a similar process, that biblical quotations and church dogmatic statements were collected, brought together, and integrated into a conceptual whole. This remained the rule up to Vatican II (1962–65). The artistic thought-patterns of earlier dogmatics and the richness of thematic associations were both forgotten. Furthermore, eschatology no longer seemed to be embedded in expressions of hope like prayers and church hymns.

Removed from its theological and liturgical context, eschatology has been reduced to a cause of the horrific vision which has long predominated regarding, for example, "orthodox" Protestant eschatology. The American theologian Reinhold Niebuhr (1892–1971) once drew the caricature of an eschatology that only has "the furniture of heaven and the temperature of hell" to offer. There is the old joke that heaven is to be preferred on account of the climate, hell for the better society. Even when eschatology *does* have more to say for itself, the chapter on the "last things" frequently remains chopped from its roots in the compendia of theological science. Many textbooks gather a withered bunch of meanings, without allowing a glimpse of the blooming and attractive interweaving arrangements that previous dogmatics had to offer. Sometimes traditional themes are rearranged and reduced to fundamental theological thought,[3] or traditional concepts are

2. For example, Heinrich Schmid, *Die Dogmatik der evangelisch-lutherischen Kirche* (Leipzig, 1843) (Eng. trans. [henceforth abbreviated ET]: *The Doctrinal Theology of the Evangelical Lutheran Church*, trans. Charles A. Hay and Henry E. Jacobs [Minneapolis: Augsburg Publishing House, 1899]); Heinrich Heppe, *Die Dogmatik der evangelisch-reformierten Kirche Deutschlands* (Elberfeld, Germany: Friderichs, 1861) (ET: *Reformed Dogmatics Set Out and Illustrated from the Sources*, trans. G. Thomson, rev. ed. [London: George Allen & Uwin, 1950]).
3. For example, Paul Althaus in his influential book *Die letzten Dinge* (Gütersloh: Carl Bertelsmann, 1926; 8th ed., 1981). Althaus attempts to understand eschatology as the development of the doctrine of justification: faith and hope de-

shrunk to leave room for a new interpretation and to make them more compatible with modern understanding.[4]

Above all, independent approaches to the doctrine of the last things tend to treat the link with Christology either insufficiently or not at all. Christology is simply assumed, giving the impression that eschatology needs only to deal with the consequences of the "person" and "work" of Christ. If the doctrine of the last things focuses on the question, "What dare we hope — *after* Christ?" the roots of our hope in Christ can become blurred. We are reminded of these roots and the interdependence of Christology and eschatology in 1 Peter 1:3: "Blessed be the God and Father of our Lord Jesus Christ! By his great mercy we have been born anew to a living hope through the resurrection of Jesus Christ from the dead."

The treatment of eschatology in Roman Catholic dogmatics also shows that traditional church teaching does not always address this deep root of Christian expectation. Rather, eschatology generally forms the closing tract in Roman Catholicism, and is dealt with in explanation of traditional doctrinal definitions. A key position is taken by the doctrine of the immortality of the soul — that the soul, when separated from the body in death, proceeds to God's judgment — as found in the Fifth Lateran Council of 1513[5] and reiterated by Vatican II in *Gaudium et Spes*.[6] In 1563, the Council

pend on God's acquittal of the guilty person *now* — and this acquittal calls the guilty person to be responsible for his own life, which God will judge at some point in the future. Christians can have confidence that the salvation, which they have already been granted through the forgiveness of their sins, will in due course become complete and reveal itself in all its fullness — but this is no guarantee of their own personal fate, which always remains God's decision. All the other themes relating to the doctrine of the last things then become perspectives on this central statement.

4. E.g., Heinrich Ott, *Eschatologie: Versuch eines dogmatischen Grundrisses* (Zollikon, Switzerland: Evangelischer Verlag, 1958). Ott tries to understand the standard eschatological concepts of "the kingdom of God," "eternal life," "death and resurrection," "the end of time," and "the last judgment" in a new way — that is, as symbols of a Christian understanding of existence, which deals with the fate of the individual in a wider context. In this sketch, Ott wanted to correct Rudolf Bultmann's existentialist understanding (see 3.2) by providing further material for consideration, without at the same time holding on to outdated or obsolete ideas.

5. "The Human Soul (against the Neo-Aristotelians)," in Henry Denzinger, *The Sources of Catholic Dogma,* trans. Roy J. Deferrari (St. Louis: Herder, 1957), 237–38.

6. "Pastoral Constitution on the Church in the Modern World in Vatican Council II," in *The Conciliar and Post-conciliar Documents,* edited by Austin Flannery, O.P., 2d ed. (Northport, N.Y.: Costello, 1980), 903–1014.

of Trent enacted a decree concerning purgatory, the place and process by which souls are purified after death.[7] This was partly but not entirely a response to Reformation theologians. According to this idea, temporal — that is, finite — sentences imposed for sin can and must be expiated through a process of purification, not least through the intercessions of the living and of the saints. Further decrees speak of the eternal damnation of those dying in a state of mortal sin. These aspects of eschatology are very closely connected with the church system of penance and care of the dying and the dead. On the one hand, then, changes in church practices have a direct influence on eschatology, while on the other hand any change or loss in eschatological understanding must have consequences. This is why no changes can be accepted by the teaching ministry of the church without considerable reaction and commentary.

The Roman Catholic presentation of the doctrine of the last things asks whether the question "What dare we hope?" relates to the continued existence of human substance, or, rather, the completion of what began with Christ. Jesus Christ completes God's creation. He redeems what God has placed in creation — something that cannot be lost, even though corrupted and deeply endangered by human sin. Therefore hope can be directed at a "fulfillment" in a quantifiable sense — at the fulfillment of what is missing. But if hope only exists as a supplement to what faith and love together have not yet been able to achieve, then hope itself can become an indication of poverty of faith, even of lack of faith.

So, for example, William Faulkner (1897–1962), in *Requiem for a Nun*, puts these last words in the mouth of Nancy, who is condemned to death and stripped of all hope:

NANCY: Because that would have been hoping: the hardest thing of all to break, get rid of, let go of, the last thing of all poor sinning man will turn aloose. Maybe it's because that's all he's got. Leastways, he holds onto it, hangs onto it. Even with salvation laying right in his hand, and all he's got to do is, choose between it; even with salvation already in his hand and all he needs is just to shut his fingers, old sin is still

7. "Decree concerning Purgatory," in Denzinger, *The Sources of Catholic Dogma*, 298.

too strong for him, and sometimes before he even knows it, he has throwed salvation away just grabbing back at hoping. But it's all right —

STEVENS: You mean, when you have salvation, you don't have hope?

NANCY: You don't even need it. All you need, all you have to do, is just believe. So maybe —

STEVENS: Believe what?

NANCY: Just believe ... [8]

Does hope in this way threaten to become some sort of rear guard? Faith and love insist on acting as the vanguard, taking priority. Opposed to this, there is a decisive question that needs to be answered: why, if faith and love take priority, should it be the responsibility of Christians (according to 1 Pet. 3:15) to give an "account for the *hope* that is in you" before all men, and *not* to account primarily for either faith or love? How can it be made clear that Christians can unceasingly thank God that they have received "a new birth into a living hope" (1 Pet. 1:3, see John 3:3: "being born from above"), and that in this hope a new life comes into being?

The Roman Catholic system of penance and the doctrine of sin and grace were among the most important targets of Reformation theology. The Reformation doctrine of justification of the sinner taking place "without God in the world" (Eph. 2:12) — occurring through God's grace alone — therefore had a direct influence on eschatology. It had the effect of cutting back lengthy eschatological themes, directing them toward the forgiveness of sins and the promise of redemption, which is accepted by faith. The believer can place hope in this doctrine, and such hope cannot be cut off by death. There is no state of existence in which the individual soul can find purification between death and judgment. The last judgment, which is also the end of the world, reveals the final separation of the saved and the damned. Before this takes place, all

---

8. W. Faulkner, *Requiem for a Nun* (New York: Random House, 1951), 272–73.

are resurrected as they have been and as they will have been for all eternity, according to faith or lack of faith and actions; that is, according to whether they have lived in faith and acted accordingly, or whether they have remained close to God.

It is the scene conveyed on so many church portals dating from the Middle Ages: the saved and the damned standing opposite each other. The viewer is confronted with the question, "Which side are *you* on?" God's judgment has the character of final separation. The picture on the church portal invites the viewer to go beyond the division, the judgment, and to step into the sphere of faith and hope. This was what the Reformation proclamation was seeking to emphasize: the verdict on what we have done and have failed to do rests solely in the hands of God. Therefore, we must restrain from judging ourselves and keep on going.

The main eschatological themes remain, then, much the same in both the Reformation church and in Catholic doctrine. Admittedly, the themes are concentrated particularly on the defeat of sin and death through the words of life, in which the themes demonstrate another fundamental form of the action of the church through preaching and pastoral care.

Even in this first outline it has become clear that the doctrine of the last things is something of a touchstone for the relationship of dogmatics to the Bible and to the preaching of the church. More than this, the systematic unity of theology comes into question: what conclusions can theology, in its wisdom, come to? What conclusions can theology draw from statements that have their roots in speech acts with their own specific functions: words of comfort and encouragement, calls to penance, exhortations? Does theology possess grounds enough to claim knowledge about the future, about what comes "after," after death and at the end of all things?

There are several cases in which the doctrine of the last things becomes particularly problematic:

1. When there is an attempt to describe the last things as events in space and time — even if in another point in time and in another place — and these events are seen as the continuation of the history of life in this world.

2. When there is an attempt to base the doctrine on guaranteed knowledge and on philosophical views that are not theologically

established and attempts are made to claim biblical texts as transcendental knowledge rather than as witnesses to hope. In this process, the texts are applied mostly on one level. No account is taken of inner tensions and different weights of various texts.

3. Where the doctrine lays claim to knowledge of a "double" end to the history of humanity, that some will be raised to heaven while others are banished to hell. This idea ignores the fact that Christians are called to hope without knowing for certain what lies in store for those who do not share in the same hope or who have rejected it. Anyone who constructs a personal idea of the end of history and of his or her own personal destiny by imagining God's judgment according to his or her own experiences attempts to disregard a boundary that *cannot* be disregarded.

Therefore caution, if not contradiction, should be exercised to counteract the claim that it is possible to say something credible and definite about what is to come. This claim is present in all three cases. However, there are different ways of presenting this caution. It can be seen as an expression of the reservation that we as humans can know nothing definite about the "hereafter." Alternatively, the caution can be understood as the expression of expectation that relies on the essential Christian "confession of our hope" (Heb. 10:23), which is always a response to God's promise.

1.2.2. Theology of History: The "Final Goal" (Telos) of History

The doctrine of the last things is disputed with similar fundamental skepticism in a second type of theological treatment of the future. This type refuses to step beyond the boundaries of the world of human experience, but does not sacrifice hope. This method directs interest toward the historical future, and asks what can be hoped for — not just with a view to waiting for the future, but with a view to helping it along the way. Hope should lead to action, to action directed at the future; accordingly, the true character of hope can only be discerned through this action. That the time for action allotted to each human comes to an end with death serves only as an impetus to ensure that the time is properly used. What counts is using the possibilities of that time to the full, attempting to contribute to a general good that corresponds as nearly as possible to the will of God. Only in concern for this future can human hopes find satisfaction.

This form of eschatology attempts to understand history according to its "end." This "end," however, is not to be seen as an abrupt cutoff point, a sudden end to history; rather, this form of eschatology deals with the end *state* of history, that is, the "end" of a changing, progressing, imperfect history in need of completion. There is no need for a vision that reaches beyond this end — it is not possible to see beyond history, since "history" itself is the coherence, the context of all happening. Attention is directed toward meanings which ultimately combine to form history in its entirety, but at the same time toward the whole mix of human deeds and suffering. The decisive question is whether future generations will also be subject to the same suffering that has until now constituted so much of human existence, if the suffering may increase, or if the chance of better times exists, if only the possibilities that exist are used to bring about improvements.

In this view, history must not fail to reach the goal — that is, it must not fail to produce what is destined to be produced. What is supposed to happen and to be achieved is a definite task. History provides milestones to mark the way. It is important to look ahead, but not simply to be content with what has always happened and what will probably always happen. Rather, one must contemplate the possibilities for change, because if possibilities are to be realized they must be imagined.

One can argue whether all this really deserves to be called "eschatology." The "end" of history (and this goes for history as a whole as much as for the history of an individual) is not the same thing as the telos of history. The telos is the purpose of history, the goal at which history aims, provided that not too many humans stand in its way, indifferent to the course of events because the only direction they can look is backward. Humanity can aim toward a final goal — but that end does not stop the course of history. If the end that puts the seal on a fulfilled history is formed out of history itself — that is, does not create a break in the course of events — then it is the result of a development that has to be seen in coherence with all happening. This ultimate goal has to be properly fought for, because it would not develop if left to itself. It is the final balance that takes precedence over everything that has preceded it, over experiences and failures and suffering, over what has been done and what has been neglected.[9]

The telos of history can be understood as the "end" of history only in the sense that nothing else can be conceived of as exceeding it. Therefore, this "end" is the ultimate form of all human hopes. Eschatology becomes a *teleology* of history — teleology as the unfolding of all that which is to be achieved in history, because it is part of the destiny of history. Destiny should certainly not be understood in this context as determination, as a framework of cause and effect into which human action fits. It is not a fate imposed on humanity. Nor does history work like a clock continually ticking, or like an alarm clock, wound and set by God to ring at the end of all things. Destiny means, rather, the dynamic ordering of movement that constitutes the relationship of events in which humanity exists. We have to adapt ourselves to this scheme, and can learn from it something about our personal and collective future. The end of each life is part of history. In this sense, then, eschatology is turned into teleology.

This end-of-history eschatology is problematic because of the implicit idea of development. This idea sees the continuity of history guaranteed only by a continuous state of change. The difference between earlier and later is often stylized as the difference between old and new, the opposition of bad and good. Death and life are, in this scheme, reinterpreted metaphorically: death means that which has been overtaken and outdated by history; life means that which has future, or that which at least points to the future.

This second type of eschatology can develop in different ways using the general mold that has just been described. Such eschatology is particularly effective if it is joined to a philosophy of history. Philosophy of history, a product of the modern era, promises to deal with the world as history — as a network of events complete and unified in itself, to be understood only from the perspective

---

9. Paul Althaus distinguishes in his book *Die letzten Dinge* between "teleological" and "axiological" eschatology; "axiological" eschatology lends eternal meaning to the present. In later editions he moved steadily further from this differentiation, because it seemed to him to be conceptually inappropriate. This distinction should be seen as a method of drawing attention to the present and future aspects of Christian hope.

of its final goal. Philosophy of history aims to guide humanity —
until now continuously divided by religion, culture, race, and social
caste — toward its true unity. That is, it aims to guide humanity
toward a general, all-embracing good. Philosophy of history prepares for the process of integration, whose aim is to create a human
culture that is the sum of all human achievement.

Can eschatology be part of this process? (Many theologians
would put the question differently, asking whether philosophy of
history has inherited the content of Christian hope.) Anyone convinced that God has given history a purpose and, further, that God
has let us know the final goal in order that we can aim at it, can
scarcely shy away from contact with teleology. Rather, such a person would probably intensify the concept of the end, and say that
history is the process through which the world is saved. Justice,
peace, and the prosperity of nature have been given to humanity by God; salvation and perdition are in our hands. The human
race will be responsible if life on earth in the end ceases forever, in
which case humanity has sentenced itself to destruction. God's will
is this final goal of history. The history of the world becomes the
judgment of the world.

In this sense teleology takes on the characteristics of a *theology
of history*. Concepts of the goal of history are qualified theologically; far-reaching historical events or decisions affecting the future
are explained as willed by God. When advocates of this theology
of history wish to play a convincing part in the confrontation with
their more progressive contemporaries, they attempt to outdo philosophy of history by explaining the end-purpose of history as an
unconditional obligation, as a decision between death and life, and
by doing so to establish an ultimate moral claim.

Anyone who supports this claim might soon find that the price
is too high. It usually is *not* the case (certainly in the long term)
that things change for the better. Experience has shown repeatedly
that the drive toward better conditions is in fact bought at the cost
of spiritual and material damages. At the very least, all groups that
stand in the way of the wished-for goal are excluded.

For this reason, supporters of this idea of a divinely ordained
telos of history generally do not wish simply to build up on a theological level what already is widely hoped for. Their aim is rather

to defend against the resignation that easily sets in following a period of new ideas — resignation prevalent among those who cannot keep up. Or they wish to stop hopes from becoming too short-sighted or too far-reaching. A faith perspective should be able to maintain the right balance. With trust in God's will, that balance will ultimately lead to the goal, even if one is faced with resistance, suffering, temptation, and affliction (*Anfechtung*).

Although it often seems that this second type of eschatology displaces eternity in favor of time, and heaven in favor of the earth, this is not the case. This eschatology is carried along by currents of expectation of God's kingdom, which is awaited both as the comprehensive renewal of historical existence and as the transformation of all human powers of imagination. These currents stretch back to Jewish messianic conceptions. In the history of Christianity these ideas constitute a hidden spring, which sometimes seems to disappear completely. But the ideas always come back to the surface, mostly in times of crisis or directly following times of crisis. They break in and swamp some Christian groups, sweeping them up and occasionally bringing them to rest on new and foreign shores. The motivating force is hope in better times and the perfection of Christianity in a changing world. The kingdom of God exists as a dynamic "final state," closely tied to goals of action intended to build up the kingdom of God.

Theology of history shows many faces. The vision of the perfection of Christianity in a better world is found in the European Enlightenment. In the United States it is even today a deeply rooted idea, due to the sense of election and mission brought to America by Puritan settlers and proudly adopted by the young republic. Reinhold Niebuhr has dealt heatedly with this belief in progress on many occasions,[10] pointing repeatedly to the ambiguous nature of everything that has been and can be achieved in history.[11] But even his eloquence has not succeeded in weakening the conviction that divine providence has its home in the society and history of Amer-

---

10. See James H. Moorhead, "Engineering the Millennium: Kingdom-Building in American Protestantism, 1880–1920," *Princeton Seminary Bulletin*, Supplement 3 (1994): 104–28.

11. For example, see *Faith and History: A Comparison of Christian and Modern Views of History* (New York: Charles Scribner's Sons, 1949).

ica. The fixed idea of carrying out the work of God belongs to the religious elements of American public life, as in, for example, the closing words of John F. Kennedy's inaugural address on January 20, 1961: "...knowing that here on earth God's work must truly be our own." This thought was transmitted on a worldwide scale through the ecumenical movement, and is today perhaps the most subtle form of American imperialism.

This is, however, by no means the only form that theology of history takes. There have, for example, always been people convinced that they must help bring about the end of history appointed by God by rooting out the evils that exist on earth, even at the cost of worldwide destruction. In another scheme, the signs of the end of the world are identified with events in world history, and are believed to be designed by God to show God's plan to the world. For this reason it is impossible to reduce ideas concerning the telos of history to a common denominator. However, certain characteristics can be mentioned, which at times connect: the conviction, for example, that (*a*) God has a plan for humanity and its history; that (*b*) this plan is somehow perceptible; and that (*c*) Christian action must converge with this plan. In the plan, our cooperation, if not our active participation, is essential in deciding the course of events.

The role of the Bible in the perception of this plan varies. Some supporters of theology of history, particularly those of a liberal slant, limit themselves to finding the general direction of history in the hope in the kingdom of God. Others — and this includes those of a revolutionary disposition, not just "conservatives" — call on the Bible as the source of knowledge about history. God has made God's plan known in the Bible; it is for us, by comparing this plan with history, to come to the right conclusions. We must point out the signs of the times, which indicate imminent divine intervention in the world. In this way, the Bible is used as an atlas of world history — an atlas which also includes all the important maps of the future.

Such thinking becomes particularly disastrous if biblical texts are used to interpret present-day conflicts as part of the drama of the end of the world. Extracts from the Apocalypse of John, in particular, are often used for such a purpose; moreover, these texts then come to form a kind of canon for understanding the Bible in its entirety. Persecutions or political harassment of believers are regarded as clashes between forces friendly with and at odds with God. Humanity is separated into two factions: those who are saved and those who are not. A decisive battle is imminent, in which simply *being* "on God's side" is not enough — "being on God's side" has to include *fighting* on God's side. Those who accord ultimate meaning to such confrontations probably count themselves among the elect!

These last two modes of thought are clearly of fundamentalist pedigree.[12] The Bible is taken as the unshakable foundation of human knowledge concerning all events, whether events taking place between God and humanity or between humans themselves. This fundamentalism is strong not only within groups which in Europe would be considered "sects" (Seventh-Day Adventists, Jehovah's Witnesses, Pentecostalists), but also within the so-called free churches (Methodists and Baptists) and "evangelical" Protestant circles. In America, fundamentalism is the hallmark of some Christian communities on the right wing of the Protestant spectrum. Fundamentalist groups have increased rapidly both in membership and religious influence in the last three decades. It now forms a political pressure group of considerable proportion. That Ronald Reagan during his first term not only saw a nuclear war as inevitable, but stylized it as the last battle against the powers of evil, raises questions as to the religious background of his worldview. These trends have led to wider publicity for the political effects of apocalyptic ideas about the end of time. The idea that the future is unchangeable or predestined by God, and that humanity must gear itself to that future, is no longer the private opinion of individuals on the fringes of society. These ideas now have to be brought into the political equation.

Typical of this attitude toward time and the world is "dispensational thinking," a historico-theological reference to what God has planned for a given era and put at the disposal of people living during that era.[13] This view of history synchronizes historical events

---

12. Ernest R. Sandeen, *The Roots of Fundamentalism: British and American Millenarianism, 1800–1930* (Chicago: University of Chicago Press, 1970).

13. Clarence Bass, *Backgrounds to Dispensationalism: Its Historical Genesis*

with biblical texts concerning the end of history, particularly the visions in Daniel 2 and 7 and Revelation.[14] What is decisive for the attitude toward present and future is the proclamation of the millennium: the thousand years of justice and peace — of Christ's rule on earth (Rev. 20:2, 4, 6) — which are to follow the decisive battle of Armageddon (Ezek. 38:1–39:26; Rev. 16:16–21) and Christ's second coming. Within this framework, the establishment of the state of Israel takes on a particular significance, and disturbances in the Middle East are viewed accordingly.[15]

The development of the relationship between Jews and Christians often has been assessed as belonging to the turbulence created by the approaching end of time, notably by the Plymouth Brethren under leadership of Irish immigrant John Nelson Darby (1800–1882), whose ideas continue to have effect today, not just in the United States. Darbyism's apocalyptic expectation is partly based on a critique of the decrepit state of the Anglican Established Church of the time. Such internal criticism of the church has repeatedly inspired speculation as to God's plan of salvation. Darbyists[16] see both Israel and the church as the preferred objects and instruments of God's work. Jewish history is equated with the

---

and Ecclesiastical Implications (Grand Rapids, Mich.: Eerdmans, 1960); C. Norman Kraus, *Dispensationalism in America: Its Rise and Development* (Richmond: John Knox Press, 1958); Timothy P. Weber, *Living in the Shadow of the Second Coming: American Premillennialism, 1875–1982* (Oxford and New York: Oxford University Press, 1979; exp. ed., Chicago: University of Chicago Press, 1987); George M. Marsden, *Fundamentalism and American Culture: The Shaping of Twentieth-Century Evangelicanism, 1870–1925* (Oxford and New York: Oxford University Press, 1980); Paul S. Boyer, *When Time Shall Be No More: Prophecy Belief in Modern American Culture* (Cambridge: Harvard University Press, 1992); James M. Efird, *End-Times: Rapture, Antichrist, Millennium* (Nashville: Abingdon Press, 1986).

14. An example of the reporting of historical events "in the light of the Bible" can be found in Hal Lindsey, *The 1980s: Countdown to Armageddon* (New York: Bantam Books, 1981). See also Hal Lindsey with Carole C. Carlson, *The Late Great Planet Earth* (Grand Rapids, Mich.: Zondervan, 1970).

15. John F. Walvoord and John E. Walvoord, *Armageddon — Oil and the Middle East Crisis: What the Bible Says about the Future of the Middle East and the End of Western Civilization* (Grand Rapids, Mich.: Zondervan, 1974). In view of the Gulf War, this book was revised and became a bestseller. See also Kurt Emil Karl Koch, *The Coming One* (Grand Rapids, Mich.: Kregel Publications, 1972); Anis A. Shorrosh, *Jesus, Prophecy, and the Middle East* (Nashville: T. S. Nelson, 1981).

16. Harold H. Rowden, *The Origins of the Brethren, 1825–1850* (London: Pickering & Inglis, 1967); Charles F. Baker, *A Dispensational Theology* (Grand Rapids, Mich.: Grace Bible College, 1971).

hands on the clock of world history. Christians can read from the historical role of the Jews how far the world is from reaching the maturity crowned by the second coming of Christ. Such considerations have strongly influenced British and American policy in the Near East since World War II.

Historians and sociologists of religion often are interested in the interaction between religious convictions and political ideas. Special attention is given to the influence of the interaction on international affairs, since denominations and sects which see signs of the end of the world in political affairs have spread enormously in recent times. This has been the case even in Eastern Europe and Latin America. However interesting these phenomena may be from the point of view of statistics, however dangerous humans can be when they consider themselves executors of the divine will, the concept of history which lies behind such ideas still needs to be considered and judged according to its theological content.

Theology of history raises the question of *how the expectation of God's action relates to the action which is open to us and demanded of us.* Theology of history usually works with the assumption that God reveals Godself in history to demonstrate God's values and aims. In order to reach what God wishes we have to fulfill what God has revealed. This normally leads to a fusion of hope and action.

Church history, however, contains numerous examples showing that an awareness of history developed with help of the biblical differentiation between "promise" and "fulfillment." The differentiation is particularly clear in the New Testament. Historical affairs are perceived as what in a determining way *have been* and as what, thereby, create the horizon of expectation — what is accepted by Christians to be God's promise, and what leads to consideration of past events. In this way, a breadth of vision can be reached which does not need to lose sight of that which is "next." This representation of history often shaped Christian communities.[17] The theologically decisive question is whether one is paying attention

---

17. See Ernst Benz, "Verheißung und Erfüllung: Über die theologischen Grundlagen des deutschen Geschichtsbewußtseins," in *Endzeiterwartung zwischen Ost und West: Studien zur christlichen Eschatologie* (Freiburg: Rombach, 1973), 38–89.

to God's promises, or whether one is distracted by concentrating on one's own expectations.

Orientation according to a telos of history comes into sharp conflict with the doctrine of the last things whenever the latter doctrine appears as a simple evasion of the present. However, it would be misleading to see the doctrine of the last things as purely restricted to the individual, including a view to an end of cosmic proportion, while seeing philosophy of history and its related eschatology as related to society. Rather, the difference in the second approach is that the place of the individual in the world is of a different type.

According to the doctrine of the last things, the fate of the human is a microcosm whose existence is both created and ended by God, just like the cosmos itself. What makes humans different is that they are explicitly called to faith and hope, and that their answer to that call does not, unlike their lives, have an end in time. During the course of life humans are in the world and can make their mark in it, but they have no power to decide over the existence or nonexistence of the universe. However destructive they may attempt to be, they have as much power to destroy the universe as they had to create it — none.

In view of an eschatology based on theology of history, on the contrary, the individual can understand him- or herself as part of an all-embracing process of transformation. Each human being makes a contribution to the course of events and in doing so can find a meaning and purpose in life — not only in this world, but also, due to the individual's creative power, in a form of life that transcends individual existence.

1.2.3. Radical Eschatology

Is it possible to deduce God's will for history from the course of events and their presumed consequences? Can we, in fact, identify God's judgment with historical events?

This question has led to the development of a third type of eschatology. This third type accuses teleology of world salvation and of similar perspectives on the future, and of no longer hoping for God's deliverance and new creation. Such approaches, it is said, invoke dynamism and speak of a capacity for change or "ultimate" decisions within history. That is, they are accused of failing to mention *what God alone can bring about*. It is precisely this happening that cannot be deduced from what we call "history" — at least, not unequivocally.

For such a radical reconsideration of eschatology it is not enough to refer to the doctrine of the last things. What is needed is a different direction of thought. Eschatology is radicalized in order to bear witness to God as the "wholly other," who cannot be deduced from the world or history, nor even from radical changes and apparent new beginnings. God is far more "the Coming One," confronting humanity in humanity's history. "New" is not a state that follows from the "old" or that cancels it out, even if that state were so different from our own conceptions that our conceptions must change with it. The decisive question must be: what is so disproportionately different, so completely new, that we humans can never deal with it properly — not even if we can put it into words?

Radical eschatology no longer looks ahead to the last things or ahead to better times to come. It also does not ask questions about what comes "afterward" or encourage spiritual visions of the future which bring a different perspective on the present, and on present activity. The third type of eschatology offers, rather, an incomparably intensive awareness of the present; what is present does not "pass away," but stands in relation to eternity. Each and every point in time is equally embedded in eternity. Eternity is not something that comes "after" time, nor is it something that gives motive power to time itself. Rather, eternity "encounters" us as our limitation — and we must be open to that limitation, we must confront it. We may not evade it. Every moment is weighed according to this limitation; it is this limitation which decides whether each individual moment will pass away or endure.

One can question whether the term "eschatology" is being overstated and even misused. This third type certainly has nothing to do with the last things, because it no longer limits itself to "things"; indeed, its tendency is to radically question *every* "thing." This radical approach tears habitual ways of thinking to pieces, making traditional expectations appear obsolete. The ultimate questions are reduced to one question: how can we *begin* to ask questions and what should be asked first? "Eschatology" is not used to designate the closing chapter of dogmatics, nor to christen a philosophy of culture and history whose main task is the reconciliation of the Christian heritage of hope with contemporary consciousness in the field of common action. On the contrary, the intent of radical eschatology is to be *theo*logy from its very roots (hence "radical"). It talks about God by looking only to God and proclaiming God as "the Coming One," by becoming itself a sign of hope in everything it tries to say — the sign of a hope that can only be received. The intent is to point out the life that comes from God, a surprising gift to be received. However, it would be wrong to say that every surprise comes from God.

Radical eschatology cannot, therefore, proceed from a human relationship to God that promotes historical progress and cultural betterment. On the contrary, it points to what is so wholly "other," so different from every conceivable future, that no one can come to terms with it. Tangible explanations, illustrations, and suggestions for action are therefore avoided.

Does this explanation treat all the important aspects of radical eschatology sufficiently? It is true that we can only talk about God because God encounters us, but we cannot simply make God the personification of surprises, coincidences, and diversions from the norm. If God's actions were simply random happenings, then in a subtle way the future could once more be "brought back into line."

In order to avoid misunderstandings of this order, the Bible speaks of *the* hope granted to humanity against all expectation, contrary to all hope. Stories are told — like the Abraham story in Genesis 15:1–6 — in order to prepare the readers to recognize this "unhoped-for hope" itself, to be open for the unexpected but promised.

"Unhoped-for hope" (*unverhoffte Hoffnung*) is a dialectical term. It means that hope cannot be spoken of as something on which we can base our ideas. This hope is not something that we "possess," however many hopes we may have within us. It is a miracle, like being born again: "born again, born anew into a living hope" (1 Pet. 1:3). Hope is a sign of redemption, of freedom — that is, of the freedom to hope, of an expectation that is sensitive to God's action and that therefore remains in the character of hope and cannot go beyond hope.

These two points must be made about the nature of hope. No one can "have" hope; rather, when someone is "seized" or "grasped" by hope, that person *lives in* hope. Only one of these two things can be said with clarity at any one time, but at the same time the other must not be forgotten. This is why "hope" is a concept in dialectic theological discourse. It is the hope of those "having no hope and without God in the world" if they are not adopted into the community of God's promise (Eph. 2:12). This is an inheritance that can never become a possession.

No eschatology, however forcible and far-reaching, can ever talk such a hope into being or "make" it convincing. But when Paul writes of the hope that calls faith into being, of the "hope against hope" (Rom. 4:18), he calls to mind the incomparable and un-changing hope granted Abraham through God's promise. Paul's intent is to convey the idea that Abraham, without knowing it, comes to stand under the cross of Christ because of this hope, since God, "who gives life to the dead and calls into existence the things that do not exist" (Rom. 4:17), encounters him. In this way, Abraham's hope reaches out to the resurrection of the crucified Christ. The person whom God meets experiences God's judgment, which decides what is and what was and what will be. Such an experience happens to us through Christ's death and life, so perceptibly that we too may hope that "we shall also live with him" (Rom. 6:8). The encounter with God is a matter of life and death and at the same time exposes us to Christ's victory over sin and death. This brings us back to themes of the doctrine of the last things.

1.3. Tensions and Controversies

Up to this point I have sketched these three types of eschatol-ogy somewhat idealistically, without mentioning specific names or theological positions. This is because I did not want the different types to be memorized only in connection with prominent names, or with the idiosyncrasies or circumstances of a particular histori-cal period. It is true that such methods make organization easier, but in the process they generally do nothing but divert attention from the real issue.

Nevertheless, it is no coincidence that the three forms mentioned in this summary follow from each other. This sketch corresponds to a striking phase in the recent history of German Protestant theology — a phase, developing between 1890 and 1930, that is worthy of consideration. The most significant ideas that came to expression in those years will be dealt with in the following two chapters. Even outside of this historical period, the same combination of ideas has come together time and time again. Such a meeting generally occurs when hope in God is accompanied by an intense personal experience that is either overwhelmingly simplistic or completely inconceivable. In these situations, responsibilities are seen, but it is impossible to comprehend their causes or consequences, let alone come to grips with them. The hope, the experience, and the responsibilities must somehow be harmonized, but without simply being reduced to a common denominator.

Even when the three types come to expression in sequence, they do not rule each other out. Each has a corrective effect on the others, indicating the overlapping areas within the problem and the points at which unanswered questions act to correct each other. This is why it is not possible to fit the different perspectives together to form an overall view. Rather, an introduction to eschatology has the task of presenting examples of how the interaction of the three contrary types can create a theologically fruitful discussion ground.

The combination of conceptions present in German Protestant theology between 1890 and 1930 is therefore only *one* example, even if an extremely illuminating one. It is an example that deals with questions and insights that, under different sets of circumstances and in other church contexts, may still be worthy of serious consideration or may need to be completely rethought.

Roman Catholic theology remained almost completely untouched by these developments before Vatican II. The fight against modernism called for by Vatican I had the effect of hindering the growth of a new consciousness in the doctrine of the last things. The faithful were not to be made uneasy by changing worldviews or to have their hope in eternal life paralyzed by a view of history committed purely to purposes of the secular realm. Historical criticism was not permitted to confuse exegesis; exegesis was committed to the service of church doctrine. Inside this seemingly solid or even rigid framework remained, however, room for individual inquiry concerning themes important in the development of doctrinal pronouncements: for example, purgatory and hell. In this inquiry, the ecclesiastical and magisterial tradition was thoroughly considered. Yet expressions of Christian piety were scarcely considered, despite the fact that traces of lived hope reaching back to the original sources — traces which church teaching often bypassed — could have been found. This criticism is just as applicable in Protestant circles.

Could we say that Protestant theology, with its concerns in eschatology, may have had a head start on Catholic theologians? Certainly the theological and philosophical debates of the nineteenth and early twentieth centuries had formed within Protestant theology an enhanced sensibility in the realm of eschatology. Such sensibility is able to create both insecurity *and* increased awareness.

The idea that this debate gave Protestant theology a head start is, however, only true insofar as revisions in theological thought are considered. As far as such revisions are concerned, it is only since Vatican II that there has been a change in Catholic theology. The Council gave a higher profile to the role of biblical exegesis in theological doctrine than it had previously been accorded, and in doing so contributed to the remodeling of eschatology. In particular, the openness of the church leadership suggested new paths for intellectual theology. New understandings, not just of individual doctrines but of theology as a whole, made their way forward. The impression is that Catholicism is rapidly catching up with developments that took place within Protestantism over a long period of time (and that to some degree have already been disposed of).

But this impression is deceptive if it is not recognized that, as far as Catholicism is concerned, eschatological questions are closely bound to the church's self-understanding. Eschatological matters are therefore involved in thematic contexts that Protestant theology does not address with the same intensity. The exception proves the rule: in his *Glaubenslehre*, Friedrich Schleiermacher (1768–1834) develops eschatology with a view to the perfection of the church as a spiritual fellowship (*Geistgemeinschaft*); everything that the individual believer experiences as salvation is grounded in that fellowship.[18]

Just as the combination of the three eschatological types formed a point of intersection for Catholic theology in the mid-1960s, such dialogue had a similar role in Protestant eschatology, not least in connection with the ecumenical movement. For example, we will see how radical eschatology in ecumenical contexts becomes displaced in favor of a theology of history, whereas in the United States it has long ago taken the lead, albeit with necessary modifications (4.5.1 and 4.5.2).

Since the 1960s, new fronts have developed in both Roman Catholic and Protestant churches and theologies. The atmosphere has changed and interest has shifted. But certain questions continue to present themselves or even to break out again in unexpected places.

For these reasons, it seems reasonable to direct attention toward the state of the debate three decades ago — that is, in the mid-1960s (chapter 4) — and in such light to look at the changing points of view and the questions that prove constant. But before this can happen, we must acquaint ourselves better with the grouping of the three types themselves. As mentioned, this classification belongs to the more recent history of German Protestant theology, but around the middle of the twentieth century came to be considered equally from the Catholic perspective.

> Eschatology is the center in which the theological weather of our time develops. It is in eschatology that the storms that threaten the whole landscape develop, capable of either unleashing destructive hail or refreshing and rendering the whole landscape fruitful. If Troeltsch's comment that "the bureau of eschatology is generally closed these days" was true for the liberalism of the nineteenth century, it is on the other

---

18. *Der christliche Glaube*, 2d ed. (Berlin: Reimer, 1830–31), §§157–63 (ET: *The Christian Faith*, ed. H. R. Mackinthosh and J. S. Stewart [Edinburgh: T. & T. Clark, 1928]). See Eilert Herms, "Schleiermachers Eschatologie nach der zweiten Auflage seiner 'Glaubenslehre,'" *Theologische Zeitschrift* 46 (1990): 97–123.

hand true that the same office has been working overtime since the turn of the century.[19]

This is how Hans Urs von Balthasar (1905–88) introduced his treatment of the problem *Eschatologie* in 1957.[20] This treatment should be taken as the framework of our consideration of the subject. It is a work of exemplary clear vision, even if von Balthasar sometimes contents himself with simply hinting. The details of the storm front that he only touches on must be more precisely described. Above all, the storm front must be researched as closely as possible. It is useless just to contemplate storms that lie far in the past. How do the storms develop? Are they perhaps the results of climatic change, the causes of which must be investigated in order to prevent more damage?

Storms bearing the name "eschatology" have developed at least three times in the past hundred years. The first storm that should be mentioned occurred at the turn of the century, with so-called *konsequente Eschatologie (consistent eschatology)*. Its target was the optimistic Christian belief in progress. It confronted this belief with Jesus' proclamation of the kingdom of God, Jesus' strangely anachronistic proclamation of God's coming. The second storm developed after the end of the First World War. This was dialectical theology's *radical eschatology*, which saw the crisis of Christianity in the light of the turning point of history — *the* turning point that God's advent in Jesus Christ created once and for all time. In the 1960s came a new departure with *theology of history*, which appealed to the meaning of the world-event that took place at Easter, at which the end of history comes into view and history is considered anew.

The third weather change could scarcely have been foreseen by von Balthasar in 1957. Many experienced the far-reaching effects of the history-of-theology outbreak as a whirlwind, which left be-

---

19. "Die Eschatologie ist der 'Wetterwinkel' in der Theologie unserer Zeit. Von ihr her steigen jene Gewitter auf, die das ganze Land fruchtbar bedrohen: verhageln oder erfrischen. Wenn für den Liberalismus des 19. Jahrhunderts das Wort von Troeltsch gelten konnte: 'Das eschatologische Bureau ist meist geschlossen', so macht dieses im Gegenteil seit der Jahrhundertwende Überstunden."

20. Published in *Fragen der Theologie heute*, ed. Johannes Feiner, Josef Trütsch, and Franz Böckle (Einsiedeln, Switzerland: Benziger, 1957), 403–21.

hind a trail of destruction. The ground was left bare, either for new growth to spring up or to run wild. What was lost in the wreckage, and what was salvageable as building blocks for the new construction? Were new foundations laid? If so, how strong have they proved to be? These three decisive developments will be presented in the next chapters along with consideration of their internal tensions, consequences, and unanswered questions. It is not my intention to reconstruct a complete history of the problems in order to discover how one should think about the term "eschatology." The discussion presents, on the contrary, a *question* that is itself of great significance for an understanding of eschatology: do external stimuli provide impetus for theology? If so, what are these external stimuli, and how do they relate to the dynamic that results from the three types of eschatology and that is kept alive by eschatology's lasting questions?[21]

---

21. See also Milard J. Erickson, *Contemporary Options in Eschatology* (Grand Rapids, Mich.: Baker Book House, 1977); and Hans Friedrich Geisser, "Grundtendenzen der Eschatologie im 20. Jahrhundert," in *Die Zukunft der Erlösung: Zur neueren Diskussion um die Eschatologie,* ed. Konrad Stock (Gütersloh: Gütersloher Verlagshaus, 1994), 13–48.

– Chapter 2 –

Jesus of Nazareth, "Bearer of Hope"?

2.1. "The Kingdom of God": A Distant Prospect?

If Troeltsch's comment that "the bureau of eschatology is generally closed these days" was true for the liberalism of the nineteenth century, it is on the other hand true that the same office has been working overtime since the turn of the century.[1]

Hans Urs von Balthasar refers to the clash between the so-called consistent eschatology and ideas of cultural-historical development found in German liberal Protestant theology at the end of the nineteenth century.

What is the point at issue? One of the spokesmen of liberal Protestant theology, Albrecht Ritschl (1822–89), understood the kingdom of God as the "final purpose of the world" (*Endzweck der Welt*).[2] The kingdom of God is personal community with God, and toward this goal it energizes an unbroken development of humanity's maturing toward moral perfection. Christianity leads all other religions and social groups in responsibility for this development, since such community alone is able to agree without constraint to the will of God. Ritschl's friend Adolf von Harnack (1851–1930) considered that the kingdom of God comes "inwardly" when God in power penetrates the soul;[3] in Jesus' parables

---

1. Hans Urs von Balthasar, "Eschatologie," in *Fragen der Theologie heute*, ed. Johannes Feiner, Josef Trütsch, and Franz Böckle (Einsiedeln, Switzerland: Benziger, 1957), 403.

2. "Instruction in the Christian Religion," in *Three Essays*, trans. Philip Hefner (Philadelphia: Fortress Press, 1972), 226.

3. A. von Harnack, *What Is Christianity?* trans. Thomas Bailey Saunders (New

of the kingdom, "everything that is dramatic in the external and historical sense has vanished; and gone, too, are all the external hopes for the future."[4]

Therefore for von Harnack and others as well, "the bureau of eschatology is generally closed these days." Ernst Troeltsch (1865–1923) used this phrase, taken from an unnamed contemporary, in his lectures on Christian doctrine,[5] and adds: "This is because the ideas that undergird such eschatology have lost their roots." The bureau is closed because it has nothing left to administrate.

The only assets remaining to the bankrupt bureau are mere "thoughts." These thoughts are occupied solely with textbook-style answers to the question, "What *dare* we hope?" The answer apparently contents itself with listing what "comes next," i.e., what follows a world stamped by misery and menaced by death. Such thoughts attempt to grasp what awaits us on the other side of the historical life we know. This conception is built on what Jewish and Christian traditions have to say about that "other side" — about the end of the world and last judgment, heaven and hell, eternal blessedness and eternal damnation.

All this is outdated, according to Troeltsch and many of his contemporaries. Such thought has nothing to do with either the modern world-view or with the content of religious expectation as it is to be gathered *critically* from the Bible.

What *are* — or, if Troeltsch is to be followed, what *were once* — the roots of the way of thinking that formed the foundation of eschatology in the old sense? On this subject, Troeltsch remains silent. He may be thinking of a graphic picture of the world, full of biblical prospects of the future: the spectacular end of history and a miraculous but nevertheless conceivable descent of a new and different world from a higher sphere. In this picture, history is not determined by its own latent purpose, which can be developed with the help of humanity. History appears as the field of battle between supernatural powers which intervene in human fate. Reli-

---

York: Harper & Brothers, 1957), 56: "The kingdom of God comes by coming to the individual, by entering into his soul and laying hold of it."

4. Ibid.

5. E. Troeltsch, *The Christian Faith*, trans. Garrett E. Paul (Minneapolis: Fortress Press, 1991), 38.

gious hope feeds on the desire that this drama should speed toward a glorious end, when those who hoped will be singled out as victors over the world.

Troeltsch and kindred spirits no longer deal with the traditional doctrine of the last things, because they believe it to be ideologically outdated. It appears to them to have nothing to do with specifically Christian ideas, but rather to be a relic of late-classical religious syncretism. They cite research into the history of religions, which shows an abundance of parallels in neighboring religions: expectation of a catastrophic end to the world, of final division of humanity between those who are saved and those who are damned. The division of humanity, like the rest of reality, will occur between what belongs to "this" world and what belongs to "the other" — i.e., the "new" — world. The historical circulation of these thoughts is enough in itself to make it highly suspicious, according to a critic like Troeltsch. Is it not true that such thoughts are part of the common property of the late-classical world, and as such perished with the end of the late-classical era, because new powers capable of forming history took their place, bringing with them different views of the future? The content of religious expectation must — so runs the conclusion — be thought out anew, in the light of the philosophy of religion.

Troeltsch provides more precise information in his encyclopedia article on eschatology.[6] According to Troeltsch, eschatology is concerned with the history of the development of the human spirit, the merging of the individual and the individual's creative activity into the universe of life — and thereby with the immortality of humankind. In this, historical responsibility — something that Troeltsch is convinced of — can find new roots, and these roots reach right into the "divine," into eternity.

Liberal Protestant theology, then, *does* develop eschatological ideas, but these are confined to ideas of activity worthy of humanity for the sake of cultural development. Such activity has eternal value, because no exertion for the sake of human culture can ultimately be lost. Or, expressed in religious terms, humans enter

---

6. "Eschatologie: Dogmatisch," in *Die Religion in Geschichte und Gegenwart,* ed. Friedrich Michael Schiele et al. (Tübingen: J. C. B. Mohr, 1910), 2:622–32.

eternity if they make themselves part of the historical whole — not just passively or even against their will, but consciously and creatively in line with the coherence and meaning of the whole. "The life beyond this world is, in very deed, the inspiration of the life that now is."[7] This strength provides motivation for formation of culture and involvement in educational and social spheres.

This human activity has little to do with exalted "ultimate goals" to be found in an ideal historical condition; rather, the idea is that, if possible, all humans should be engaged in cultural activities so that history might remain continuously in flux. When this happens, history can develop what lies hidden within it, and that has already proved promising for the future. Given such participation, every contribution is of importance in the fabric of world history. Moreover, each contribution is of infinite importance in the unforeseeable interaction of all historical moments.[8] Only in this way can — must — humanity be approached. It is no coincidence that some of Troeltsch's students tended to shy away from taking on active ministerial work. This may have been because they did not know what they would talk to the dying about other than grateful remembrance of their lives' achievements. Instead, Troeltsch's students preferred to dedicate themselves to educational tasks — the harder, the better.

This transformation of eschatology paved the way for a passionate appeal to bring the developmental-historical view of life into harmony with "moral-religious" expectation, instead of allowing both to be disrupted by hope in an afterlife. The critical point is to be found in the motivation of hope discovered in the course of research into religious history. The critical question is as follows: Does this hope refer to imminent divine intervention, capable of sweeping aside all hindrances? Or is this hope based on the power

---

7. E. Troeltsch, *The Social Teachings of the Christian Churches*, trans. Olive Wyon (Chicago: University of Chicago Press, 1981), 2:1006.

8. This teleological eschatology crops up again in another form in the works of Pierre Teilhard de Chardin, *Le Phénomène Humain* (Paris: Editions du Seuil, 1955) (ET: *The Phenomenon of Man*, trans. Bernard Wall [New York: Harper & Brothers, 1959]); idem, *Le Milieu Divin* (Paris: Editions du Seuil, 1957) (ET: *The Divine Milieu: An Essay on the Interior Life*, trans. Bernard Wall [New York: Harper & Brothers, 1960]); idem, *L'Avenir de l'Homme* (Paris: Editions de Seuil, 1959) (ET: *The Future of Man*, trans. Norman Denny [New York: Harper & Row, 1964]).

of life and cultural formation, confident because its roots rest in connection to God?

This either-or seems critical. It makes certain questions necessary: Can we still hope in the same way as Jesus' contemporaries? If so, do we really live according to our hope? Anyone who answers "yes" must allow all the more for the additional question, "Can — may — we still wish to act within the boundaries of that hope?"

Liberal Protestant theology of history sees history as a universal whole, as a tissue into which each individual participant is individually responsible for composing a piece, either large or small. What is therefore decisive is participation in this process, not just the possibility of future gain; it is always meaningful to be involved in history. The future presents itself as the catalog of all progress that is humanly possible; if we are to extend existing lines of development into the future, it is obvious that there are boundaries to expansion that must be crossed, but no insurmountable barriers.

"Future" is limited by these views. Anyone expecting the future to bring surprises, interventions, disturbances, or even an earth-shattering catastrophe should be careful that these expectations do not suffocate hope or stand in the way of the urgent tasks of the day. That person should also not create a notion that in effect destroys itself when the feared events either do not happen or turn out to be manageable, perhaps precisely *because* they function as an incentive for us to master life itself that little bit better.

Can, then, this harmony of culture, development, and religious openness still refer to Jesus of Nazareth? That is, to the Jesus of Nazareth who really lived and acted, up to the point of his death? Some liberal Protestant theologians in the last decade of the nineteenth century came to doubt that it could, even to deny it. Their wish was to make Jesus' proclamation of the kingdom of God heard again and to show the offensive nature of his preaching, if understood within the context of its conceptions of God and humanity, of the world and time. This preaching, they emphasized, was imbued with Jesus' immediate expectation of the end of the world; God would very soon destroy "this world," and build on its ruins something completely new — another world. Jesus' thought and action were directed at the advent of the new world. What remains to be completed in this world, doomed as it is to destruction, only interests Jesus insofar as it serves to prepare the way for the kingdom of God or to bring it into being — as far as that is humanly possible! Does this "rediscovery" of Jesus' preaching constitute a hurricane warning for theology and the church at the end of the twentieth century? Or is it just a tempest in a teacup?

2.2. Jesus' Proclamation of the Kingdom of God: Summer Lightning?

Albert SCHWEITZER, *Von Reimarus zu Wrede: Eine Geschichte der Leben-Jesu-Forschung* (Tübingen: J. C. B. Mohr, 1906) (2d ed.: *Geschichte der Leben-Jesu-Forschung* [Tübingen: J. C. B. Mohr, 1913]; ET: *The Quest of the Historical Jesus: A Critical Study of Its Progress from Reimarus to Wrede*, trans. William Montgomery [London: A. & C. Black, 1910; reprint, New York: Macmillan, 1968]); Johannes WEISS, *Die Predigt Jesu vom Reiche Gottes*, 2d ed. (Göttingen: Vandenhoeck & Ruprecht, 1892, 1900) (ET of the 1st ed.: *Jesus' Proclamation of the Kingdom of God*, trans. Richard Hyde Hiers and David Larrimore Holland [Philadelphia: Fortress Press, 1971; reprint, Chico, Calif.: Scholars Press, 1985]).

Consistent eschatology is the term Albert Schweitzer (1875–1965) used in 1906 to describe the interpretation of the historical Jesus that sees Jesus' preaching and his life as based completely — i.e., consistently — on the *imminent expectation of the kingdom of God*.[9] In 1892, Johannes Weiss (1863–1914) described the eschatological character of Jesus' proclamation of the kingdom of God as pointing toward the breaking into history of a catastrophic end, which would call into being a new world in which God reigns.

In this, Weiss and Schweitzer contradict the historico-theological ideas of development and emergence represented by liberal Protes-

---

9. Montgomery translates *konsequente Eschatologie* as "thoroughgoing eschatology." Schweitzer's use of language is not clear. He describes Jesus' position as *konsequent eschatologisch*. Looked at more closely, however, it is in fact the *reconstruction* of this position that is to be understood as *konsequent eschatologisch*, by which consistent eschatology becomes a theological position. The aim is to show the inconsistency of previous eschatologies historico-critically, and thus to dispose of them neatly.

In Roman Catholic theological handbooks, consistent eschatology is registered as *Eschatologismus* (eschatologism). It is not a pretty word and is used to designate a questionable theory. See Franz-Josef Schierse, "Eschatologismus," in *Lexikon für Theologie und Kirche*, 2d ed., ed. Josef Höfer and Karl Rahner (Freiburg: Herder, 1959), 3:1098–99; André Feuillet, "Eschatologismus," in *Sacramentum Mundi*, ed. Karl Rahner et al. (Freiburg: Herder, 1967), 1:1193–97.

tant theology of which they otherwise knew themselves to be part. They remind their readers that the kingdom of God signifies a complete break between the time of "this" world and the time which operates in the next, at least as far as the prophetic preaching of Jesus of Nazareth is concerned. That the kingdom of God does not "grow" out of history, but rather breaks into history, and that this "catastrophe" is close at hand has been a challenge for Christian theology from the very beginning. Von Balthasar had this in mind when he spoke of the growing demands placed on the "eschatological bureau": the office is now open round the clock, because eschatology has taken over all aspects of theology.

Consistent eschatology is a construction of historical research into atmospheres of crisis. When the course of history is interrupted, when coherence falls apart and every foundation disappears into chaos, the motto "only participation counts" no longer has anything to hold on to. Only the prospect of triumph after the destruction can lend meaning to the state of history. Only that person who is certain that he or she has a part in the victory over history can proclaim the world-catastrophe. Did not Jesus of Nazareth understand himself in this way? And is it not the case that his confidence was possibly the only explanation for what he said and did, even up to his readiness to die for his hope?

Weiss and Schweitzer are convinced of this. Their wish is to expose the roots of Christian eschatology by investigating the question of the historical Jesus. What did Jesus of Nazareth want to achieve? By what ideas was he driven? What temporally conditioned targets had he set himself? And how did he react to adversities and opposition? Methodologically, Weiss and Schweitzer are at one with Troeltsch. Jesus' expectation, as documented by the Bible, should be taken out of its imaginative packaging and should be reconstructed so that it is clear which aspects of his way of life resulted from his expectations.

Weiss and Schweitzer came to the conclusion that Jesus' expectation (and also that of the first Christian generation) can no longer be a sustainable hope today. Such hope does not, therefore, represent the beginning of an evolving moral and religious world organization, the continuation of which is still the work of Christianity today. Jesus expected the imminent end of history, or at least the end of the previous history of suffering, misery, and godlessness — and he expected that end within the foreseeable future.

This expectation inspired Jesus, but also — according to Schweitzer — drove him to his death. Jesus promised his disciples that the Son of Man, herald of the kingdom of God, would come before they had finished their mission to Israel (Matt. 10:23). This verse was for Schweitzer the key to Jesus of Nazareth's consistent eschatology. When the kingdom of God failed to come Jesus staked his own life on an attempt to force the judgment of God and to hasten the coming of the new world. But confronted with Jesus' death, God still did not act; the world was not transformed with a roll of thunder. What is there then to hope for, after Jesus' death?

From the point of view of consistent eschatology, further development, which should also be the driving force of modern Christianity, is presented in this way. Jesus' disciples wished at first to preserve Jesus' hope in its entirety. They even went on to strengthen it, by turning their master (after he had been taken away from them) into part of that hope, and reckoning with his speedy return, the *parousia*. But as the world catastrophe was further delayed, the hope must, of necessity, sooner or later have become invalid. The early Christians waited in vain for the coming of the kingdom of God in the immediate future, as Jesus had described it, so to speak, with drums and trumpets, but also accompanied by the advent of Jesus himself coming on the clouds of heaven. However, in order for their religion to survive, the Christians, now more sober and thoughtful, found it necessary to give up their expectations in favor of an approach that could help them become established on a long-term basis.

The imminent expectation of the kingdom of God (Naherwartung) is based on a presumed event. The kingdom of God is "near" in the sense that it is, admittedly, not here today, but that it *could* tomorrow or in the immediate future be "here." "Nearness" means a rapidly dwindling distance in time. Therefore it is part of the essence of this expectation that it can only be maintained for a certain period of time. Such an expectation is used up, or exhausted, in the passage of time. If what is proclaimed does not come to pass, the disappointment must somehow be dealt with.

People either bring themselves to new hope by moving that which has not yet taken place further into the future, *or* rework the expectation so that it can now be brought more into harmony with the course of events. In this process, however, the hope of God's sudden intervention in the course of time dwindles.

Jesus' second coming is delayed. Can it be that it will never come to pass? If that is the case, it is all the more important to continue to work in his spirit. From the perspective of consistent eschatology, *the delay of the parousia comes for this reason — to constitute the key to the history of Christianity.* Christianity has in the main — apart from a few incorrigible enthusiasts existing on the margins — corrected its over-hasty expectation. It has gradually come to understand how to adapt itself to the world, not merely to come to terms with it — and in the course of this adaptation it has for the first time developed a culturally creative capacity. This is, and remains, Christianity's chance for the future.

Franz Overbeck (1837–1905), a contemporary of Weiss and Schweitzer, follows the reconstruction up to this point; that is, to the establishment of the survival strategy by which "early Christianity" became a "church," at the price of its expectation of the *parousia.* Overbeck resolutely disputes the idea that Christianity carried on in Jesus' footprints. Rather, Christianity lost its true Christian character and became nothing more than a constituent part of ancient culture when it converted the expectation of the *parousia* into the idea of the end of the world that will "someday" take place. One can wait quite peacefully for the end of the world; it doesn't need to disturb daily life. In this manner Overbeck criticizes both the church norm of his day and — more strongly — the *Kulturprotestantismus* of a liberal stamp. (This he also does in his polemical work *Concerning the Christlikeness of our Contemporary Theology*[10]).

Advocates of consistent eschatology, on the other hand, come to a different conclusion. The more Christianity attempted to exercise an influence in Jesus' sense, though detached from his pressing hope, the less it had to concern itself with apocalyptic thoughts.

---

10. F. Overbeck, *Über die Christlichkeit unserer heutigen Theologie,* 2d ed. (Leipzig, 1903; reprint, Darmstadt: Wissenschaftliche Buchgesellschaft, 1963).

Only in this way could Christianity follow Jesus: admittedly contrary to his hope, freed by his death from the excesses that made Jesus sacrifice himself — freed from hope of immediate divine intervention. Christian theology, then, grew out of the *transformation* of Jesus' failed expectation. Since Schweitzer, the cause for this gradual relaxation of Christian hope has been designated by the term *Parusieverzögerung* (delay of the *parousia*).[11]

The parallel within Roman Catholicism on the subject of consistent eschatology is the unwittingly ironic phrase used by the modernist Alfred Loisy (1857–1940): "Jesus annonçait le royaume, et c'est l'Église qui est venue" (Jesus foretold the kingdom, and it was the church that came).[12] The tradition of the church is the evolution of the gospel. Church dogma has developed beyond the gospel and its messianic idealization, searching to determine "its providential meaning, the universal scope, its transcendent efficacy."[13] But this realization changed the gospel. This is what the Protestant New Testament scholar Erik Peterson (1890–1960) addresses.[14] He refers specifically to the basis of consistent eschatology, to which Loisy alludes, explains the origin of the church through the failure of the eschatological expectations of the Jewish Christians, and converts to Roman Catholicism. A consistent consequence of consistent eschatology?

Berthold LANNERT, *Die Wiederentdeckung der neutestamentlichen Eschatologie durch Johannes Weiss* (Tübingen: Francke, 1989); Rolf SCHÄFER, "Das Reich Gottes bei Albrecht Ritschl und Johannes Weiss," *Zeitschrift für Theologie und Kirche* 61 (1964): 68–88.

2.3. What Remains of the Hope of Christ?

What significance does consistent eschatology have for a reconsideration of eschatology?

---

11. For the consequences for the history of doctrine, see, e.g., Martin Werner, *Die Entstehung des christlichen Dogmas, problemgeschichtlich dargestellt* (Bern: Paul Haupt; Tübingen: Katzmann-Verlag, 1941).

12. A. Loisy, *L'Évangile et l'Église* (Paris, 1902), 155 (ET: *The Gospel and the Church*, trans. Christopher Home [Philadelphia: Fortress Press, 1976], 166).

13. Loisy, *The Gospel and the Church*, 46.

14. E. Peterson, *Die Kirche* (Munich, 1929); reprint in *Theologische Traktate*, ed. Barbara Nichtweiß (Würzburg: Echter, 1994), 247–57.

To the present day, it has repeatedly been asserted[15] that consistent eschatology "rediscovered" the eschatological character of Jesus' message, and by doing so won back eschatology for the purposes of theology.

This initial observation may in fact be true as far as it concerns historical reconstruction of the New Testament prior to Albert Schweitzer and Johannes Weiss, particularly regarding the eighteenth- and nineteenth-century quest for the historical Jesus. The quest portrayed Jesus as a "human like you and I" but with some heroic, or at least exemplary, features. This image of Jesus was strongly corrected by Weiss and Schweitzer.[16] Consistent eschatology has, indeed, brought Jesus of Nazareth closer in his "foreign-ness," precisely in that aspect of his message that is distant for the modern reader and that therefore alienates him. This statement conforms to genuine historical research, which cannot just cut the documents it deals with to suit the shape of what is already known, let alone treat them merely as reflections of the spirit of their own age. But doesn't this last caveat apply just as much to consistent eschatology itself, at least in its deepest logic?

Weiss and Schweitzer contradict a developmental-historical eschatology and its farsighted certainty of knowledge concerning the final purpose of history. They make it clear that the end of Jesus' life, as well as the experiences of his followers in relation to their hope in him, speak against such farsightedness.

What now? Weiss contents himself with the statement that we can no longer hope as Jesus did; we have to live and act according to the prospect of a purified religious conception of the world.

---

15. See Rudolf Bultmann in his introduction to the reprint of Johannes Weiss, *Die Predigt Jesu vom Reiche Gottes*, ed. Ferdinand Hahn (Göttingen: Vandenhoeck & Ruprecht, 1964), v.

16. Not long after Weiss, Richard Kabisch represented Jewish eschatology as also being the center of Pauline theology. "The consciousness that *the whole of Christianity is a piece of eschatology* for Paul, who not only expected the end of the world order, but even the world's end from eschatology (from the appearance of the Lord), had the most profound effect on his wholly practical way of life." [Das Bewußtsein, daß das *ganze Christentum ein Stück Eschatologie* ist, (hat) für den Paulus, der nicht nur das Ende der Weltordnung, sondern der Welt Ende von der Eschatologie, von der Erscheinung des Herrn erwartet, auf seine ganze praktische Lebensrichtung die allertiefste Wirkung.] *Die Eschatologie des Paulus in ihren Zusammenhängen mit dem Gesamtbegriff des Paulinismus* (Göttingen: Vandenhoeck & Ruprecht, 1893), 317.

Schweitzer wishes to go in a different direction by closing the gaps between Jesus' expectation and our hope. He seeks to prove that Jesus' death itself obligates us to live in the power of Jesus' trust in God, and as far as possible to act meaningfully. The result of Schweitzer's thinking is the same as Weiss's, but Schweitzer's treatment is grounded more deeply.

Both, however, agree with significant points of the cultural-ethical outlook of Albrecht Ritschl and Ernst Troeltsch. Christians are, in memory of Jesus of Nazareth, called especially to work toward the perfecting of humanity in cultural development — but with the difference that Schweitzer no longer takes as his source Jesus of Nazareth's conception of the world and its future, but the consequences that can be drawn from his death. To Schweitzer the kingdom of God can no longer be the final purpose of the world. Apart from these differences of opinion, the protest of consistent eschatology against teleology of history remains a family argument within the house of theological liberalism. In the case of Johannes Weiss, the conflict is with his father-in-law, Albrecht Ritschl!

Consistent eschatology has had the effect for the New Testament of directing attention once more to the word "eschatology" — but it spotlights the peculiar cosmic-dramatic elements of Jesus' expectation only to store them in the history of religion's collection. For the overtime worked by the eschatological bureau, Jesus' consistent eschatology is now only necessary as far as it serves to declare futuristic views to be exaggerated, misleading, or obsolete.

For this reason, consistent eschatology extends the term "eschatology." Now it is used to describe almost every aspect of the New Testament though it may show, on closer perusal, no relationship to objects of hope, a temporal future, or a radically expectant discourse concerning God. The term "eschatology" has become a "black box," not to be looked into if it is to be used. This is also part of the inheritance left to us by consistent eschatology.

The eschatological bureau is busy because it can claim a right to use the trademark "eschatology" for every convincing historically supported opinion about the life of Christ. Consistent eschatology positions itself as the historically correct awareness that has definitively decoded Jesus' own state of consciousness. For this very reason, it allows people in cases of doubt to go different ways rather than to follow Jesus' own way, since the latter was evidently destined to fail.

Consistent eschatology understands itself in opposition to traditional dogmatic theology, particularly the cosmic characteristics of the doctrine of the last things. The destruction of the world and ensuing New Creation should be eliminated — without replacement — in favor of the *evolution of Christian responsibility*. In this way, consistent eschatology expropriates eschatology from the dogmatics that follows the tradition, and reclaims it for a reconstruction of the development of early Christian history that — so the theory runs — could only transitionally have been "consistently" eschatological.

Consistent eschatology, then, ushers us politely away from eschatology — and away from all the variant meanings of eschatology mentioned above[17] — instead of introducing us to it. And yet it nevertheless offers a lesson unusually rich in consequences for theology.

To what extent many of the ideological assumptions and methodological principles used by the advocates of consistent eschatology have come to nothing or proven obsolete need not concern us here. However, the concept of history should at least be mentioned — history as a coherence of facts, shaped by humanity with human values and purposes — in which expectations of the future within a framework of time are so defined that they are dependent on the fulfilling of predicted events.

This concept of history seems to make it possible to return to the "historical Jesus" and to claim his legacy as the legitimizing authority for piety. What Christians can believe, hope, think, and do *has* to be traceable to what was without doubt historical *fact* in the life of Jesus or to what can be shown to be a reconstructible motive for his actions. Weiss and Schweitzer have certainly contributed to rendering questionable any transference of contemporary character idealization onto Jesus of Nazareth. Jesus can no longer be seen as an inwardly mature self, reflecting on the conditions of life, supe-

---

17. Despite loud protests against German liberal Protestantism's theology of history, the suggestions of consistent eschatology remain within that framework — but come across as more tired and skeptical.

rior to the world because of his freedom, and immune to everyday adversity.

Another prejudice from consistent eschatology is still particularly hardy today: the idea that what humans believe and hope must find expression in what they do, and therefore that beliefs and hopes can be read from their actions or lack of action. Further, faith and hope have, strictly speaking, no object. Besides that, they depend on a worldview made up of conceptual "material" that can therefore be analyzed in its elements, elements that themselves can be placed in a fixed literary tradition and pursued back to their cultural origin. Religion and theology function as manufacturers of "conceptions of the world," and use new fabrics or different patterns to weave new results.

All this is of little help for eschatology. A guiding point for reconsidering eschatology is that consistent eschatology runs into difficulties when it attempts to follow the clues of Jesus' life right to the end. This is particularly evident in Schweitzer, who is more logical in this than his predecessors. His presentation should be considered once again:

Jesus of Nazareth set all his hopes, in an almost supernatural way, in an imminent intervention on the part of God that would bring a new world into being — and he brought his own life into play for the sake of this expectation, hoping to help bring God's new world into being, indeed to *force* God to act. In the process he himself, it is true, perished — *but his religious message did not,* since its roots are in community with God and shine even in the end of his life, communicated as the paradoxical fruit of his death.

Is Jesus, then, a *"bearer of hope"?*

Yes and no, answers Schweitzer. The lesson that he draws from the fate of Jesus runs as follows: anyone expecting God to intervene spectacularly in the fate of the world will fail. He must change that hope. He must place himself within the course of events, without, however, allowing himself to be controlled by them. Then, free from the world, he can have a meaningful effect in the world. Religious development needs this balance to prevent it from being derailed by false hopes. Only someone who reflects on his responsibilities and, further, who understands within which boundaries such responsibilities can hope to prosper, can contribute to the moral completion of the world and in doing so fulfill the task that God has given to every human being. With this insight, Schweitzer takes his leave from Jesus in the Garden of Gethsemane. At Golgotha, Schweitzer remains a spectator, and, having learned the lesson of the tragic end of Jesus' life, hastens speedily away.

The sum of Jesus' life and death according to consistent eschatology brings us to this conclusion: *We can no longer hope as Jesus hoped — but we can continue to work in his spirit.*

Is the statement an illuminating summary, which can open the way to a lot more? It has, anyway, come to be a widespread standard for Christian behavior. For that reason it is worthwhile to trace the thought-patterns of consistent eschatology, and to come to grips with them.

The slogan "Onward! in the spirit of Jesus!" admittedly has the effect of heading off the strongest critique of contemporary Christian "progressive" ideas. The thought of the "completion" or "perfection" of Christianity as Jesus understood it, and with it the "completion" of the world, is once more becoming somewhat dominant. Since consistent eschatology has connected hope in the kingdom of God to the achievements of Jesus' life, that hope is dashed to pieces by the cross. Now consistent eschatology clings to that death as if it were an insurmountable obstacle, and declares this death to be the foundation of enlightened behavior of good middle-class citizens, according to the maxim: "Act always so that you cannot be disappointed because you set your hopes too high." Schweitzer draws this logic from consistent eschatology, even if he did later find his way as a physician into the African jungle — a vocation representing anything but the behavior of a "good middle-class citizen."

2.4. Hoping for Christ

At this point, we face a crucial decision. The historical method (as used by Schweitzer) leads to the cross of Jesus, but can view his death only as the end of his life. Schweitzer wishes to pursue Jesus' life to its end, and to understand his death as the final event of his life. What happens to Jesus on Golgotha between God and Jesus remains beyond the perspective of history. Therefore consistent eschatology, in order to proceed further, passes the cross of Jesus at a respectful distance.

Consistent eschatology can only note Jesus' preaching of the kingdom of God insofar as it expresses *Jesus' hope.* At no point in the New Testament, however, is there any discussion of "Jesus' hope." This may be a coincidence. As far as the evangelists are concerned it seems clear that they wish to retell what Jesus proclaimed, including God's judgment (Matt. 5:12; 10:22), and what he brought before God in prayer. The evangelists, however, do not comment on Jesus' hope in relationship to his behavior.

Jesus proclaims the kingdom of God. This preaching is so closely bound to the person preaching that his execution inevitably raises the following question: *Has Jesus anything to do with the God that he proclaims, even and especially in his death?* Schweitzer also poses this question, but believes that only if God intervenes in world history in a wholly incalculable way can Jesus' hope be fulfilled, and his preaching endorsed.

Here lies the decisive question about Jesus Christ: *How do we perceive his death?* As a final attempt to bring his life to completion, to win meaning for his life despite all previous failures? This is how Schweitzer, following the methodology of the "quest for the historical Jesus," sees it. Or do we, faced with the cross of Jesus, take note of God's verdict on the truth of Jesus' proclamation, indeed on his *existence,* before and with God? Does God's will reveal itself through, with, and in what happens to Jesus Christ? If so, we are called to hope against hope, to believe in the one who brings the dead back to life, and who "calls into existence the things that do not exist" (Rom. 4:17). Anyone who agrees belongs in the ranks of those who say, in response to God's affirmation of God's promises in the person of Jesus Christ, "Amen! Yes — it is so!" (2 Cor. 1:20).

This is the theological ground for speaking of "hope *in* Christ" rather than the "hope *of* Christ" as the example of our hope. It is the name that is important — not just "Jesus of Nazareth," but "Jesus Christ," the one that God has made Christ, Messiah, in whom all hopes of deliverance and expectations of salvation are united. And for this reason there is also "hope *with* Jesus Christ," the hope that comes from accompanying him on his way — and that is not a path that somehow skirts death, but a route that leads *into* the death of Jesus itself.

A real "rediscovery" of Jesus' eschatological message and of the early Christian expectation of Christ must therefore reveal that all hopes only related to patterns of behavior were buried with the crucified Jesus. What Jesus hoped in cannot be portrayed as targets or purposes. Jesus Christ's death on the cross cuts off every hope for world-shaking action. In the unearthly silence following Jesus' cry from the cross there is a contradiction, a silent rejection of every intervention whose purpose is to build up, to bring about, or even to prepare a way for the kingdom of God.

Jesus' death on the cross contradicts religious hopes in a unique way. Schweitzer considered the warning against continuing to hope as Jesus did to be all that could be taken from the end of Jesus' life. Jesus Christ is, despite that conclusion, the "bearer of hope" because of his proclamation of the coming of God. In this way, *he becomes the bearer of hope, in that he takes humanity's hopes on himself, and carries them with his cross, frustrating the highest expectations for God's renewal of the world and redeemed life.* The crucified one does not only carry the sins of the world and in doing so take them away (John 1:29) — he also carries the expectations of the world. These hopes hang on the cross at Golgotha.

Looked at from the opposite angle, Paul considers remaining in sin and a hidden lack of hope, which will not hold to the Easter promise, to be closely related (1 Cor. 15:16–19). For this reason, Paul deduces from Christ's resurrection that the victor over sin and death determines the range and degree of our hope: "If for this life only we have hoped in Christ, we are of all people most to be pitied" (1 Cor. 15:19).[18] The most to be pitied? Is there not something decisive to be gained from a hope directed at "life's reality," a hope that is full of enthusiasm? Paul, in any case, sees the opposite. Anyone who only has hope for this world has passed by the empty tomb but doesn't see the resurrected one. Anyone who hopes only for his own life also passes by the crucified one and re-

---

18. Paul is not just trying to outbid a hope that lasts only for our lifetime by offering a hope that reaches beyond this life. "To hope in Christ" means a lot more — to be in him, to remain in him. If he had remained in death, that would also mean the end of those who believe in him.

turns to the normal daily agenda, as if nothing had happened. The misery of hope can only be measured in relation to what is promised and from what it turns away, whatever reasons lie behind that rejection.

In 1 Corinthians 15, the apostle turns against a pseudo-Christian hope that attempts to condense the expectation of Jesus Christ — that is, hope in Christ and, through that, in God — to mean merely a fulfilled life. All that remains in this view are the cooling ashes of eschatological ardor, in which the experience and expectation of salvation have been welded together. Paul's intention is not simply to encourage his audience to believe in an "afterlife" — rather, he sees Christian hope to be completely tied up with Jesus' resurrection. In the resurrection, God, on whom Jesus called, has established God's own divinity[19] and proved that God is Lord even over death. For this reason, Jesus' resurrection is the promise of our life with God; therefore, it is the foundation of our hope. This idea is found in the doxology of 1 Peter 1:3: "Blessed be the God and Father of our Lord Jesus Christ! By his great mercy we have been born anew to a living hope through the resurrection of Jesus Christ from the dead."

Albert Schweitzer was perfectly right. No continuing hope can be won from the demise of Jesus. However, Schweitzer comes to this conclusion because he fits the historical observation of Jesus' death into the scheme that he presupposes for Jesus of Nazareth and for all future generations. Since he judges hope to be an achievement of life and the staking of one's own life for the kingdom of God to be the most extreme exertion, he sees this hope irrevocably buried with Jesus. But we cannot look beyond the cross of Christ, let alone "get over it."

We are not able to pass by the cross of Jesus Christ, because God *judges* the dead Christ. God represents him as other than that which humanity sees. God cuts him off from everything that humanity has done to him, all the judgments that lead to his death, including the hopes, desires, and disappointments that were pinned to him — and who knows which of those things led him to perse-

---

19. That this action affects God's self was to become one of the themes of the patristic doctrines of the Trinity and of Christology.

cution and condemnation? But God gives saving affirmation of the path that the human Jesus took among humans. For this reason, the New Testament emphasizes that *the crucified Christ was not annihilated, but remains our hope.*

The resurrected one is, according to the continuous witness of the New Testament, the newly realized existence at God's side. This is not a further step but a new reality, and therefore also a different way. For this reason, it is not possible to add the events of Easter to the death on the cross, as if it were a simple matter of arithmetic: cross + resurrection = Jesus Christ. Rather, God's creative affirmation creates a new existence for the crucified Jesus Christ, for humanity. This affirmation is so final and all-embracing that from now on no hope in God can bypass Jesus Christ.

How is all this understood? The answer to God's affirmation of Jesus Christ, as it runs through the New Testament, is the voice of those broken and still becoming. The world order, for these individuals, comes irrevocably to an end, and they see themselves exposed to that end, with no alternative ideas to help them come to terms with the situation. The form of this world is passing away (1 Cor. 7:31) — the lines and the figures for orientation, the norms used to measure what is above and below, near and far, the notches for grasping hold of reality. The memory of Christ is included in what is passing away (see 2 Cor 5:16).

Jesus Christ must himself impart this memory to those who belong to him. He intervenes to convince Thomas, the skeptic. All that the disciple could deduce from the reports of his friends was that they had met with some sort of resuscitated corpse. He wished to be sure of that, to touch it. The resurrected one permits him to touch the wounds — but Thomas, who had only wanted to be sure of the identity of the Master, to be able to put his trust in him as he remembered him, suddenly recognizes that Jesus is the "wholly other." He stutters out the confession, "My Lord and my God!" (John 20:28). Only by seeing Jesus as the wholly other has Thomas recognized him.

That the disciples' ideals fall apart, leaving room for the figure of Jesus Christ to emerge — the resurrected one himself must bring that about. He meets two of his followers on their way to Emmaus, while they dwell on their disappointed messianic hopes: "But we had hoped that he was the one to redeem Israel" (Luke 24:21). Jesus replies: "Was it not necessary that the Messiah should suffer these things to enter into his glory?" (24:26). Then he interprets the scriptures for them, those that point toward Christ. Only later, when the disciples recognize the stranger as their teacher, do they ask, "Did not our hearts burn within us while...he opened to us the scriptures?" (24:32).

We would very much like to know the specific texts that Jesus might have quoted. But it is not a "proof" that is being considered, in which Christ is prophesied in arid words. The Law and the Prophets in their entirety are being considered as witness to the living will of God. With this act begins a new reading of the Holy Scriptures, and the New Testament is to a large extent a reflex of this reading.

To an outsider, this interpretation may seem like a violent confiscation of texts belonging to Judaism, aggressively reducing the Jewish holy scriptures to the common denominator of messianic expectation. This hermeneutic is further complicated by the fact that it is difficult to find an expectation from the Jewish scriptures that the coming of Jesus Christ simply affirms, without altering or reinterpreting the expectation. Because of this, one cannot approach Jewish scriptures as a checklist of items to be crossed off with the comment, "Done! Finished!" (see John 19:30). The reading of the Law and the Prophets in the light of Good Friday and Easter means, rather, that what God has *already* done and said must be learned anew (see Luke 24:27).

God's action in the crucified Christ is the decisive act, God's final word, which every discourse concerning God must now acknowledge. What is God's righteousness? How is the peace of God established? What is life, and what is death? Previous answers are now subject to the judgment of God spoken over Christ. In this act, the scriptures are "opened up" — disclosed as the declaration of the will of God, open for all. What had previously been important in the relation of God to God's people and to the Gentiles no longer exists. In this understanding the form of this world passes away; above all, it passes away in recognition of Jesus Christ. Judging Christ, the Messiah, according to the standards of the death-destined world is now past. Christ is not constrained by space or time — that is the meaning of the empty tomb. Whoever now recognizes Christ does not stand opposed to him, but is "in him"; he already belongs to the New Creation (2 Cor. 5:17).

2.5. Jesus Christ: The Final One, the Coming One

Behind the New Testament shines the event of the crucified Christ's resurrection, with its message of his "oneness," his unity with God. The biblical texts divide the event into a spectrum of many colors. And the more the scriptures remain transparent, allowing this message to shine through, the clearer they are as witnesses to hope.

In what the writers of the New Testament say, in what they put forward as arguments and responses to questions of lifestyle and orientation in time and space, they proclaim the death of Jesus "until he comes." This is how Paul (1 Cor. 11:26) characterizes the Lord's Supper, the table fellowship in which the community experiences the presence of Christ. Through this, the community is called to hope in Christ, and the community must perpetuate that hope in receiving and sharing the body and blood of Christ. Other forms of testifying to Jesus Christ equally proclaim his death, until he comes. It is not intended that Christ should be merely "proclaimed" — that is, declared, "shouted about" — for a period in which he cannot call attention to himself. Rather, the death of Jesus should be proclaimed. God did not simply take the one rejected by humanity out of humanity's hands, but rather gave him over to death, allowed him to die, and then, incomprehensibly, saved him, tore him away from death. In this way, God showed him to be the Coming One. The Jewish term "Messiah" means now for Jesus' followers the one who lives entirely in God's way, wholly removed from the grasp of humanity, but equally devoted to humanity.

That Christ is coming does not mean that he is not "here." But what does "being here," as referred to by the New Testament, actually *mean?*

2.5.1. Expectation as Confession of Christ

Jesus Christ is referred to as being at God's side, because God stood by him. He is one with God, without being absorbed into God.

In Revelation 1:8, God is referred to as the one "who was, who is, and who is to come," and a little later in the terrifying vision Jesus speaks, in much the same words: "Fear not, I am the first and the last, and the living one; I died, and behold I am alive for evermore, and I have the keys of Death and Hades" (1:17–18). The last one, the *eschatos, comes as the Savior.* He comes and saves, but only in God's own way. Christians have to be prepared for this unexpected, unhoped-for way of transformation, and therefore they must exist in a state of expectation of the coming. They become transformed *into* the hope of Jesus Christ, called to the way that Jesus himself went, full of expectation, which is now the way to Jesus Christ himself.

The New Testament is intended to be read with this expectation of Christ in mind, and to be a witness leading ever more deeply and intensively into the "hope against all expectation" (Rom. 4:18). This hope cannot be anticipated. On the contrary, its promise sharpens the sense of what is to come, or rather of the *one who is to come.* What points the way is by no means what lies in the future, or a summing-up of history, but everything that, in Jesus Christ, has finally, definitively, been promised — as promised to humanity in the proclamation of his death and the power of his resurrection.

The "one who is to come" and the "final one": these are not the sole predicates of Christ, and therefore may not be allowed to be considered by themselves, leading to one-sided discourse concerning Christ. But they may not be pushed aside or relegated to the sidelines of theology. Understanding eschatology depends heavily on not dealing merely with some kind of *eschaton* (end) or *eschata* (last things) existing on the horizon of theology — whether that horizon appears to be near or far — but on treating Jesus Christ as the *eschatos,* and, ultimately, on a consideration of God. To God alone does Jesus Christ subordinate everything, including himself, so that God may be all in all (1 Cor. 15:28).

The consequences for Christology should only be touched on here. The theology of the early church was to a large extent tied to the question, "Who is Jesus Christ in relation to God?" After long internal and external struggles for clarification, the answer that earlier theologians came up with was the statement that Jesus

Christ is true human and true God, "really [*alēthēs*] God and really human being" (Definition of Chalcedon, 451), "of the same essence [reality] with the Father" (Nicene Creed/Creed of Constantinople, 325/381). This is how the "*coming of Christ* for our salvation" was paraphrased.

In a certain sense, this is an answer to the question which John the Baptist's disciples directed at Jesus: "Are you he who is to come, or shall we look for another?" (Matt. 11:3; Luke 7:19–20). Jesus does not answer with a simple "yes" or "no" — he points instead to what has come to pass through his preaching and his actions, and adds, "Blessed is he who takes no offense at me" (Luke 7:23), referring to the way in which he acts for humanity.

When the evangelists relate this story, readers and listeners feel that they are asked how *they* would answer. Would they say, "Yes, you are indeed he who is to come"? Or would they have to confess that they are waiting for someone, or something, else? Or do they secretly belong to those who hail Jesus as "the one who is to come" when he enters Jerusalem, and hold out the symbols of their hope for peace and perfection (Matt. 21:8–10), but then desert him at Golgotha, their hopes bitterly disappointed; they will turn away from him, and perhaps even mock him. Thus the hopes that they direct toward God are put to the test!

The crucified one as the "one who is to come," who brings in the time of salvation — that is a scandal that can scarcely be reconciled with any known expectation of salvation and perfection. If he, and no other, is the Savior, that means that humanity can only be saved the way he was saved, through which he became the Savior. He has, as expressed in Hebrews, followed the path that he was led along and on which he was brought back from the dead (Heb. 12:2–3; 13:20). On this path he *remains the Coming One* and is the Final One; we can expect nothing from God greater than him.

This is what the early church's Christologies were trying to convey in their own ways and with their linguistic resources. Certainly, their discourse concerning the Coming One remains colorless and more limited than what was laid out in the New Testament. Jesus Christ is "the one who will come, to judge the living and the dead" (Apostles' Creed). This sounds like a return from tempo-

rary absence, a return for the crowning end — and leaves open
the question of what lies between, what could happen in the
meantime.

In John, where Jesus' "coming and going" is a crucial, recurring
theme, the idea is more concise. Jesus will come again. That is, he
will come "anew," when he has prepared the place for his followers, "that where I am you may be also" (John 14:3). Concerning
the disciple that Jesus loved, Jesus expresses a hypothetical wish
for him "to remain until I come" (John 21:22). The evangelist re-
marks that this statement was misunderstood as a promise that the
disciple would not die before Jesus came. But this, it is explained, is
not what Jesus promised (21:23). Every additional question is thus
ruled out. When Jesus Christ promises his coming he promises not
to leave his followers, whatever may happen.

The title of Coming One for Jesus Christ is not an appendix
to Christology that can be surgically removed if it starts to cause
discomfort. Rather, the title forms Christology as a whole. Without eschatology, Christology would not only be incomplete, but it
would run the risk — as can be seen in many examples taken from
the history of theology — of limiting the coming of Jesus Christ
to history, simply looking at his legacy and how humanity can
use it.

Eschatology does not add a conclusive chapter to Christology,
but contributes to the expectation of Jesus Christ as the one to
come. It therefore shapes Christology, without smoothing it out or
giving it a more manageable form. *The task of eschatology is to
keep alive the question, "Are you the one who is to come?"* Eschatology may neither suppress this continual, pressing, and irritating
question, nor dramatize it by providing misleading expectations.
Eschatology should teach and above all consider what form an
answer can take.

Let us compare this task once more with the details of consistent eschatology. Consistent eschatology is the swan song of
Leben-Jesu-Forschung, of the quest for the historical Jesus. It is
the method's final lamentation, even if some would be inclined to
praise consistent eschatology as the overture to a new theological
direction. The question of the historical Jesus is designed to replace
early church Christologies by going to the historical foundations,

to Jesus of Nazareth without theological whitewash, to the picture of Jesus provided to the observer and that speaks to him or her directly. Albert Schweitzer's *Quest of the Historical Jesus* itself shows and embodies the fact that this picture of Jesus is too often just a mirror of the observer's own expectations — the portrait of his or her idealistic vision of an exemplary man, in touch in every way with God. Jesus virtually becomes a projection of religious hope, the expectation for human beings in their behavior and relationship to God. Weiss and Schweitzer came to the opposite conclusion. Jesus is *not* close to modern humanity, but is distant precisely *because* of his strange and alien hope. That the meaning of Jesus for the present can only be preserved if Jesus' strange hope is abandoned — and that that hope was what logically gave rise to his death — is what Schweitzer wanted to prove beyond anything else.

Consistent eschatology works with the theme that New Testament theology grew above all out of the process of overcoming the disappointment of immediate expectation. This "crisis management" had its beginnings in the early church and led to its theology. Jesus' announcement that the end-events would take place within the lifetime of his disciples (Mark 13:30; Matt. 16:28) constitutes the key to this development theory. For the young Christian community, the announcement spurred an expectation of the *parousia*. The community finally freed itself of this immediate expectation, relaxed and contented itself with the spirit of Jesus, because it felt this spirit would be enough to lead to "perfection," and so to progress. Thus was the Christology tied to an imminent *parousia* abandoned.

Even if the "information" presented by consistent eschatology is somewhat threadbare, and leaves easily discernible the marks of "crisis management" designed to defend contemporary German liberal Protestantism, its strength is that it does not pass over unwieldy texts such as Mark 13:30: "Truly I tell you, this generation will not pass away until all these things have taken place." It is right to ask about the state of the hope of Christianity when it can no longer deal with these words of Jesus. Many would be content with the explanation that it is part of Jesus' true humanity that he should be subject to a contemporary conception of the world and its expectation of an immediate cosmic catastrophe,[20] according to the adage, "to err is human, to forgive, divine."

The center of the critical questioning for which consistent eschatology sees itself as advocate is not, however, to be found in the time factor of immediate expectation[21] — what is expected becomes invalid if it doesn't happen immediately — but in the *content of the hope*, which in consistent eschatology is presumed unquestionable. The hope is the claim that Jesus proclaimed a salvation in which the world falls apart. Since this event did not arrive, it can no longer be hoped for.

Consistent eschatology leads us to believe that imminent expectation has to die out, and for that reason we can no longer expect anything. All we can do is follow the prospects that the life of Jesus has left.

Let us look at the question: *What is different after the crucifixion, and how different is it?* Opinions differ on this question, and from this point paths diverge.

Between Good Friday and Easter, nothing seems to have changed. The empty tomb — the open wound of the world — is eliminated. Humanity forgets the scar and gets on with the daily agenda. But not all humanity. Despite the fact that the world remains the same, one small group of humans searches for traces of Jesus. The search changes them, and in the long term could change the face of the world.

This perspective points to a decisive either-or. If salvation is something that should visibly, palpably, and with universal effect reshape the world, then we must wait for it anew, *unless* we give up that hope because it is exaggerated or too external. We instead could content ourselves with what remains of Jesus, particularly

---

20. See Leonardo Boff, *Vida para além da morte* (N.p.: Editora Vozes Ltda., n.d.) (German translation: *Was kommt nachher? Das Leben nach dem Tode*, trans. Horst Goldstein [Salzburg: Otto Müller, 1982], 100–101).

21. Werner Georg Kümmel relativizes this: "The imminent expectation [*Naherwartung*] is . . . not merely the timebound form of expression for the certainty of the present beginning of God's rule; rather Jesus speaks within the conceptions of his age of the *nearness* of God's rule, so as by it to establish *under current circumstances* the certainty of the completion of the intended saving action of God" (*Verheißung und Erfüllung: Untersuchungen zur eschatologischen Verkündigung Jesu*, 3d ed. [Zurich: Zwingli Verlag, 1956], 144).

with the warmth of his love. "Onward in the spirit of Jesus!" can then be the refrain.

Waiting for salvation anew would have the effect of tying Christian eschatology once more to Jewish messianism,[22] in order to recover both stability and vigor. Consistent eschatology points in the other direction. A compromise would, however, also be conceivable, if it kept hold of the expectation of salvation — perhaps with reference to 2 Peter 3:13[23] — but in the main insisted that the decisive salvific event had already happened. In Jesus Christ salvation has appeared. Humans have been saved — even beyond the boundaries of the "old" people of God — and can be certain of resurrection to eternal life. They can be certain even if this "completion," along with the fulfillment of all other expectations, remains to be hoped for. Is this compromise not the norm in Christian theology?

Consistent eschatology refuses to content itself with this compromise — and that is good. Insisting on the ideological framework it discovers surrounding the historical Jesus and his proclamation of the kingdom of God, it repeats the question, "What has changed, and how?" Consistent eschatology intensifies the question further by allowing a *change of consciousness* to count as an alternative to the *world-scale catastrophe* that is awaited in vain. The world has not changed — who can deny that? But since Jesus, humans have been able to live and die differently. Their attitude to the world has changed drastically. On the basis of this change of attitude, they can bring about much that leads to long-term spiritual, social, cultural, and political change. Change is achieved, even if not suddenly and overwhelmingly. Christianity becomes an "assistant" to eschatology.

The external world has not changed. What has changed is the inward nature of men and women who have come to maturity through Jesus' death. With this information gleaned from enlightened eschatology, schematizations are unavoidable. One from von

---

22. Friedrich-Wilhelm Marquardt pleads for this in his work, *Was dürfen wir hoffen, wenn wir hoffen dürften? Eine Eschatologie*, 3 vols. (Gütersloh: Chr. Kaiser/Gütersloher Verlagshaus, 1993–96).

23. "But according to his promise we wait for new heavens and a new earth in which righteousness dwells."

Harnack was cited earlier: God's kingdom comes "inwardly," he wrote, and the external concept of expectation for the future is gone. On the other hand, the realism — not to mention material-ism — of the biblical expectation of the kingdom of God can be used to attack his explanation. Such a dilemma was not created by consistent eschatology, but consistent eschatology has allowed it to gain prominence: One must either hope as Jesus hoped, attempt to force convulsive changes, and fail. Or one must act in the spirit of Jesus and reshape hopeless relationships inwardly.

This either-or seems as old as Christianity. It has lasted at least as long as we have used the named schematization to interpret the New Testament and later Christian writings. If the texts are read using this conceptual framework, they cannot easily present any other conclusion. Impartiality, or, put differently, a developed awareness for theology, is necessary if one is not to be led by these schematizations. That exegetical and systematic theological literature is full of these schematizations[24] only promotes linguistic confusion. Yet it must be considered that although the expectation of Christ has indeed been, both in early Christianity and now, a problem for Christian churches and for their theology, it has never, as far as we know, led to a fundamental crisis. Schweitzer seems to be unaware of this; at least he does not respect the complex tradition of Christian eschatology.[25] From his point of view, the Christian church simply transformed the initial imminent expecta-tion of the end of the world into a mere dogmatic statement about last things. Therefore, the church was not aware of the thin ice on which it had been skating through eighteen centuries. There is a ballad told by the German poet Gustav Schwab (1792–1850) of a rider who traveled safely across the frozen Lake Constance. Though safe on the solid ground of the opposite shore, he died of shock when he realized the danger from the thin ice over which he had already passed. A comparison can be made to Schweitzer's and others' "cultural historical" understanding of the church: The

---

24. See Albrecht Oepke, "Parousía, páreimi," in *Theological Dictionary of the New Testament,* ed. Gerhard Friedrich, trans. Geoffrey W. Bromiley (Grand Rapids, Mich.: Eerdmans, 1967), 5:858–71.

25. Gerhard Sauter, "Eschatologie IV. Dogmengeschichtlich," forthcoming in *Religion in Geschichte und Gegenwart,* ed. Hans Dieter Betz et al., vol. 2 (Tübingen: J. C. B. Mohr, 1999).

church had gone through eighteen centuries of apparently solidly frozen expectations regarding the return of Christ. Though the church had now made it safely to the saving shores of a "cultural historical" eschatology, it might now die upon realizing the danger from which it was now delivered.

It has, however, often been difficult to keep the church on the right course of hope in Christ. Two typical deviations into extremism are found in the New Testament itself. There is first the question that lies closest to the problem of consistent eschatology: "Where is the promise of his coming? For ever since the fathers fell asleep, all things have continued as they were from the beginning of creation" (2 Pet. 3:4). The author of this letter imputes to the questioners unfair intentions — he considers that they are led by their passions — but perhaps they really do suffer in this respect. Second, one finds the assertion that the resurrection has already happened, which is branded as a false teaching in 2 Tim. 2:18. It is said that the resurrection can be found in what has been granted to those who believe in Christ, and that they need not expect anything more. Faith is turned around by this assertion. Every hope becomes invalid unless it is built within the boundaries of what one can hope to achieve.

The first error searches for the purely futuristic. What is expected is the "wholly other" — measured by what has always been and still remains. The "wholly other" to come would be the equivalent of "what has never been," and would be designed to remove everything that had existed up to the present. Yet what is to come is measured according to what has always been, in that what has always been is the standard for determining its opposite. The second erroneous approach circles around the ecstatic, immortal present and suns itself in its own fulfillment. This extinguishing of hope in saturated sleep rates, in the New Testament, as the most extreme danger to faith, more seductive even than the previously mentioned aberration, which nevertheless roots itself to "what remains."

The swallowing-up of hope is described in all its paralyzing consequences: hunger for power, opinionatedness, egocentricity, lack of feeling, and withdrawal into self-fulfillment (2 Tim. 3:1–5). The list goes further than the resignation, lethargy, or escapism that might characterize lack of hope these days. Lack of hope denies

the action of God in the crucified Jesus Christ. It dissolves all
relationship to space and time.

This can be said with such definite and far-reaching effects because *hope belongs inalienably to the lordship of Jesus Christ and
to his victory over the powers of corruption.* Hope is the gift
granted to those who belong to him. For that reason hope is the
absolute positive — neither a changeable mood, nor an orientation
toward indefinite time, nor the power that comes from wishing.
Christ's hope does not leave us with the ambiguity of hopes born of
desires and disappointments. It is rather the place sought by those
who "have fled for refuge . . . to seize the hope set before us. We
have this as a sure and steadfast anchor of the soul, a hope that
enters into the inner shrine behind the curtain" (Heb. 6:18–19).
What Christ has given drives us to hope — to hope in him! Hope,
therefore, does not bridge the gap between present and future; it
does not simply allow life to carry on, by preventing stasis or regression. Rather, hope reaches into the present, into *today,* to open
it for the full dimension of what God intends.

2.5.2. The Sending of the Spirit at the End of the World

The "absolute positive" has a name: the *Spirit of God.* It is experienced as the promise of Christ, sealed by his death and empowered
through his resurrection, of his presence and his second coming
(*parousia*).

The Spirit that Jesus promises "will teach you all things, and
bring to your remembrance all that I have said to you" (John
14:26). It makes sure of Jesus' words, not just by jogging the disciples' memories and saving the memory of Jesus from oblivion.
This is the promise that remains with the disciples and stays with
them at all times. The Spirit does not need to "reactivate" anything, or to conjure up a blissful past, since "he will guide you into
all the truth . . . and he will declare to you the things that are to
come" (John 16:13). *The Spirit will bring to perfection what Jesus
has accomplished.* The Spirit will "convince the world concerning
sin and righteousness and judgment: concerning sin, because they
do not believe in me; concerning righteousness, because I go to
the Father, and you will see me no more; concerning judgment,
because the ruler of this world is judged" (John 16:8–11). The

statement represents an unexpected new outline of familiar concepts, portraying sin as failures and mistakes that are to be brought back to order, righteousness as an embodiment of the perfected social world, and judgment as the divine weighing and reckoning. What these concepts meant previously does not count. The end has irrevocably come!

With the coming of the Spirit who keeps Jesus' promise comes another promise, that Christ will be glorified (John 16:14). But it is necessary first that Jesus "goes to the Father." This sounds almost as though Jesus stands between God and humanity, and therefore that he must disappear from the scene after having removed obstacles on the path to God. Going to the Father, however, is part of his way — in it, his oneness with God is perfected. This oneness is communicated by the Spirit. The Spirit is "all ears" for what comes from God and what leads to God (John 16:13–15). Therefore, *God's Spirit,* who comes to humanity, is the *gift of hope,* because the Spirit brings hope to, and unites hope with, what is of God. Precisely because of this action, the Spirit *remains* the gift of hope in God. The Spirit does not merely constitute a relationship between God and humanity. The Spirit makes us aware of what Jesus said and did in a way we could never build from reference to the historical Jesus. For this reason, the existence of Jesus is not limited to memories. It is only in the coming of the Spirit that Jesus' words, his works, and the character of his death — indeed Jesus himself — are opened and made accessible. For the message of Jesus' death is not to be drawn from his dying, nor from the circumstances that led to his execution, nor from the intentions of the men who caused it, nor from Jesus' presumed ambitions and from others' reactions to those ambitions. The message must be spoken and confirmed; for that, the Spirit is necessary, God is necessary. Only God can pronounce the divine verdict over Jesus' existence.

For this reason, references to the role of the Spirit in John do not announce a time for the Spirit "after Christ." Historical epochs are not part of the discussion. He who comes is marked only in relation to that which is no more.

With a slightly different nuance, Hebrews 9:26 speaks of Jesus being sacrificed once and for all "at the end of the age" to take away the sins of the world. He will come again "to save those who are eagerly waiting for him" (Heb. 9:28; cf. 10:37). This end does not correspond with traditional concepts of the end of the world that may form the horizon of expectation for many readers today. The end of the world cannot be defined by naming what must give way before God can come. Nor can "completion" be defined by the imaged "perfection" for which, deep inside, we long. And even less is the end the crowning balance of all that effort can achieve, which requires only God's favorable acknowledgment. The end is shown in Jesus' death and resurrection and can neither be repeated nor sublimated into a transition to a different spiritual state.[26] On Golgotha, the world order ends, as indicated by the evangelist Matthew. Heaven holds its breath, the earth trembles, the stones themselves shatter. The world can neither contain the Son of God, nor exclude him. What had seemed part of the eternal order is torn apart. The temple curtain is rent asunder, revealing the darkness of the Holy of Holies — and the emptiness. Whoever is looking for God should look to the crucified Son of God, who is recognized by a pagan (Matt. 27:51–54; Mark 15:39).

What no longer matters is separated from what is *true and therefore remains*. The new beginning defines the end of what had existed previously. No one in whom this new beginning has been consummated can return to the previous state, just as no one can return to the state before birth. Therefore Christians praise God as the one who has brought them through a new birth to living hope through the resurrection of Jesus Christ from the dead (1 Pet. 1:3). Nothing is as it used to be.

Paul describes the gift of the Spirit as the guarantee of incomparable future glory that will have no need to make up for past misery (2 Cor. 1:22; 5:5; Rom. 8:23). God's binding commitment is the promised Spirit, the "seal" that places believers under God's protection, the "down payment" for the *promised* inheritance (Heb. 9:15). Gentiles become co-heirs of the promises made to the people of God. Through Jesus' death, their alienation from

---

26. See on this subject Dale C. Allison, Jr., *The End of the Ages Has Come: An Early Interpretation of the Passion and the Resurrection of Jesus* (Philadelphia: Fortress Press, 1985).

God and enmity toward Israel are erased. They are freed from god-lessness and lack of hope (Eph. 2:12). This inheritance is not a tradition that one merely makes one's own, nor is it an attitude of expectation. Whoever has been declared an heir is now a member of the household of God. Being an heir means inviolable "belong-ing." The inheritance — unless specifically withdrawn — cannot be lost in the long term, even through misbehavior.

Experience of the Spirit has awakened hope in Christ, which is the hope of faith. The question of the "when" of Christ's *parousia* is not warded off, but the question does not lead to a crisis. However, crisis is only prevented as long as Spirit does not come to replace hope. The latter case presents the misunderstanding that experience of the Spirit has to balance a loss of confidence. Spirit is, however, the form of God's action in a world marked by the death of Christ. The face of the world changes, and its form becomes obsolete in making way for God's creative will. God's ultimate, all-embracing will is no longer contested by creaturely selfishness. With the Spirit, God intervenes and creates a wholly new situation in his relationship to the world and to humanity — not just to the chosen few.

"What has changed? And how much has it changed?" So run the suggestive and vexed questions advanced by consistent escha-tology. Consistent eschatology did not invent the questions — they are inevitable if an end is to be conceived, and if this hereafter is to be "the other" in relation to the here and now. God's Spirit, however, is also experienced as "the other." The Spirit lends an *intuitive sense* that God is other than our expectations. There is no longer time nor space to think about what might happen. The Spirit gives the strength to be *prepared* and to keep one's eyes open. To use New Testament terminology of hope in Christ, the Spirit grants us the capacity to "watch." Vigilance only makes sense if a startling and unpredictable coming is to be expected. "The day of the Lord will come like a thief in the night" (1 Thess. 5:2; 2 Pet. 3:10; see Matt. 24:43). Therefore, "besides this you know what hour it is, how it is full time now for you to wake from sleep. For salvation is nearer [!] to us now than when we first believed; the night is far gone, the day is at hand" (Rom. 13:11–12).

Preparation does not entail general openness, which would im-

ply an attitude of "always being ready,"[27] or — even worse — make
it imperative to be constantly awake, a sleep deprivation that could
become torture. The state of readiness involved in expectation of
Christ is rather directed toward God's action as revealed in and
through Jesus Christ, conveyed as promise. *Hope is therefore an-
chored in its context in God's action.* The Spirit enables awareness
of the correlation of God's action in creation and redemption, of
the sending of Jesus Christ into the world, of his death, resurrection, majesty at the right hand of the Father, action in judgment
and salvation, and necessary coming.

As gift of hope, the Spirit forms human awareness, which can
glimpse other dimensions than those glimpsed by memories and
foresight. The field of perception is thus broadened and given new
horizons. Suffering that had previously been tolerated or overlooked comes to light. The cry is heard, the plea of a creation
caught in emptiness, a creation calling for salvation and not just
for solutions (Rom. 8:22–23). "World" can be differentiated from
"creation" without the two being separated. "World," caught up
in itself, capable of rebelling against God and contesting its own
rights to ownership, becomes obsolete. Anyone aware of "creation" looks to the creator, who defends the creator's rights over
everything through action that reshapes creation. "New creation"
is no longer coupled to destruction of the world, but is the symbol
of "being in Christ" (2 Cor. 5:17). The Spirit prepares us for unity
with God, for the community from which the Spirit comes and in
which the Spirit finds fulfillment.

"Experience of the Spirit" is a helpful piece of terminology,
meaning a reality that cannot be thought up. God's Spirit fills humans so they can no longer remain alone, imprisoned in their own
ecstatic powers. Therefore, to give account for the hope that fills
you (1 Pet. 3:15) means to appeal to God's Spirit and not to one's
self. The call to reckoning is preceded by the cry, "In your hearts
reverence Christ as Lord!"

What can be said about the Spirit as gift of hope is found in

---

27. Günter Klein speaks of a "transformation of imminent expectation into 'always being prepared' (*Stetsbereitschaft*)," "Eschatologie IV: Neues Testament," in
Theologische Realenzyklopädie, ed. Gerhard Krause and Gerhard Müller (Berlin
and New York: Walter de Gruyter, 1982), 10:270–99; quotation is from p. 296.

doctrinal elements already present in the New Testament. Doctrine is necessary for the orientation of Christian living, for the sake of clarity of hope. As the heart of the gospel's origin is the person of Jesus himself, necessitating a narrative dealing with him as the "one who is here," so the heart of Christian dogma is the remembrance of the death of Christ "until he comes." Dogma points toward Jesus' coming but without setting down ideas that must be carried out. Just as it was necessary for the Gospels to question who Jesus really was, so it is necessary for theological dogma to say who Jesus really *is.*

These doctrinal elements, the beginnings of which are recognizable in the New Testament, admittedly do not correspond to the building blocks of eschatology as the subject has so far been introduced. Anyone trying to prove a New Testament eschatology transfers the variant meanings sketched in chapter 1 to the biblical texts, creating more puzzles than he or she solves. The impression could be given that theological dogma can be traced to historical bases, to traditions that in history came to be developed and of necessity reformed. In the question of the biblical reasons for hope, however, we encounter something completely different — the terra incognita that lies between Good Friday and the confession of the Christian community: "We await..." It was not that the hope of Jesus' followers went astray for those three days, after which they were able — miraculously — to hope that the expected world-scale catastrophe would come to pass after a delay, and that it would bring Jesus with it. It is also not the case that the disciples decided after Jesus' death that they had to carry on his cause in his Spirit.

What do we know about the time between Jesus' death and the confession of hope in the New Testament? The Easter narratives hardly answer this question — on the contrary, they lend it increased urgency. What happened when the disciples encountered a Jesus who met them yet who, at the same time, was removed from them? How do the nuances of these stories present themselves in humanity and in what we see in communities united in faith, whose hope does not derive from traditional hopes? Even if the Christian confession of faith came to remember certain expectations, *the faith did not come into being through those expectations.*

Doctrine that clarifies the inner logic of the Christian confession of faith does not intend to overcome embarrassments or deficits. The doctrine is too weak for that. It would be easier to say that God wished to cause a change in consciousness through Christ, or to say that humanity's lack of energy for radical change is to blame for the awaited future not having come to pass. This either-or option presented by consistent eschatology is not a solution to the problem; on the contrary, it poses its own question about *how* ultimate questions should be asked.

Study of the New Testament leads to eschatology, as far as it creates familiarity with the insoluble *inner tensions* that pervade the texts. The texts demonstrate the inconsequential nature of: what no longer is in the light of what is coming to be; the passage of time in the visible world in the light of the unexpected way in which God acts; the tendency to cling to certainties on the way in the light of the symbols of hope.

Zachery HAYES, *Visions of a Future: A Study of Christian Eschatology* (Wilmington, Del.: Michael Glazier, 1989); Anthony A. HOEKEMA, *The Bible and the Future* (1979; Grand Rapids, Mich.: Eerdmans, 1991); idem, *Zukunftserwartung in biblischer Sicht: Beiträge zur Eschatologie*, ed. Gerhard Maier (Wuppertal: Brockhaus, 1984); idem, *Eschatology and the New Testament: Essays in Honor of G. R. Beasley-Murray*, ed. W. Hulittgloer (Peabody, Mass.: Hendrickson, 1988); Petr POKORNÝ, *Die Zukunft des Glaubens: Sechs Kapitel über Eschatologie* (Stuttgart: Calwer Verlag, 1992); Ben WITHERINGTON III, *Jesus, Paul, and the End of the World: A Comparative Study in New Testament Eschatology* (Downers Grove, Ill.: InterVarsity Press, 1992).

2.5.3. *The Unheard-of Surprise of the Kingdom of God*

Let us deal specifically with one component of Jesus' proclamation — the kingdom of God — considering the parables that Johannes Weiss, for example, passes over with suspicious ease. In his presentation of Jesus' proclamation of the kingdom of God, Weiss in fact refers only to the parables as examples of the "effusions of a soul buffeted by storms and battles."[28] The parables, Weiss writes, attempt to express the fact that God will soon appear to establish God's rule

28. J. Weiss, *Die Predigt Jesu vom Reiche Gottes*, ed. Ferdinand Hahn (Göttingen: Vandenhoeck & Ruprecht, 1964), 53. See the English translation of the first edition, *Jesus' Proclamation of the Kingdom of God* (1892) (Chico, Calif.: Scholars Press, 1985), 78–79: "[T]hese are moments of sublime prophetic enthusiasm, when an awareness of victory comes over him. It is noteworthy that these expressions are uttered in a context of fiercely hostile attack, and in response to scoffing questions (Luke 17:20 [Matt. 12:25])."

and to conquer God's enemies, who at present hold this world in their thrall. Even in his parables — according to Weiss — Jesus wishes to stress the contrast between this world and the next world, and by doing so to prepare for a future which he, in moments of prophetic enthusiasm, feels has already dawned.

The opposite position is held by Charles Harold Dodd (1884– 1973). He designates Jesus' proclamation of the kingdom of God as *realized eschatology,* as eschatology that has become reality. For Dodd, Jesus' proclamation has less to do with perfection, with fully achieved realization, than with the fact that divine *reality* has actually appeared. God confronts humanity. God steps out of a distant dwelling, and humanity comes to feel God's powerful sovereignty:

> Something has happened, which has not happened before, and which means that the sovereign power of God has come into effective operation. It is not a matter of having God for your King in the sense that you obey His commandments: it is a matter of being confronted with the power of God at work in the world. In other words, the "eschatological" kingdom of God is proclaimed as a present fact, which men must recognize, whether by their actions they accept or reject it.[29]

What is eschatological is "the wholly other." The eschatological rule of God is God's judgment and salvation which humanity has until now been awaiting. In Jesus' proclamation, these events have been realized. "Realized eschatology" means that the powers of the future world are gradually "realized," made real, as a series of unprecedented and unrepeatable events in Jesus' activity.[30] Humanity must come to terms with this fact and can no longer evade it.

Why does Dodd name this event, in which eternity breaks into time without being absorbed into it, "realized eschatology"? It is a symptom of the fact that the word "eschatology" is already so hackneyed, so worn out, that it can be virtually synonymous with "salvation." In that case, all that remains is the question — and Dodd answers in the affirmative — whether salvation is "here." Behind this question, however, lies the differentiation between the

---

29. C. H. Dodd, *The Parables of the Kingdom* (1935; Glasgow: Collins, 1988), 36.
30. Ibid., 41.

absolute and the historically relative, between eternity and time, between idea and appearance. What is presented in the Gospels as temporal progression can only be a symbolic representation of eternal realities. Salvation cannot exhaust itself in historical event, and therefore salvation exists in the "here" and the "to come." What is considered "earlier" or "later," when confronted with eternity without change, is not important. What matters is that what happens is of eternal validity.

"Realized eschatology" is therefore a monstrous term that hides the fact that eschatology no longer has to do with the future. The future appears as a boundary of the world of experience, surrounded by eternity, shrouded by eternity as the earth is shrouded by its atmosphere. Therefore Dodd does not have to argue whether realized eschatology involves a fully accomplished event or an event in the process of being accomplished, or whether he is thinking of an act or a process. He means both, and could for that reason accept the amendment to the term suggested by Ernst Haenchen, *sich realisierende Eschatologie*[31] — eschatology in the process of being realized. The term, however, is not any clearer. How is an eschatology supposed to "realize itself"?

One can find fault with Dodd's explanations in that they interpret the New Testament using Platonic modes of thought, which have particular associations in the English linguistic field. The terms "this" and "the other" world translate into time and eternity. God's power is taken as the Absolute, the coming of God as a crisis experience, and the eschaton as a point of decision that can take place over and over again. However valid this objection, it points to a deep-rooted problem, which even the early church attempted to answer using Platonic thought. How is it possible to bridge the chasm between Jesus' proclamation of the kingdom of God and the church's representation of that proclamation? Can we, *may* we, still expect the kingdom of God in such a way that "its expected coming closes the long vista of the future"?[32] Given Jesus' proclamation of the proximity of the kingdom of God and Jesus'

---

31. Taken up by Joachim Jeremias, *The Parables of Jesus*, trans. S. H. Hooke (New York: Charles Scribner's Sons, 1963), 230.
32. Dodd, *The Parables of the Kingdom*, 40.

parables about the kingdom of God, is there a waiting period before it is realized? The problem evidently ceases to exist if Jesus were announcing an eschaton in which eternity and time, transcendence and immanence, come into contact with each other in such a way as to bring about a "now" that cannot be marked on a time line. Confronted with eternity, the difference between the arrival of the kingdom "earlier" or "later" would be insignificant.

This interpretation would mean that Jesus had broken through familiar conceptions of time — provided that he did not simply fall prey to a fundamental error that would have made his proclamation unreliable. But in this solution, in which Dodd is also taking a stand against consistent eschatology, another dilemma presents itself. How does the early Christian *expectation of the coming of Jesus Christ,* contained in the creeds of the church, relate to the *perception that the kingdom of God has already come,* as Jesus describes in his parables? Asked more pointedly, is it not the case that the one belief must fall away if the other is to survive?

That is how Dodd sees it. He believes the early church reconstructed the concept of time that Jesus had broken, in order to be able to hope in Christ. With its return to a schematic understanding of time, the church fell prey to an obsolete apocalyptic expectation, and for that reason came to see a necessity to hope in something over and above what had come to pass in Jesus Christ. The church began to read the parables differently than Jesus had preached them, and "reworked" them as preparations for the "second and final world-crisis."[33] Therefore, Dodd demands a "purification" of the consciousness of time. He could have referred to Paul — "the form of this world is passing away" (1 Cor. 7:31) — but Paul, unlike Dodd, does not mean that this world has always been decaying while remaining receptive to the "eternal realities" that it can never fully grasp. To Paul, the form of this world that is passing away includes the illumination of time by eternity. For this reason, Dodd's revision only goes halfway; he replaces one form of this world with another.

Nevertheless, Dodd's construction contains a question that we

---

33. Ibid., 130.

should keep in view. Are we so caught up in a warped concept of time that we do not notice what is coming toward us?[34]

With realized eschatology, Dodd does not refer to an event that lies behind us; rather, he means an occurrence that, so to speak, comes over us. He refers to God's judgment and God's salvation as unexpected, without precondition, and as set into action by God. Salvation realizes *itself*. One of Dodd's disciples, William David Davies of Duke Divinity School, is alleged to have answered the objection that realized eschatology is not in accordance with the New Testament with another question: Is not the justification of the sinner realized eschatology? In such justification, God's judgment is carried out. Even if the term "realized eschatology" may not satisfy sharpened linguistic sensitivity, it still points rightly to the idea that eschatology is not dependent on familiar concepts of time, but that it bears witness to God's activity by irrevocably replacing the old with the new.

The term "inaugurated eschatology"[35] has been proposed to refer to the way of Jesus' proclamation. The parables, with their metaphorical language, are characteristic of such proclamation. Metaphors, which for Weiss are an exaggerated means of expression and therefore to be understood literally, are for Dodd symbolic paraphrases of truth that bring the kingdom of God near.[36] They are understood in the current conception of the parables as representations of divine truth that are being disclosed to us, not as mediators of factual meaning. Jesus describes how God unexpectedly and incomprehensibly approaches humanity. He does not depict God as an example of ideal human behavior, not as a tolerant father, a careful merchant, a farmer dependent on nature, or a businessman who cares more about his people than profit. Jesus talks about what God is like and how God acts: un-

---

34. Arthur Rich draws attention to the difference between future as *adventus* (coming) and *futurum* (futurity) in *Die Bedeutung der Eschatologie für den christlichen Glauben* (Zurich: Zwingli Verlag, 1954), 5.

35. A corrective suggestion made by Georges Florovsky and mentioned approvingly by Dodd in *The Interpretation of the Fourth Gospel* (Cambridge: Cambridge University Press, 1953), 447.

36. E.g., Hans Weder, *Die Gleichnisse Jesu als Metaphern: Traditions- und redaktionsgeschichtliche Analysen und Interpretationen*, 3d ed. (Göttingen: Vandenhoeck & Ruprecht, 1984), 58–98, 275–301.

expectedly, contrary to good business practices; wastefully, so full of goodness that God must necessarily appear unjust. Values are turned on their head; a remission of debt of inconceivable proportions is mentioned. God wants humanity to entrust themselves to God and to get involved in God's actions. God breaks through humanity's expectations of God and of everything that humanity imagines about "life with God." In this way, expectations are directed toward the living God.

The parables, especially the parables of the kingdom, are

> stories which shatter the deep structure of our accepted world and thereby render clear and evident to us the relativity of story itself. They remove our defenses and make us vulnerable to God. It is only in such experiences that God can touch us, and only in such moments does the kingdom of God arrive.[37]

Do the parables steer away from Jesus' death and resurrection to draw attention to hope in and awareness of God? In that, they belong to the secret of Jesus Christ that is revealed on Golgotha, admittedly only in that they call us to hope in the hidden God. To that extent, Jesus' parables are inalienably bound with his death, and can only be heard properly in the shadow of the cross. Jesus' proclamation of the kingdom of God, therefore, is most closely bound with the proclamation of his death, until he comes.

---

37. John Dominic Crossan, *The Dark Interval: Towards a Theology of Story* (Sonoma, Calif.: Polebridge Press, 1988), 99–100.

– Chapter 3 –

THE ACTIVITY OF GOD
IN HUMANITY AND IN ITS HISTORY

Following the analysis of Hans Urs von Balthasar, the second "storm" involving eschatology is dialectical theology's clash with German liberal Protestantism. The criticism raised by dialectical theology clearly reveals the expanse of spiritual rubble left by World War One. As far as many central Europeans are concerned it was during the war that the phantom "God in history" met its end. With it perished the idea that God's plan for world history had been entrusted to humanity (specifically to Western Christendom) to put into practice. The war also deeply disturbed another fixed idea — that God's power can be translated into power over nature and social structures, as a sign of the cooperation of all "religious" humans with God's plans for humanity. Liberal supporters of society and revolutionary-minded social critics had been able to agree with such convictions.

What did so-called dialectical theology, represented by Karl Barth (1886–1968), Rudolf Bultmann (1884–1976), Friedrich Gogarten (1887–1967), and, more distantly, Paul Tillich (1886–1965),[1] offer in this crisis? What *could* it offer? Dialectical theology offered nothing less than the word "eschatology," admittedly with a different and more intense meaning than previously. *"Eschatology" became a boundary marker (Grenzbegriff).* The word no longer referred to the horizon of prospects. Instead, it limited theological insights possible for human understanding,

---

1. To the same circle belongs Emil Brunner, *Das Ewige als Zukunft und Gegenwart* (Zurich: Zwingli Verlag, 1953) (ET: *Eternal Hope,* trans. Harold Knight [London: Lutterworth Press; Philadelphia: Westminster Press, 1954]). See also Adrio König, *The Eclipse of Christ in Eschatology: Toward a Christ-Centered Approach* (Grand Rapids, Mich.: Eerdmans, 1989).

demonstrating at the same time what the foundation for theological insight can be. This is why such theology is radical: it reaches to the roots of theology. It does not encourage an apocalyptic atmosphere or fears of catastrophe, nor, unlike a 1920s Expressionist series of books, *Der jüngste Tag* (The last day), does it announce a new age or describe a turning point in history. Dialectical theology intends to be prepared for *God's reality alone,* God as the "wholly other," whose reality is *totaliter aliter* in relation to the world.

3.1. Eschatology as Boundary Marker of Theology

Karl BARTH, *Die christliche Dogmatik im Entwurf,* vol. 1: *Die Lehre vom Worte Gottes: Prolegomena zur christlichen Dogmatik* (Munich: Chr. Kaiser Verlag, 1927); 2d ed., ed. Gerhard Sauter (Zurich: Theologischer Verlag, 1982); idem, *Church Dogmatics* [CD], vol. II/1: *The Doctrine of God,* trans. T. H. L. Parker et al. (Edinburgh: T. & T. Clark, 1957, 1980); idem, *Der Römerbrief,* ed. Hermann Schmidt (1919; Zurich: Theologischer Verlag, 1985) (ET: *The Epistle to the Romans,* trans. Edwyn C. Hoskyns [London: Oxford University Press, 1933]).

Direct communication from God is not communication from God. A Christianity that is not wholly and utterly and irreducibly eschatology has absolutely nothing to do with Christ. A spirit that is not at every moment in time new life from the dead is in any case not the Holy Spirit.

This passage from the second edition of Karl Barth's *The Epistle to the Romans* (1922),[2] with its unparalleled predilection for sharply formulated diametric opposites, marks the clash between God's action and the history of Christendom. Barth's statement was something of a shock for a Christianity, which thought it would see the kingdom of God growing visibly within Christendom and had anticipated its own perfection. Such Christianity is convinced that its world should be formed according to the kingdom of God, and that it is able to accomplish the task through the Spirit. The Spirit is understood as a relationship to God, deeply rooted in every person. Such Christianity asks if it is not true that the Spirit, which comes from God and leads to God, changes

---

2. Barth, *Der Römerbrief* (1922), as cited and translated in idem, *CD* II/1, 634–35. E. C. Hoskyns's translation of the text, "If Christianity be not altogether thoroughgoing eschatology" (*The Epistle to the Romans,* 314), is not reliable at this point.

reality, so that forms with eternal value — cultural, spiritual, and sociohistorical achievements that outlast transitory life — can be created in the world. What else can be done?

Such were the sentiments of the "commonsense" German liberal Protestantism in which Barth grew up. It was such thought that he was trying to overcome in his first interpretation of Romans (1919), using the concept of world transformation, which is stronger and more drastic than a cultural evolution. According to Barth, a new consciousness of the biblical concept of God's Spirit was needed. God's creative Spirit is the dynamic of life. Only the movement of the Spirit brings into existence history worthy of the name, meaning an event in which the new comes into being by overcoming the old, which is prey to death.

In 1922, Barth went further. Is that Spirit, the alleged personification and driving force of all life, really the Spirit of God, the Holy Spirit? *That* Spirit can only be *God's* presence and God's new creation of life from death. The Spirit is the power of the resurrection that breaks through everything that can be thought, said, and hoped under the spell of death. The boundary of death is and remains the horizon of the world, which means that it is possible only to speak of "life" as the "strict beyond" of death. God's Spirit can only be spoken of as God's activity toward humanity and its history. We can only *await* the coming of the Spirit and allow it to happen; the Spirit cannot be claimed as motivation for our attempts to radically change the world. Only in this way can there be talk of "Christianity," of Christianity waiting for the Spirit.

In the passage quoted above, Barth is not just attacking German liberal Protestantism as represented by — among others — Troeltsch, Weiss, and Schweitzer. He is also amending his earlier attempt to outdo that position. Those earlier efforts had brought him near to the Swiss religious socialists and their "battle for the kingdom of God."[3]

---

3. Hermann Kutter, *Sie müssen! Ein offenes Wort an die christliche Gesellschaft,* 2d ed. (Jena: Eugen Diederichs, 1910); idem, *Gerechtigkeit: Ein altes Wort an die moderne Christenheit* [Römer I–VIII], 2d ed. (Jena: Eugen Diederichs, 1910); idem, *Die Revolution des Christentums,* 3d ed. (Jena: Eugen Diederichs, 1912); Leonhard Ragaz, *Der Kampf um das Reich Gottes bei Blumhardt Vater und Sohn, und weiter* (Erlenbach-Zurich, Munich, and Leipzig: Rotapfel-Verlag, 1923).

With this background, it is noteworthy that Barth's comment concerning "Christianity as eschatology" relates to Romans 8:23–24, in which Paul speaks of the "redemption of our bodies," and continues: "For in hope [or, by hope] we were saved!"[4] Barth intensifies this wording in his translation, "By hope we are saved,"[5] because the coming of Christ into the world — the "invisible, inaccessible, and impossible"[6] — meets us *as* hope. Hope shines over the unredeemed world, tearing apart every concept of the world; reality breaks through every bond. This breakthrough happens when we humans find ourselves suddenly before God in the midst of world events that we cannot escape. Hope is what remains for humans in the face of God's self-representation. "All that is not hope is wooden, hobbledehoy, blunt-edged, and sharp-pointed, like the word 'Reality.' "[7] Barth comments on Romans 12:12, "Rejoice in hope!" as follows:

> The great hope which God sets before men compels them to demonstrate against the course of this world.
>
> To *rejoice in hope* means to know God in hope without seeing Him, and to be satisfied that it should be so.[8]

Barth uses the key word "eschatology" to identify the crisis of humanity — especially humanity's attempts at right living and actions — *in the face of the advent of God.*

It is no longer the case, as it was for Troeltsch, that the "hereafter" is the power of the "here and now." Rather, the "hereafter" is the crisis of the "here and now." But that is going too far already, as far as Barth is concerned. *God's* "hereafter" can never be claimed as the crisis of the "here and now," lest theology becomes nothing more than one way among many of talking about the crisis.

---

4. "Hope" outlines, so to speak, the space in which the saved life exists. The RSV reads "for in this hope we were saved."

5. Barth, *The Epistle to the Romans,* 314: "*By hope we are saved* — inasmuch as in Jesus Christ the wholly Other, unapproachable, unknown, *eternal power and divinity* (1:20) of God has entered into our world."

6. Ibid.

7. Ibid.

8. Ibid., 457.

This is the same approach taken by Barth some years later when he came to deal with traditional linguistic usage concerning the "last things":

> Last *things*, as such, are not *last* things, however great and significant they might be. He only speaks of *last* things who would speak of the end of all things.[9]

Strictly speaking, we humans are not in a position to talk about something "final" as God's reality. Such talk would no longer be eschatology, which is our dilemma. We can either talk about last things — in which case we remain in the realm of "things" and never progress further — or we can take "last" as the linguistic expression for what is "different from all things," in which case we cannot say more.

This is why Barth tries, in his *Epistle to the Romans,* to put fundamental theological terms such as "Spirit" and "life" back into their theological context. Only when understood anew in light of that context can such terms be won back for theology and the message of the church. This recognition applies particularly to the term "eschatology," which is more often used as a campaign slogan than to designate an aspect of theological doctrine.

Barth is obviously no longer interested in what the term may have meant in theological tradition. The term seems to have no content. That was largely the case for most of Barth's theological contemporaries, due not least to the influence of consistent eschatology. The desire for changing the linguistic meaning of "eschatology" had created a vacuum. Apart from "outsiders" such as Martin Kähler (1835–1912),[10] theology seemed at a loss for words regarding eschatology. With Barth, the term could at least be used to mark the boundaries of the "impossible possibility" (*unmögliche Möglichkeit*) of discourse concerning God.

Instead of a detailed eschatology, what concerns Barth is the relationship of time and eternity as a conceptual framework for talking about God. Such discourse is shaped by expectation. God's

---

9. K. Barth, *The Resurrection of the Dead,* trans. H. J. Stenning (London: Hodder and Stoughton, 1933), 110.

10. M. Kähler, *Dogmatische Zeitfragen: Alte und neue Ausführungen zur christlichen Lehre,* vol. 3: *Zeit und Ewigkeit,* 2d ed. (Leipzig: A. Deichert, 1913).

eternity is not within time. Rather, it breaks into time, but does not become a passing moment. In adapting to this idea theology may not concentrate on any point in time, whether past or future. The eternal God touches the passage of time at every point at which God acts — that is, at *every* point in time. What we conceive as past, present, and future is of equal value before God.

Theology must be prepared to be interrupted by God, to have its web of words cut. Theology's purpose is to highlight this process. Paradoxically, the more theology attempts, the less it achieves. Theology may even end up pointing away from God.

Should theology, then, begin with eschatology? That is, should it begin with radical eschatology instead of a doctrine of the last things or Christian expectation for the future? In the Göttingen lecture *Unterricht in der christlichen Religion* (Instruction in the Christian religion), Barth rejected this course, along with the idea of constructing dogmatics from a different starting point, such as baptism.[11] That Christianity worthy of the name can be nothing but eschatology through and through must not lead to theology being read backwards.

Barth does not leave eschatology out of his outline of dogmatics,[12] but develops the relationship between eternity and time by considering that the inexpressible nature of our existence will one day be superseded. This promise of "becoming" determines our future. Barth deliberately keeps at a distance from the doctrine of the last things. Indeed, he keeps away from any finality in order to speak of Christ as *the* "final," *the* "ultimate." Christ is also the Coming One, but that title conveys only that Christ's glorification at God's side is not yet accessible to us, just as God's reality is not yet accessible. With the theme of "becoming," Barth recapitulates nearly all dogmatics about an expected salvation that will put us in direct contact with God. It is precisely because of a coming salvation that theological discourse must remain dialectical as long

---

11. K. Barth, *Unterricht in der christlichen Religion,* vol. 2: *Die Lehre von Gott/Die Lehre vom Menschen,* ed. Hinrich Stoevesandt (1924–25; Zurich: Theologischer Verlag, 1990), 7 (ET: *The Göttingen Dogmatics: Instruction in the Christian Religion,* trans. Geoffrey W. Bromiley [Grand Rapids, Mich.: Eerdmans, 1991], 1:322).

12. This part of his lecture, which was completed in Münster in the winter of 1925–26, has not yet been published.

as it remains within time. Traditional topics of the doctrine of the last things, such as resurrection, judgment, eternal life, and eternal damnation, illustrate the problematic nature of theology — the necessity of speaking of the end of all things while calling people to hope in God!

How do our concepts of time relate to the reality of God's eternity? Barth pursues this question in more detail in the third version of *Church Dogmatics,* particularly when discussing the doctrine of God. Eternity, Barth emphasizes, is not an endless continuation of time. Rather, it is God's time. Our discourse concerning God therefore remains connected to God being revealed, which for humans always remains in the future — external to our consciousness and reckoning of time.

But God does not just belong to the "hereafter" of our time. Rather, God acts in breaking through our concepts of time. In speaking of God, we do not expect an event within time, nor do we refer to something timeless. On the contrary, God comes as sovereign over time, not just from age to age but in every moment.

In emphasizing God's will to be present at every moment, Barth is not trying to stress the present as a unit in time or to reserve the future as a mode of time for God. That God is always the Coming One does not allow us to locate God in the future, ignoring both past and present, or to see past and present as the prehistory of the future. That Christianity is "thoroughgoing eschatology" cannot be allowed to concentrate attention on what might come to pass or be brought to pass. Barth saw himself thwarted by this misunderstanding of theology as devoted to the future. Twenty years later, he attempted to place the well-known comment from his commentary on Romans within the context of his doctrine of God.[13] It is not just that God *will* be; God *was* and *is* God. The emphasis lies on *being God.*[14]

Barth is not afraid to speak of teleology on occasion,[15] of the passage of time toward an end that is real. That discussion, however, cannot be allowed to divert attention from the fact that God, the eternal one, is "beyond time." God does not come to an end

---

13. CD II/1, 634–35.
14. Ibid., 608–40.
15. Ibid., 635.

with time. That is why God determines what comes "before" and "after" in our temporality. On the other hand, such reasoning does not mean that God exists solely "above" time. That God may be called on as the one who is God yesterday, today, and tomorrow has its origin in *God's very own history,* in God's being, which "produces" Godself. At this point in the argument, Barth makes use of the *doctrine of the Trinity,* which he had already dealt with in detail. He uses this doctrine in two ways:

First, God is in relation to Godself as Father, Son, and Spirit. The three persons of the Godhead stand in a living relationship to one another, in constant and inexhaustible movement toward each other. Human concepts of temporality cannot grasp that God's eternity is not outside of time, but exists as an "immanent Trinity."

Second, the doctrine of the Trinity says that the triune God creates history by emerging from and giving of Godself to call the world into existence. God directs its fate in a mysterious way and intervenes in the actions of creatures in order to save and perfect what God wills. This doctrine describes God as an "economic Trinity." God's action begins, continues, and reaches its end; in that respect, it can be said that God "has time." The beginning, middle, and end of God's activity are not separated from one another, but rest in God, in God's eternity. God's eternity and omnipotence point to each other. In God's actions, God remains true to Godself and promises to be faithful to humanity.[16]

By acting in this way, God reveals Godself to humanity. God shows us at the same time both *how* God acts and *what* God does. This activity has a name: Jesus Christ. The foundation of theology is God's act of making Godself present in Jesus Christ. This act at the same time involves God's self-revelation in God's Word. For this reason, the *history of Jesus Christ is the focus of all history.*[17] In Christ the relation of all events to God is perceptible, which allows a glimpse of the *universal perspective.* Through,

---

16. See Robert Jenson, *God after God: The God of the Past and the God of the Future, Seen in the Work of Karl Barth* (Indianapolis and New York: Bobbs-Merrill, 1969), 110–13, 125–28.

17. See David Ford, *Barth and God's Story: Biblical Narrative and the Theological Method of Karl Barth in the "Church Dogmatics"* (Frankfurt: Peter Lang, 1981).

with, and in Jesus Christ, everything of lasting worth for humanity and the world in relation to God has taken place. Therefore,
theology derives from the Christ-event alone; it is based wholly
on Christology. Theology, for Barth, refers to what was accomplished between God and man through Jesus Christ, who is true
God and true man. This accomplishment is of relevance for all humanity. The entirety of this theology — in the *Church Dogmatics*
at an almost overwhelming scale — is influenced by the perception
of the *christological perfect*: "It is accomplished!" (John 19:30).[18]
Jesus Christ has completed everything that he came to do, right
to the bitter end. He dies as one cursed and rejected. But in this
end God has achieved God's purpose — the salvation of the world,
which God chose to accomplish through God's Son. Jesus Christ
has become the reconciler. It is accomplished.

What remains? For one thing, the universality of this revelation should become so all-embracing that no one can escape it.
Jesus' resurrection and transformation into God's glory remain to
be "accomplished" for the rest of humanity. Is another eschatology
necessary to place alongside the idea of christological fulfillment?

At this point Barth runs into linguistic difficulties. Occasional
experimentation with teleology or the idea of a threefold effectivity
of the presence of Jesus Christ — his *parousia* in "the resurrection, the outpouring of the Spirit, and the final return of Jesus
Christ"[19] — cannot solve these problems. They also do not constitute the heart of Barth's argument. But who would not run
into linguistic difficulties when trying to claim that Christ has accomplished all while saying that what remains to be done is the
occasion for further hope?

In the *Church Dogmatics*, Barth went to much trouble to avoid
that alternative. Moreover, he was concerned to prove the alternative misleading while ensuring that no vacuum could develop
between christological fulfillment and hope in fulfillment. The
meaning of eschatology emphasized earlier — limitation of human
discourse concerning God through time — supported him in his

---

18. Translator's note: The NRSV reads, "It is finished." I have chosen to use the
more traditional "It is accomplished" on the grounds that the latter is more closely
related linguistically to the theological concepts being discussed here.

19. *CD* IV/3, 294.

task. In my opinion, Barth clung to this characterization of eschatology in his understanding of dogma. Dogma is an "eschatological term" or concept, Barth stated in 1927 in *Prolegomena to Christian Dogmatics*.[20] This raises the decisive question of how we can talk about God, the *wholly other,* who is removed from our conceptual possibilities but who at the same time determines the beginning and the end of our discourse including the conditions of our conceptual possibilities. The most that we can aspire to is an *approach* to God's truth. This statement applies specifically to theology and its pronouncements, which will never be able to reach God's actual truth.

Eschatology, in this fundamental meaning, is concerned with the human attempt "to do theology" and with the foundations of theology, since theology addresses concepts to which no human can testify directly. Theology is in that respect dialectical (and remains so in the *Church Dogmatics*), because theology must always remember that God contradicts all human attempts to grasp divine reality. Theology must be placed under God's verdict. That is why theology as a whole is eschatologically oriented. Theological discourse is wholly dependent on *God's* justification of what is said. Only if directed to God's judgment can theology produce responsible discourse concerning God.[21] Theology is a process of "continual approach" toward God's truth, but always remains an approach.

To come into and to remain in motion, theology must subject itself to continual self-examination, to ensure that its discourse leaves room for God. In this belief Barth remains true to his earlier comment that Christianity must be completely, utterly, and unabatingly eschatology, even if the phrasing fell into disuse. Only eschatology can make clear that Christianity would exist only as a historical phenomenon with shadowy beginnings and an extremely uncertain future if it were not concerned with Christ, with him alone.

Barth's reasoning emphasizes a question that he shared with

---

20. Barth, *Die christliche Dogmatik im Entwurf,* 150, 162, 489, 583; repeated in CD I/1, 269.
21. On this perspective see Hinrich Stoevesandt, *Gottes Freiheit und die Grenze der Theologie: Gesammelte Aufsätze* (Zurich: Theologischer Verlag, 1992).

his friend Eduard Thurneysen[22] as well as with Rudolf Bultmann and Friedrich Gogarten. Despite rhetorical virtuosity, all four were forced to struggle for words. "How can we speak of God?" they asked, in order not simply to talk *about* God or to summon God's help in history. Eschatology epitomizes this language problem.

Barth distances himself increasingly from this hesitance. If his initial intention was to use the term "eschatology" to designate the frontier of all theology, the idea was to point to God's transcendence. Eschatology cannot be a restricted theme within theology, but must embrace the entirety of theology. Barth never abandoned this conviction. But in the light of the christological perfect, the grounds for the conviction are clearly different. The conviction is based no longer on the painful insight that if we want to talk about God we *cannot* start from our own shortcomings. The *Church Dogmatics* gives a feeling of freedom from all such shortcomings. In his Whitsun prayer, Barth expressed this feeling in the following way: May God make us capable, he prayed, "to risk the small, yet still so significant, step — away from comfort with which we can comfort ourselves and to hope in you."[23]

It is strange that Barth can describe this hope as a "veil" which will fall away in the "post-temporal eternity" (*nachzeitliche Ewigkeit*), when the human sense of time no longer applies.[24] According to this statement, the perfection that is lacking in life will reveal the reconciliation that has already happened in all its dimensions. This fulfillment is the telos of all things and cannot be found in developments within time. *The eschaton brings complete recognition* of what is already "real" in God because it has conclusively happened in Christ.

This is as far as Barth addresses in the *Church Dogmatics* what he planned to include in the prospective fifth volume, *Lehre von der Erlösung* (Doctrine of salvation). One might ask whether eschatology has anything specific to say if it deals with salvation in this manner, that is, as an understanding of fulfillment as the

---

22. E. Thurneysen, "Christus und seine Zukunft: Ein Beitrag zur Eschatologie," *Zwischen den Zeiten* 11 (1931): 187–211; idem, *Kreuz und Wiederkunft Christi* (Munich: Chr. Kaiser, 1939).

23. K. Barth, *Gebete* (Munich: Chr. Kaiser, 1963), 40.

24. *CD* II/1, 631.

disclosure of what has been completed by Jesus Christ.[25] Is hope reduced to the expectation that all limitations on our perception will vanish? Yet "perception" cannot be limited to the intellect. Rather, the term refers to becoming aware of truth in its full scope, in the wealth and abundance of human existence, created and reconciled by God. This is the truth that we can never really be aware of during life. Hope is necessary, because we continue to live in sin — in arrogance, lethargy, and deception.

In what, then, can we hope? What can hope help us endure, so that what we endure does not become the final word? Barth preferred to express himself anecdotally rather than dogmatically on this point. He looks forward to a vantage point from which he can argue theology with people like Wolfgang Amadeus Mozart and Friedrich Schleiermacher without necessarily squabbling. Barth was once asked whether we will see our loved ones again one day, to which he is alleged to have answered, "Certainly, but we'll see the others as well!" That is Barth's doctrine of election — his doctrine of the universality of reconciliation — in a nutshell. It stands in continual tension to the traditional idea of a general resurrection from the dead followed by the separation of the saved from the damned. In Christ such differences no longer exist.

"Why eschatology at all?" The question begs an answer. Could not Barth's understanding of eschatology, for example, reduce to a pneumatology of the presence of God, for which we only can hope? Or is eschatology not already sketched in the doctrine of election, that in Jesus Christ all humans are chosen and have escaped damnation? What is the necessity, one might ask, of a future judgment? The last judgment is just the revelation of what God long ago decided in Christ: We cannot yet claim knowledge of this judgment since that would completely contradict divine election.

Such issues remain open in Barth's dogmatics. It is idle to speculate as to whether — and how — Barth would have answered those questions, since the work remains a fragment.

---

25. CD III/2, 624, 632–33. Barth raised this point again in a letter to Helmut Gollwitzer on November 7, 1967. See K. Barth, *Briefe 1961–1968*, ed. Jürgen Fangmeier and Hinrich Stoevesandt (Zurich: Theologischer Verlag, 1975) (ET: *Letters, 1961–1968*, trans. Geoffrey W. Bromiley [Grand Rapids, Mich.: Eerdmans, 1981], letter #272, pp. 274–76; quotation is from p. 275).

Kjetil HAFSTAD, *Wort und Geschichte: Das Geschichtsverständnis Karl Barths*
(Munich: Chr. Kaiser, 1985); Gotthard OBLAU, *Gotteszeit und Menschenzeit: Es-
chatologie in der kirchlichen Dogmatik Karl Barths* (Neukirchen: Neukirchener
Verlag, 1988); Gerhard SAUTER, "Why is Karl Barth's *Church Dogmatics* not a
'Theology of Hope'? Observations on Barth's Understanding of Eschatology," forth-
coming in *Scottish Journal of Theology* (1999); Tjarko STADTLAND, *Eschatologie
und Geschichte in der Theologie des jungen Karl Barth* (Neukirchen: Neukirchener
Verlag, 1966).

3.2. Eschatological Orientation of Christian Existence

Rudolf BULTMANN, "Die christliche Hoffnung und das Problem der Entmythologisierung," in *Glauben und Verstehen* (Tübingen: J. C. B. Mohr, 1960), 3:81–90;
idem, "Die Eschatologie des Johannes-Evangeliums," in *Glauben und Verstehen*,
vol. 1 (Tübingen: J. C. B. Mohr, 1933) (ET: "The Eschatology of the Gospel of
John," in *Faith and Understanding*, trans. Louise Pettibone Smith [New York: Harper & Row, 1969], 1:165–83); idem, "Geschichte und Eschatologie im Neuen
Testament," in *Glauben und Verstehen*, 3:91–106; idem, *The Presence of Eternity: History and Eschatology, the Gifford Lectures, 1955* (New York: Harper &
Brothers, 1957).

Like Karl Barth, Rudolf Bultmann also places eschatology in the
center of Christian theology. His conception of eschatology is even
more radical, not to say reductionist, than Barth's. In his essay on
the eschatology of the Gospel of John (1928), Bultmann writes:
"The concept of faith is . . . defined eschatologically."[26] Eschatology
does not answer the question of what is to come, but designates
everything that can be said about faith. It sets the direction of
faith. Bultmann's position was already so fully developed that it
only needed fine-tuning later on.

In 1954 Bultmann described the eschatological character of
Christian faith as taught in the New Testament as follows:

> The "now" receives its eschatological character by the en-
> counter with Christ and the word that preaches him, since
> in the encounter with him the world and its history come to
> their end and faith as the new creature is freed from the world
> [*entweltlicht*].[27]

Bultmann does not consider what he presents as John's eschatology to be just one of the evangelist's themes. He understands it

---

26. Bultmann, "The Eschatology of the Gospel of John," 174.
27. Bultmann, "Geschichte und Eschatologie im Neuen Testament," 105.

to be the essence of Johannine theology. At the same time, it is a summary of Bultmann's central theological idea.

Jesus Christ, the one who reveals, confronts anyone who hears him with a decision. The choice is to understand oneself from the perspective of God's all-defining reality and through that to come to a new understanding, or to continue to understand oneself from a human perspective and the possibilities open to it. The inheritance of revelation — eternal life — is the destiny of anyone who follows the call of Jesus. Anyone who follows him is freed from the bondage of death of this sinful world, a world subject to the fullness of God's judgment. The individual is freed from his own past, to which he was in danger of falling victim. What counts from now on is whether that person lives according to the freedom that has been prepared for him, or whether he sinks back into self-reliance, and by doing so delivers himself again as hostage to the world.

What lies ahead for this world may be revealed tomorrow or the next day, or at a distant point in time. Anyone who believes is freed from that worry, and therefore can be content to let it be. For the believer, salvation — the eschatological "now" — is present in the sense that it is there to be received in faith through continually repeated acts of choice. Salvation is not something that can be "possessed" by the believer.

For this reason, a believer understands the future differently from someone with no belief. A nonbeliever is concerned to keep hold of what he has achieved — what he has "become" — for all time. The nonbeliever is therefore not free for the future, although everything that he does is based on the assumption that he can reckon with an indefinite amount of space and time. Although dependent on freedom, he cannot create freedom for himself. It is only God's grace that can grant freedom and, with freedom, future. If humans — including and perhaps especially theologians! — wish to know and to say more about the future, they will find themselves less able to say things with certainty, and perhaps unable to say anything at all.

Bultmann, then, concentrates on the idea that *faith grants another temporality*, different from the one that applies to our existence in the world. From day to day we reckon according to the type of time that flows from the future into the past. What has happened determines the present and at the same time reaches into the future, which holds the balance of our actions and sufferings. We see the result in front of us, because we can never put it behind us. We are subject to existence within time, a transient existence that has no power of redemption but instead involves us increasingly in a struggle to hold on to something, and by doing so, to save ourselves.

God's promise of freedom saves us from this struggle. This happens when the kerygma, the message of the God's unconditional grace, approaches us. This "approach," *futurity that has its roots in the proclamation,* turns normal concepts of time upside down. In the same way that every conscious human being is aware of the certainty of one's end even though one does not continually meditate on death, *those who hear the kerygma are placed under the cross of Christ.* This frees them from the course of time that ends in death. With the death of Christ, the curse of this transient existence comes to an end. Although those who hear the word must at some point die, what lies before them is no longer death, but life (see John 5:24). "Life" is therefore not the result of a collection of experiences to which death will one day be added.

Eschatology is the experience of passing a boundary, the "determining of a particular *now.*"[28] What we experience as "now," a scarcely perceptible transitory moment, gains permanence when God uses it to speak to us. The word — the *kerygma* — comes to us "here and now," approaching us from outside, from God. It must be said *to* us; we can never say it to ourselves. It calls us to a decision about life and death that no human is able to make, but to which every human is called, either to accept or reject. It proclaims that the hour has come. To paraphrase Paul: Now, when you hear God's voice, *now* is the time of salvation, so do not cut yourselves off (2 Cor. 6:2). At the same time, the kerygma relates to those for whom the hour has come: you have already died, God's word of grace has definitively ended your old lives. Anyone who accepts this message has chosen the promised future and a new understanding of self. He now lives in the presence of promised salvation, and at the same time the perfection of salvation remains

---

28. Bultmann, "The Eschatology of the Gospel of John," 178.

yet to come, since it is beyond our comprehension. To use Paul's imagery again, we cannot see what we hope for (Rom. 8:24) — therefore it always remains in the future for the believer, as long as he exists.

"Eschatology," therefore, talks of how the human self can relate to itself in a new way in view of its temporality. This reduction of eschatology has the consequence of making time something inward and historical events unimportant. What has happened or could happen no longer matters. Rather, what counts is whether the human, who has to answer for his own history, loses himself in the course of events or exists according to futurity.

Bultmann disposes of the doctrine of the last things with one fell swoop. Eschatology, in his definition, deals with the presence of salvation in the encounter with Christ as the one who reveals. In line with this, eschatology is the symbol of the existence, the "lived life" that results from this encounter. Apocalypticism is therefore no longer relevant for Christian faith. Bultmann simply cuts out apocalyptic elements in the New Testament, dismissing them as later additions.

An example can be taken from John. God's judgment takes place whenever humans hear Jesus' word as the word of revelation and either accept or reject it as decisive for their existence. In this sense, judgment is an eschatological event. But how can this be reconciled with the fact that the same Gospel proclaims judgment as an historic event at the end of time? All humans will come forth from their graves to be judged according to their deeds and rise to the "resurrection of life" or the "resurrection of judgment" (John 5:28–29). For Bultmann it is inconceivable that the theologian who wrote John's Gospel could have thought so illogically. He explains the discrepancy as resulting from the intervention of church editors who "smuggled" traditional ideas into the text.[29] Bultmann considers this smuggling to be the work of a reactionary censor who was only willing to pass certain difficult passages after toning them down with additions designed to reestablish the moral of the story. In the process, the provocative train of thought was de-

---

29. R. Bultmann, *The Gospel of John: A Commentary,* trans. G. R. Beasley-Murray, R. W. N. Hoare, and J. K. Riches (Philadelphia: Westminster Press [1971]), 261.

stroyed. Bultmann reacts to such revision in the same way that he responds to traditional dogmatics and eschatology: it is secondary and surplus to requirement, if not downright misleading.

It is only the "faith event" that really deserves the title "eschatology." That is, the event in which the old self comes to an end and the new, immortal life of freedom in the power of God's grace begins. This moment of revelation is not a date on a time line, to be enriched and perhaps even surpassed by subsequent experience. All we can do is be continually prepared for it, because it is an encounter which must continually take place anew.

Now, several decades later, it is difficult to make Bultmann's conception of eschatology accessible, let alone to give an idea of the fascination it held in his day. The existential pathos, the "understanding of oneself" in the light of the "here and now," the monotonous plea for "historicity," the insistence on the *unverfügbar Kommende* ("coming not at one's disposal"); all this is as much out of fashion nowadays as it was "in" at the time.

What appeared particularly attractive was the radicality of Bultmann's presentation of the essence of Christian faith: directed toward God alone, with ears attuned to the gospel message of God's unconditional grace, with no further safeguards, independent of any compulsory ideas about world and history. In this formulation, Bultmann repeats a motif that he had developed very early on, that the root of religious existence lies in the transcendence of God's reality, which renders existence invulnerable in the face of the snares and temptations of the transitory realm of appearances.[30] Religious development must maintain the balance between the present as it is experienced and the future we await, without allowing itself to be led astray by false hope.

In conjunction with dialectical theology, Bultmann emphasizes that faith is called into existence by God's word. The basis of faith is not to be sought in a "religious constitution" that is part of humanity, but in the external nature of God's word. God speaks to us from outside ourselves, and comes to us in God's word. The word of God can be reduced to the kerygmatic call to decision; per-

---

30. See Martin Evang, *Rudolf Bultmann in seiner Frühzeit* (Tübingen: J. C. B. Mohr, 1988), 257–62, 266–76.

ception, faith, and hope reduce to a change in self-understanding. Faith is intrinsically hope, since it allows itself to be drawn into what is *unverfügbar,* not at one's disposal and beyond human planning and control. Hope means openness to transcendence; transcendence itself is understood as a futurity that time cannot catch, and therefore always belongs to the future.

The moment of truth for Bultmann's radical eschatology is *that we do not expect something, but rather are spoken to by the word from the cross in a conclusive manner which awakens hope.* The notion has proven extremely resistant to criticism. The attraction lies in the fact that Bultmann subjects all New Testament texts to the decision between freedom for the future and slavery to care. In this, he uses the existence-analysis of Martin Heidegger (1889–1976), his colleague and dialogue partner in Marburg who in 1927 published his groundbreaking work *Sein und Zeit* (Being and Time). Bultmann shares with Heidegger a criticism of the understanding of history that deals only with facts and the supposedly objective interconnection of given data. In opposition, Bultmann addresses how humanity creates history, whether out of fears for personal existence or freed for the challenge to live open to the *unverfügbare,* reality not at one's disposal.

This message, both in the 1920s and in the 1940s, was sown in intellectual soil that had been plowed and turned over by war. How can hope bloom again, after promises of a better future and control of life's problems have failed and even led to dreadful evil? How does one find something to hold on to in such a maelstrom?

Bultmann's conception was attractive for the generation that had lived through the war, particularly at the end of the forties and the beginning of the fifties. That generation was confronted with the necessity of starting "completely afresh," without forgetting history but without allowing itself to be suffocated by feelings of guilt. The freedom of faith means that one does not have to understand oneself only with respect to the past. This perspective helps subtly in the process of coming to terms with the past. After many years of simply receiving and carrying out orders, persons again felt self-reliant. They had to consider how they should shape their existence and what forces they would allow to lead them. The liberated self suddenly gained strength through the continual necessity of making independent decisions. The heart of Bultmann's eschatology is a message of liberation. It sounds eschatological because it deals with an *"end" that is marked by the cross of Christ.*

But what is this "end"? And what is the cross?

"Christ is the end of the law, that everyone who has faith may be justified," writes Paul (Rom. 10:4). Bultmann interprets the first part of the verse as history's death sentence: "For history has reached its end, since Christ is the end of the law."[31] But it is only a false understanding of history — faith in the potential of history — that has come to an end. God's action brings to an end humanity's false understanding of itself within time. The concept of history whereby humans, attempting to control the world, are in fact enslaved to history, is broken. This process is the essence of salvation. Freedom in grace is the common denominator to which Bultmann reduces the end of all things.

There is an obvious objection. History, with all its inherited burdens, entanglements, and confusions, is given up as lost. Is it not true that the difficulties involved in seeing what has happened in relation to what is to come are simply reduced to the single question of how the individual can relate to them? This is the opinion voiced by, among others, the Russian Orthodox philosopher of religion Georges Florovsky (1893–1979). His opinion is of particular interest since he comes from a tradition of belief and thought untouched by specific Central European considerations.

> Now, Existentialism does claim to be itself an eschatological doctrine. But it is a sheer abuse of terms. Eschatology is radically interiorized in its existentialist reinterpretation. It is actually swallowed up in the immediacy of personal decisions.... In the last resort, it amounts to the radical dehistorization of the Christian faith.[32]
>
> History is no more a theological problem.[33]

---

31. Bultmann, *The Presence of Eternity*, 43.

32. G. Florovsky, "The Last Things and the Last Events" (1962), in *Collected Works*, vol. 3: *Creation and Redemption* (Belmont, Mass: Nordland, 1976), 243–65; quotation is from p. 243.

33. Ibid., 244.

In Bultmann's thinking, the objection would be that the Christian faith runs the risk of allowing useful ideas concerning the course of events to become obsessive. Such ideas belong to the "form of this world" that is passing away (1 Cor. 7:31), and theology should be in the front line of the clearing-up operation. History is often spoken of carelessly, as though it could be overlooked — as though we were familiar with the course of events and could deduce what has happened and could yet happen from our sketchy and incomplete knowledge of events! What do we actually know about what history is, how it "happens," and how it will progress?

Bultmann does not ask this question. On the contrary, he takes humanity as the subject of history and does not want restrictions placed on the subject's freedom of action. Eschatology, he emphasizes, is the possibility of true freedom which makes responsible action possible — without the necessity of taking impersonal, anonymous contexts into consideration. The emphasis is on the presence of the salvation event, in which the individual is directly open to God. In this event, the world and everything related to the world is constantly relativized.

This nonworldly *Gegenwartsekstase* (ecstatic grasp of the present moment)[34] was a target for Ernst Käsemann (1906–98). Bultmann's Gifford Lectures on "History and Eschatology" gave the final impetus for Bultmann's self-willed disciple to distance himself from his teacher.[35]

Bultmann's ideas prompted Käsemann to the theory that the starting and finishing point of Christian theology is the turning point in history awaited in apocalypticism (according to Bultmann, this had already taken place in Jesus' death).[36] Apocalypticism rep-

---

34. Bultmann uses the term *Entweltlichung*.

35. Ernst Käsemann, "The Beginnings of Christian Theology," in *New Testament Questions of Today*, trans. W. J. Mantague (London: SCM Press, 1969), 82–107; idem, "On the Subject of Primitive Christian Apocalyptic," in *New Testament Questions of Today*, 108–37.

36. So also J. Christiaan Beker, *Paul the Apostle: The Triumph of God in Life and Thought* (Philadelphia: Fortress Press, 1980); idem, *Paul's Apocalyptic Gospel: The Coming Triumph of God* (Philadelphia: Fortress Press, 1982); idem, *Suffering and Hope: The Biblical Vision and the Human Predicament* (Philadelphia: Fortress Press, 1987).

resents an experience of history in which humans are conscious of being objects rather than subjects. Imprisoned by their fleshliness in the history of the world, they yearn — together with the world — for redemption. The advent of Christ and his rule attacks the pitiable state of the world, and every Christian is involved in the decisive battle. Apocalypticism describes humanity and the human environment as caught up in misery and sin. We are subject to history: history is not simply the battlefield on which the fight for humanity's freedom occurs, but rather the battlefield between God and evil. What matters is humanity's allegiance. The voices of those who suffer can be heard in apocalypticism — the voices of the people who hope in God's victory over God's enemies and the power of God's justice. In comparison, Bultmann's eschatology amounts to an elegant and restrained "religious" treatment of the present, with the intent of discovering salvation in a space free from fear and hope.

Käsemann's conception of history sounds more realistic than Bultmann's. It is, in any case, richer in perspectives. It also indicates why Christian hope awaits Jesus Christ as the Coming One, as Savior and Judge, as the ruler who intervenes every day in his incomparable way, in earthly powerlessness and suffering for the sake of those who belong to him, as well as for the whole world. In the end he will accomplish the all-embracing salvation which he began.

Retracing Christian theology to apocalypticism as a systematic construct and as a framing concept of theology, rather than as just a phenomenon in the history of religion, leads to a dramatic picture of history. The present situation is then interpreted accordingly. In light of the global political and social developments of the 1960s and 1970s, Käsemann's revival of apocalyptic found a wide response.

Apocalyptic eschatology as described by Käsemann is equally a message of liberation, bringing with it a call to decision. But this decision is subordinated to Christ's rule and supports a change of power, not just a change in self-awareness. Like Bultmann, Käsemann is thinking of a phenomenon that is fundamental for all theology. He remains Bultmann's disciple in that he favors predogmatic and nondogmatic eschatology and devalues all attempts at a doctrine of the last things on the grounds that they are evidence of decadence.[37]

However, both Käsemann and Bultmann run the risk of reducing hope to a repeated act, if it cannot be related to a theological context which deals with the foundations and target of hope. It must also be possible to speak and think about freedom, even if it is promised and experienced as acquittal. Theological discourse concerning God's history with humanity (the context of God's activity) is necessary precisely because the foundations of freedom and hope are external to us and cannot be generated. Such discourse would state what we might hope for — not gathered from historical reflection or foresight, but in the relationship of our discourse and thought to what is promised.

Bultmann's conception of the advent of God does not deal with what is promised and proclaimed in the word on the cross. According to Bultmann, theology consists of reflection on humans' place before God as illustrated by the Bible, but threaded carefully through the needle of existentialist interpretation, using the question of human self-understanding. It is true that Bultmann wants to avoid reducing theology to religious anthropology, as had happened with liberal theology, but he still shares the problems of liberal theology. Were he asked what has changed through the death and resurrection of Jesus (2.5.1), he would answer that human self-understanding would be different. There is little that differentiates this response from what people like Albert Schweitzer had to say. Schweitzer and others said that Jesus brought about a change of consciousness, since a believer receives new self-understanding in coming to terms with a fundamentally disturbing experience. Bultmann wishes to see God's action in this radical change in human self-understanding.

Bultmann would reject the above discussion as a misunderstanding. He sees self-understanding as a catalyst for everything that really concerns humanity; it relates to humanity's very existence, not just human thought processes and actions. But Bultmann is not convincing in his idea that existence in the world inevitably means

---

37. See his critique on 2 Peter, "An Apology for Primitive Christian Eschatology," in *Essays on New Testament Themes,* trans. W. J. Mantague (London: SCM Press, 1964), 169–95.

involvement in the matters of the world, and he does not concern himself about it. Perceptions such as those of Paul about the groaning of creation and its expectation of salvation (Rom 8:22–23) hold no interest for him. He notes them as examples of mythological discourse that attempt to depict events outside the human world as if they actually could happen.[38] Bultmann lays aside such texts with the comment "finished!" (*erledigt!*).[39] But removing all such expectation turns theology and the Christian message into a barren intellectual wasteland.

Johannes Körner, *Eschatologie und Geschichte: Eine Untersuchung des Begriffes des Eschatologischen in der Theologie Rudolf Bultmanns* (Hamburg-Bergstedt: Evangelischer Verlag Herbert Reich, 1957).

3.3. In the Darkness of Hope

Friedrich Gogarten did not use the term "eschatology" to make headlines.[40] Rather, he seems to consider the term more as an epitaph for unanswered problems. As a student of Ernst Troeltsch he deals repeatedly with philosophy of history, attempting to emphasize Christian hope in contrast to the ideas of progress that mark the new age. This is to a large extent in line with Bultmann's and Heidegger's diagnosis of the risks posed to humanity by its behavior. Gogarten, however, also stresses freedom for the future.

In 1954, a time of apparent consolidation in the Western world, Gogarten published a study on the subject of Christian hope. The study runs parallel to his larger work on the problem of secularization and secularism. The larger work was written in the postwar period; power-conscious ideas of world history collapsed and the tendency grew to control events through "planning." Gogarten deals with the crisis of Christian faith in modern (Western) culture — a crisis in which it is becoming clear that control of the world through technology and rationality is no solution. The

38. "Die christliche Hoffnung und das Problem der Entmythologisierung," 89.

39. "New Testament and Mythology," in *New Testament and Mythology and Other Basic Writings*, translated and edited by Schubert M. Ogden (Philadelphia: Fortress Press, 1984), 5.

40. See Friedrich Gogarten, "Die christliche Hoffnung," *Deutsche Universitätszeitung* 9, no. 24 (1954): 3–7; idem, *Verhängnis und Hoffnung der Neuzeit: Die Säkularisierung als theologisches Problem*, 2d ed. (Stuttgart: Friedrich Vorwerk, 1958).

"modern person," according to Gogarten — and this is a standard conviction of many contemporary culture critics — has attempted to put history at his own disposal. He plans his future in order to realize his anticipated potential.[41] But this belief in progress is the worst enemy of Christian hope, because, although directed toward the future, it avoids dependence on God or openness for the advent of the unexpected.

Future as coming (Zu-kunft) *is the theological contradiction of a planned future, which is the strategic continuation of the present.* Christian hope, according to Gogarten, seems groundless and unstable because it does not value what humans wish to achieve through their wishes. Why hope without wishes? According to Gogarten, we humans tend to find ourselves in the fulfillment of our wishes, and therefore to retreat into ourselves, even when we believe that we long for something above and beyond ourselves. If hope is to be wholly directed toward God it must be "pure" hope. When using the term "pure," Gogarten is not talking about the opposite of "impure." He speaks of a hope that is only hope, and nothing else. Only such hope can deal with reality. It is not deterred by reality's inscrutability, but can leap into the unknown. Only someone who lets go of all wishes can really begin to hope. Yet this statement is probably misleading since it is still too actively expressed. Human wishes must be destroyed as if by purifying fire — a type of purgatory — until all that remains is the core of hope.

Gogarten associates pure hope with God. In the context of his culture criticism, he ascribes pure hope to the wholly other reality that opposes reality related to human wishes. Pure hope opposes all planning aimed to guarantee one's own future. The way we hope shows whether we have fallen to the world we hope to bring into being, or whether we, bare and naked and fully ourselves, are open to God.

Gogarten considers himself to be in agreement with the young Luther. In his second lecture on Psalms, Luther speaks of "purest hope in the purest God" (*spes purissima in purissimum deum*).[42]

---

41. Such a person is depicted by Max Frisch (1911–91) in *Homo faber* (Frankfurt: Suhrkamp, 1957).

42. The comment is on Psalm 5:12. M. Luther, *Operationes in Psalmos* (1519–

But Luther sees hope as subject to God's holiness, which purifies and sanctifies our expectations so that hope is directed completely toward God. Gogarten, on the other hand, recommends puritanical purification or even destruction of all expectation for the sake of a pure attitude, for openness to the secrets of the future. A new virtue is necessary which can withstand the seductive idea of control of the future and by doing so win freedom for the unpredictable, "real" future. "Hope that comes of faith . . . leaves the future empty."[43]

While Gogarten wants to lead humanity back to the essence of hope by freeing such hope from the pressures of achievement, Luther speaks of hope in God by interpreting a psalm — that is, a prayer. Purity of hope, honest hope — not "pure hope" and "sheer hope" — requires a prayer for God to deliver us from the fear and care that distract us with self-seeking wishes. May God show us that the world is transitory, but also show us where God is present in this transitory world. This plea addresses the desire to calculate, administrate, rationalize, and control life. But it also encourages readiness to get involved in what is incalculable, inscrutable, and unforeseeable. God is not synonymous with the unexpected. Purified hope helps, however, distinguish between God and the unexpected.

For Gogarten *theologia negativa* is the basis of hope. *Theologia negativa* concentrates on what cannot be said, and in this it is different from Jewish eschatology. Gogarten attributes the "content" of expectation to Jewish eschatology, and insists that Christian theology has to be different.[44] Hope resulting from Christian faith is a pure attitude, and preserves its purity by not wanting to hope for anything.

---

21), in *Luthers Werke*, ed. J. F. K. Knaake et al., 66 vols., Kritische Gesamtausgabe (Weimar: Böhlau, 1883–), 5:166.16–19; hereafter cited as *WA:* "Adeo scilicet omnia a nobis aufferenda sunt, ut nec optima dei dona, idest ipsa merita, reliqua sint, in quibus fidamus, ut sit spes purissima in purissimum deum: tunc demum homo vere purus et sanctus est" ("Therefore all things must be taken away from us, so that even the best gifts of god, i.e., merits, in which we trust, are not left, so that there is the purest hope in the purest God: only then the person is really pure and holy").

43. Gogarten, *Verhängnis und Hoffnung der Neuzeit*, 127.
44. Ibid., 183.

3.4. The Shining of the New Being in History

Paul Tᴉʟʟɪᴄʜ, *Dogmatik: Marburger Vorlesung von 1925*, ed. Werner Schüßler (Düsseldorf: Patmos, 1986); idem, "Eschatologie und Geschichte" (1927), in *Main Works/Hauptwerke*, vol. 6: *Theological Writings/Theologische Schriften*, ed. Gert Hummel (Berlin and New York: Walter de Gruyter/Evangelisches Verlagswerk, 1992), 107–25 (ET: "Eschatology and History," in *The Interpretation of History*, trans. Elsa L. Talmey [New York: Charles Scribner's Sons, 1936], 266–84).

Paul Tillich does not talk about the last things or the *eschata*, nor about Jesus Christ as the *eschatos;* rather, he deals with the eschaton as the point of intersection between eternity and time.[45]

The eschaton comes into contact with time in the *kairos*, the moment of time that bears history, at which the distinction between continuation and end is located. At the same time, the absolute is glimpsed in the *kairos*. What is absolute cannot be found in the past or in any anticipated utopian future. The *kairos* has, then, a time-critical power — not as a negation of what has gone wrong, but because it is open to the reality of God.

It is this conception of eschatology as the coming of the eternal within time that connects Tillich with Barth and Bultmann. Like Gogarten, he takes sides against the German liberal Protestant theology of history, but, unlike Barth and Bultmann, without abandoning a theology of history. He follows German idealism's philosophy of history, although not in its full vision of world history or in its attempts to understand the course of universal history. The key consideration is *the moment at which history comes into being.* How does what we call "history" come into being? Tillich's intention is to use philosophy of religion to clarify this question and, in doing so, to help theology.

According to Tillich, history consists of an event within space and time that develops out of what has happened previously and that brings later events into being. A pure happening of this type, however, remains within the finite, closed circle of being. It is only when this spell is broken that something "new" happens and that "meaning" appears within space and time. This is the eschatological *kairos*. It does not descend on humans to force them to a new viewpoint. It breaks into and disturbs seemingly self-evident situations, leading anyone open to its power beyond the present and

---

45. Tillich, "Eschatology and History," 278–82.

beyond themselves. In this way, the *kairos* constitutes the point of contact between transcendence and history.

Tillich leaves the realm of Platonic thought in which time is the shadow of eternity. On the other hand, he also distances himself from the idea that humans are "guided" by utopias which they simply have to bring into being. Utopias make it possible for things that have not come into being to win both space and permanence. Utopias can be productive if they drive human consciousness beyond what exists at present, and to this extent Tillich welcomes such ideas. What Tillich objects to is the idea that the human is the subject of history. But he also does not want God to be understood as a similar agent. How could such an idea be conceived? History is not a question of space and time in which "subjects" are active. In contrast to a merely causal, mechanical-deterministic course of events, the meaning of "acting within history" stems from the "new" breaking through from the depths of being. God and human beings meet in the *kairos;* they grasp hold of what God makes possible.

The *kairos* brings something into being that is not the result of previous happenings. Time is torn apart to make way for a "meaning" that shapes it — but only if this "meaning" continues to point toward transcendence and is not spoiled by human beings. To put the concept another way, persons are not only influenced by God's activity in their inner religiosity. Rather, God enters into history, without being absorbed into it. Admittedly, Tillich would not formulate the idea like that, preferring an ontological vocabulary. Being enters into time, in order to give a meaning to what exists.

Tillich carries basic concepts of Christian theology into the conceptual world of philosophy of religion — an artificial linguistic world which has a certain charm, but does not really help precise understanding. Creation and grace are seen within the crisis of the visible. Tillich refers to the eternal origin of being which must constantly come into existence anew; eternal salvation, the liberation of existence, through meaning, from the unordered diversity of appearances; and eternal perfection, in which the validity of events — a validity they do not possess on their own — is made clear.

Material dealing with Tillich's application of the principles of religious fulfillment in a critical and decisive historical situation exists in the exchange of letters in 1933–34 between Tillich and Emanuel Hirsch.[46] Tillich and Hirsch (1888–1972), initially friends, had a common interest in theology of history, or — as Hirsch puts it — in "Christian philosophy of history."[47] Both use the idea that the "divine" is present in historical challenges, which have roots in previous developments but cannot be fully understood in terms of previous developments. In any case, these historical challenges that will decide the future cannot be met without divine meaning. Tillich attempts to identify socialism as the historical bearer of these challenges and as heir of the prophetic criticism of political, intellectual, and religious shortcomings. Hirsch, on the other hand, finds the salvation of the values torn apart by World War One in the nation (*Volkstum*), in which God's challenge to reform living conditions is heard and can be answered. Hirsch and Tillich agree that the last judgment begins to emerge within world history. For Tillich, however, judgment leads to the crisis of all historical activity and the communities involved in such activity. To this extent a certain reserve remains concerning the identification of God with history — a glimmer of the radical eschatology we examine next. According to Hirsch, the judgment of God that emerges in historical catastrophes sanctions political institutions — that is, the nation. The nation promises to reestablish intellectual and political powers undermining the Western world in the service of true social existence.

However great the distance between Hirsch's and Tillich's political views, however different their treatment of the judgment of God, the common denominator is nevertheless this concept of God's judgment. Judgment qualifies the course of history, and makes it possible to see divine intervention in historical events

---

46. P. Tillich, *Ergänzungs- und Nachlaßbände zu den Gesammelten Werken,* vol. 6: *Briefwechsel und Streitschriften: Theologische, philosophische und politische Stellungnahmen und Gespräche,* ed. Renate Albrecht and René Tautmann (Frankfurt: Evangelisches Verlagswerk, 1983), 137–218.

47. E. Hirsch, *Die gegenwärtige geistige Lage im Spiegel theologischer und philosophischer Besinnung: Akademische Vorlesungen zum Verständnis des deutschen Jahres 1933* (Göttingen: Vandenhoeck & Ruprecht, 1934). On the intellectual presuppositions in Hirsch's position, see Gunda Schneider-Flume, *Die politische Theologie Emanuel Hirsch's* (Bern: Herbert Lang; Frankfurt: Peter Lang, 1971).

and to use events as guides for healing shattered relationships. But how? Here, Tillich and Hirsch think very differently. The controversy prepares us for the problems of the theology of history (chapter 4).

In his *Systematic Theology*,[48] Tillich develops his idea of Jesus Christ as the manifestation of the *new existence*. His coming in time is not simultaneous with the futurity that belongs to listening to the proclaimed word, as it is in Bultmann's interpretation. God's new existence manifests itself within time by cutting through the course of time. This is the basis of the dynamic principle of history: no single expression of historical life is ultimate. If seen in such a light, events are perverted, falsified, even "demonized."

This dynamic is the leitmotif of the fifth part of the *Systematic Theology*, "History and the Kingdom of God." Tillich has a colorful palette in his hand, which he uses to illustrate where the kingdom of God — the Christian symbol of a fulfilled and completed life — can be seen: in all creative cultural achievement, which is creative insofar as it is a part of history.

> In every creative act progress is implied, namely, a step (*gressus*) beyond the given.[49]

> History, in terms of self-creativity of life drives toward the creation of a new, unambiguous state of things. And history, in terms of the self-transcendence of life, drives toward the universal, unambiguous fulfillment of the potentiality of being.[50]

Tillich establishes parameters for what is new in history, true to the idealistic philosophy that saw history as the progressive self-realization of the divine spirit.

Tillich exported European reactions to the crisis of totalitarian historical world-views to the United States. At the same time he blended in an element of puritanical politico-religious tradition, which emphasized crossing of boundaries, the continual necessity

---

48. P. Tillich, *Systematic Theology*, 3 vols. (Chicago: University of Chicago Press, 1951–63).
49. Ibid., 3:333.
50. Ibid.

of new departures for new shores. That blending incorporates another fundamental idea — that to set boundaries means to cross them. In the United States, the idea is almost tangible. The New World, reached by Europeans fleeing difficult circumstances and religious or political distress, had to be conquered. The pressure to expand soon led to the ideology of "manifest destiny" — the idea that God had chosen the American people for a destiny of territorial and cultural expansion.

Tillich's intent was to prevent these ideas of destiny from evolving into aggressive and defensive imperialism, not just in North America, but within Western culture as a whole. Here his thought meets the Christian ethics of his colleague at the Union Theological Seminary in New York, Reinhold Niebuhr.[51] Both wish to show eschatology to its best advantage in culture criticism. To Tillich and Niebuhr, all insistence on achievements, absolutes, and forms runs the risk of totalitarianism. To these cultural critics everything must become fluid again in order to point toward the transcendent being — only then can existence be endowed with meaning.

Tillich gained much influence in the United States with these ideas, not least within the civil rights movement, and indirectly within North American liberation theology.

Gert HUMMEL, ed., *New Creation or Eternal Now: Is There an Eschatology in Paul Tillich's Work? Contributions Made to the Third International Paul Tillich Symposium Held in Frankfurt/Main, 1990* (Berlin and New York: Walter de Gruyter, 1991); Ulrich SAMSE, *Der Zusammenhang von Eschatologie und Ethik bei Paul Tillich* (Th.D. thesis, Bonn, 1980).

3.5. Radical Eschatology — Theology with a New Horizon

3.5.1. The Message Specific to Eschatology

Karl RAHNER, "Eschatologie," in *Sacramentum Mundi*, ed. Karl Rahner et al. (Freiburg: Herder, 1967), 1:1183–92; idem, "Eschatologie, theologisch-wissenschaftstheoretisch," in *Lexikon für Theologie und Kirche*, ed. Josef Höfer and Karl Rahner (Freiburg: Herder, 1959), 3:1094–98; idem, "Theologische Prinzipien der Hermeneutik eschatologischer Aussagen," in *Schriften zur Theologie*, vol. 4 (Einsiedeln, Switzerland: Benziger, 1960) (ET: "The Hermeneutics of Theological Assertions," in *Theological Investigations*, trans. Kevin Smith [New York: Crossroad,

---

51. See, among other works, *The Nature and Destiny of Man: A Christian Interpretation*, 2 vols. (New York: Charles Scribner's Sons, 1941–43).

1982], 4:323–46); idem, "Zur Theologie der Hoffnung," in *Schriften zur Theologie,* vol. 8 (Einsiedeln: Benziger, 1967) (ET: "On the Theology of Hope," in *Theological Investigations,* trans. David Bourke [New York: The Seabury Press, 1977], 10:242–59).

Anyone who weighs the doctrine of the last things against dialectical theology's radical eschatology will find that the latter does not make the weight. Themes such as the resurrection of the dead, the last judgment, the end, and the perfection of the world are either left out completely or reinterpreted so radically that they lose their normal appearance. Those who support dialectical theology naturally put together a different account: didn't the traditional themes lose their meaning long ago? Is it not necessary to return to the origins of theology as dialectical theology does, and to reformulate theology on christological bases, as in Karl Barth? Or to use an existential interpretation, as in Rudolf Bultmann and Friedrich Gogarten? Or, as in Paul Tillich, to use a new religio-philosophical setting and to intensify analysis of contemporary issues to make eschatology rewarding and worthwhile?

The intent of radical-dialectical eschatology is not, however, to preserve the substance of the doctrine of the last things by reintroducing it with new attention to language. Rather, its hope is to revise the very foundations of theology by pointing to God as the wholly other, *totaliter aliter,* in relation to all human experience, inaccessible even to human wishes and desires and the expectations fueled by such wishes and desires.

Eschatology has to be radical to this degree if it is to deal fittingly with God's transcendence. "Transcendence" is probably far too pale a description for God's inaccessibility. The word gives the impression that the boundaries of human capabilities are crossed and that God is to be met on the other side, but that the ideas still remain in the realm of human thought. This is the case even when the human being considers the boundary set by finite nature. Who is in a position to contemplate that barrier? It is impossible to conceive the extreme radicality of the boundary of death during the course of life. Is it in fact — and, in my opinion, this is the important question — a boundary that we reach for the first time at the end of our life?

"Eschatology" indicates the boundary of *all* human discourse concerning reality. It marks that boundary when it speaks of *God crossing the border into this world,* coming to us in God's revelation. This is not an event that takes place at the end of time, nor is it the seal of history; rather, it is God's persistent activity in relation to humanity and humanity's history.

What lies behind eschatological radicality is the idea that God is infinitely distant from history, that God may be as absent in history as in nature — at least, according to the standards of our daily experience of nature and of history. The trauma of the First World War contributed to this dazed state. Thirty or forty years later it was not just the horrors of a second and more terrible war but, even more, the destruction of humanity in extermination camps which meant that God could no longer be found within human actions. Finitude, mortality, and "being toward death" (*Sein zum Tode*) — Martin Heidegger's phrase — are wretchedly helpless concepts in the face of mass murder. The boundless quantity of the killing threatens to become an inconceivable "quality" of death, a collective composition that threatens to swallow all individuality. Is Christian hope not also hit by these events? A history of individuals, independent and removed from collective implications, is unthinkable. The individual can scarcely save him- or herself with a hope that depends on personal identity, to be won or lost through interaction.

In such circumstances, can eschatology do anything more than indicate the absence of words? Such absence cannot mean silence, since silence could mean silence concerning the horrors. Paul Celan (1920–70) wrote thus:

We swear by Christ the New One to marry the dust to the dust,
the birds to the wandering shore,
our heart to a stairway in water,
We swear to the world the sacred vows of the sand,
we swear them gladly,
we swear them aloud from the rooftops of dreamless sleep
and whisk the white-hair of time . . .

They shout: You blaspheme!

We have known it long since.
We have known it long since, but what of it?

In the mills of death you grind the white meal of Promise,
you set it before our brothers and sisters —

We whisk the white-hair of time. You warn us: You blaspheme!
We know we do,
let the guilt come upon us.
Let the guilt come upon us of all warning signs,
let the gurgling ocean come,
the emphatic gust of reversal,
the midnight day,
let come what never was!

Let a man come forth from the tomb.[52]

This is the language of radical eschatology, even more radical than the previous examples. In the poem, philosophy of history shows more than signs of strain — it breaks completely. "Let come what never was" — how does that phrase relate to "Christ the New"? Had radical eschatology already sensed the collapse of the philosophy of history?

Jewish thinkers attempt to resist this attitude toward language. For example, the philosopher Emmanuel Levinas (1906–96) argues against the idea that what is true is identical with the whole. He is alluding to Hegel's Christian philosophy of history, which attempted to conceptualize the actualization of God's Spirit within history.[53]

Levinas sticks to the commandment against creating an image of God (Exod. 20:4). God is wholly and completely transcendent, impossible to depict, intangible, and incomprehensible. God meets humanity with an absolute claim, with strict commandments. Anyone who follows the directives in the Torah can create space for salvation. This notion of God is a touch more unrelenting than the *Unverfügbarkeit* (not at one's disposal) of God and humanity as seen by Bultmann, Gogarten, and the like. Levinas's view liberates

---

52. P. Celan, "Late and Deep," in *Speech-Grille and Selected Poems,* trans. Joachim Neugroschel (New York: E. P. Dutton, 1971), 25.

53. E. Levinas, *Totalité et Infini: Essai sur l'Extériorité* (The Hague: Martinus Nijhoff, 1961) (ET: *Totality and Infinity: An Essay on Exteriority,* trans. Alphonso Lingis [Pittsburgh: Duquesne University Press, 1969]); idem, *Le Temps et l'Autre* (Montpellier, France: Fata Morgana, 1979) (ET: *Time and the Other and Additional Essays,* trans. Richard A. Cohen [Pittsburgh: Duquesne University Press, 1987]).

theology from any objectifying view of God, the world, and humanity. Levinas sees humanity called to responsibility for salvation or perdition. God's transcendence does not allow humanity to escape; it confronts humanity, so that humanity can stand firm for the decisive moment and judgment.

But can this ethic of salvation survive without a concept of history? Walter Benjamin (1892–1940) deals with this question.[54] Benjamin attacks the perception of time as a continuously flowing current — an idea that is the basis of the Western ideology of progress (thesis 6). Within this flow of time, all moments are alike. There is no creative pause, no return to successful moments. "Progress" of this sort is devastating: it sweeps past everybody that it doesn't carry along, swallowing the sufferers, and the forgotten.

The "angel of history" sees the inexorable course of progress as it really is, as a heap of rubble rising toward heaven (thesis 9). Behind the angel the gates of paradise are barred. Therefore, the future is not a space accessible to humanity.

Against the futility of pure progress Benjamin sets his hope in the moment, in which the gates of paradise will open and salvation will come to humanity. Salvation will reconcile humanity with its past, with all those who lived and who have been forgotten. The motif Benjamin uses is both apocalyptic and messianic. God sets an end to the suffering of this earth, transforming it into happiness by redeeming those who suffer from their apparent futility and, by so doing, freeing history from its vanity. That act will occur at the day of judgment and halt the destructive progress of history; it will tear apart the "continuum of history" (theses 15–16). It is not enough simply to await this "present time" that can occur at any moment (see thesis 3); it must be brought to pass (thesis 15). A new subject of history must arise, who will draw to himself what slumbers in the forgetfulness of history — perhaps the lost paradise.

For Benjamin, messianism and Marxism must enter into symbiosis in order to bring an end to the inferno of inhuman subjugation of the world. Benjamin calls to mind the theological elements that secretly drive Marxism (see thesis 1), but his intent is above all

---

54. W. Benjamin, "Geschichtsphilosophische Thesen," in *Zur Kritik der Gewalt und andere Aufsätze* (Frankfurt: Suhrkamp, 1971), 78–96.

to revise Marxist views of history that have the effect of swallowing up individuals. Benjamin was himself a victim, but nevertheless
is not afraid of the theology of history. His messianic expectation
forces him to come to terms with it.[55]

Does messianism as the guiding star of salvation throw light on
Jesus' cry from the cross, "It is accomplished"? Or does the cry
again raise consistent eschatology's question (2.5.1) of what has
been changed by Jesus Christ — and how it has changed? How can
Celan refer to Christ as "Christ the New One"?

Referring to Jesus' cry on the cross, *what is accomplished?* even
the radical eschatology of dialectical theology does not go far
enough when faced with this question. It does not go far enough
if it can only deal with expectation of the coming Christ in terms
of what happened "once and for all" through him. For this leads
to "Christology as...eschatology in perfect tense" (*Christologie
als...perfektische Eschatologie*);[56] all that remains is to decide
what happened in Christ. No eschatology would be necessary. The
dominating motif is a retrospective view of Jesus Christ, and that
means falling victim to a false concept — not simply a false idea
of space and time but, far worse, a distortion or even deformation
of Christology. Jesus Christ cannot merely be behind us — what
would there be before us?

The question remains, Does Christianity preserve a memory of
Christ and consider this memory suitable preparation for everything that is to come? Or does Christianity commemorate Christ
by hoping in him and speaking of him as "the Coming One"? We
have already seen (2.5.1) that it is not enough to answer, "One or
the other." Church tradition had always held fast to the idea that
Jesus Christ, who came to save us, will come again. But if that idea
refers to more than the quantitative completion of Christ's work,

---

55. Benjamin's thoughts are influential especially for Roman Catholic theolo-
gians. See Johann Baptist Metz, "Hope as Imminent Expectation or the Struggle
for Forgotten Time: Noncontemporaneous Theses on the Apocalyptic View," in
Faith in History and Society: Towards a Practical Fundamental Theology, trans.
David Smith (New York: Seabury Press, 1980), 169–79; Medard Kehl, *Escha-
tologie* (Würzburg: Echter, 1986), 327–36; Josef Wohlmuth, "Zur Bedeutung der
'Geschichtsthesen' Walter Benjamins für die christliche Eschatologie," *Evangelische
Theologie* 50 (1990): 2–20.

56. Gerhard Ebeling, *Dogmatik des christlichen Glaubens* (Tübingen: J. C. B.
Mohr, 1979), 3:399.

what characterizes the *parousia?* Who do we expect the Coming One to be?

The radical eschatology of dialectical theology never or rarely, as in the case of Karl Barth, dealt with such questions. The intention of dialectical theology was, in order to talk about God, to clarify what it means to refer to Jesus Christ. Therefore dialectical theology attacked every hope nurtured only by Christianity's high-handed and self-sufficient expectations which merely proposed ways to live a better life and to conduct cultural activity.

When Barth, Bultmann, and Gogarten separated eschatology from the theory of progressive accretions of Christianity, their intention was also to attack the evidences of degeneration in church and theology. Hope arriving from Christianity's promises can quickly turn to resignation if noble Christian ideals are endangered by historical catastrophes and the destruction of cultural values. When this happens, many people refer to the motto: "Better not to hope in something that could be disappointing; better just to believe!"

In the argument *concerning the reasons for hope,* dialectical theologians pointed to the transcendence of God and to *the* hope that can only come from God — from outside ourselves. This appeal spearheads radical eschatology against all historical foundations of theology; thus, eschatology takes on a central significance for theology as a whole.

On the Roman Catholic side, Karl Rahner (1904–84) also spoke in favor of a decidedly christological reduction of eschatology. In 1960, two years before the Second Vatican Council, he proposed a complete rethinking of the doctrine of the last things. He proposed freedom from the doctrine in order to get to the most basic hope of Christianity. A clarification of hermeneutical premises, particularly in biblical texts that had only been used as proof passages to support traditional church dogmatics, laid the groundwork for this rethinking of eschatology. Rahner also found fault with the way dogmatics largely ignored the riches of insight regarding hope won in the history of the church. Dogmatic eschatology was no longer sufficiently embedded in the experience of faith, and no longer capable of dealing with false expectations within the church. As Rahner sketched in two encyclopedia articles, this was why the framework of eschatology needed to be redefined, in order to deal with tasks of Christianity in the future and with changed perceptions of the world and time.

Is it an exaggeration to suspect that Rahner, writing shortly before the Council, targeted church triumphalism as well as the self-destructive discouragement within theology? The traditional doctrine of the last things could no longer inspire hope, partly because its assumptions were hopelessly far removed from the ideas about what could be known.

Rahner develops his definition of eschatology in contrast to apocalypticism, accusing the latter of predicting a fixed future in the present:

> Christian eschatology is not some anticipating reportage of events to happen later[,]...rather for the human in his spiritual decision for freedom it is a necessary first look from himself, from the particular salvation-historical situation through the Christ event (as aetiological basis of knowledge) onto the final consummation of this person's own individuality, already the eschatological existential situation for the making possible of his individually clarified decision into the mysterious opening...[57]

Apocalypticism is presented as the opposing type to eschatology, as a fixed idea of the future that determines the present. One might ask if it is true that Christianity has no need for visions.

Eschatology, on the other hand, *unfolds* the history of Christ, regarding the future as yet to happen in time and as where the encounter with Christ will take place; apocalypticism attempts to "catch up" with future.

There is a twofold objection to anticipation of the future, according to Rahner. First, God's future is closed to human knowledge — according to Mark 13:32, not even God's Son knows the day and hour of the eschaton.[58] If we knew the end, we would see ourselves determined by that knowledge, in which case we would not be truly free. Eschatology has to guarantee the gift of freedom for history. *Freedom* is Rahner's real interest — freedom as an

57. Rahner, "Eschatologie, theologisch-wissenschaftstheoretisch," 1096.
58. Rahner, "Theologische Prinzipien," 408.

essential character of faith. Does freedom come from the New Testament, or does it stem more from a fascination for the philosophy of freedom found in German idealism, which considered human fate to be threatened by foreign heteronomy? Rahner's fear that freedom is endangered by the future is one aspect of this tendency to avoid foreign heteronomy.

Eschatology is formed through christological anticipation of "perfection," based on the idea that the believer has already reached a form of eschatological existence (*schon eschatologische Daseinssituation*). This view does not propose a gleaming future but a perspective on God's activity, even if it tends to leave possibilities open rather than defining what occurs between God and humankind. The hope that comes from faith is shaped in accordance to what happened to Jesus Christ. Eschatology offers the *perspective of the christological perfect.* There Karl Rahner is in agreement with Karl Barth.

This christological foundation differs from Christian hope derived from the historical effects of the life and death of Jesus of Nazareth. In this formulation, hope is found in the history of Jesus Christ, in what happened between the true God and the true man, in the salvific value of what is communicated and granted to those who believe in Christ through the Spirit of God. *The future of salvation is the eschatological perspective of the Christ-event.* Only this can ward off false expectations and overcome the resignation that comes from disappointed hopes.

What is accomplished? One might ask what we no longer need to accomplish since the life and death of Jesus Christ has revealed what we are unable to do. On the cross, Jesus has removed confusion between our existence and what we consider to be "God," while at the same time removing the chasm between God's "transcendence" and all human attempts to bridge the gap. Jesus Christ, the crucified one whom God has raised to life, stands before us as true God and true man. According to Hebrews,[59] he has been led along a path that now stands open to us — the path that accords with God's will (Heb. 2:4–18; 4:4–16). Jesus encourages us to ex-

---

59. This is the line followed by Bertold Klappert, *Die Eschatologie des Hebräerbriefs* (Munich: Chr. Kaiser, 1969).

pect that we will be drawn into what God wills. He is the only human who can tell us what has changed and how it has changed, because at the same time as being human he is the wholly other.

This seems to be the essence of a christologically centered radical eschatology. The price is high. Eschatology is absorbed into christologically determined theology so that it ceases to be a special doctrine. In the case of Bultmann, Gogarten, and Tillich, the traditional framework of dogmatics is either abandoned or taken up only in certain motifs.

Paradoxically, radical eschatology makes necessary the question, *why eschatology at all?* What does Christian theology lack if it lacks a specific eschatology? What can eschatology say that can be said in no other field of theology?

The specific subject of eschatology is God's activity in creating the new, which is accomplished by irrevocably bringing the old to an end or by perfecting what is brought to an end. God deals with what already exists by transforming it. In this activity of judging and redeeming the character of God's judgment can be seen. *God will pronounce judgment over what is, what is no more, and what will remain.* This verdict allows for no repeal. The verdict does not reject creation, but makes a creative call to new being. The verdict does not "restore" anything.

Although we still await God's judgment, judgment takes place whenever God constitutes hope. This happens when God calls us to the incomparable hope that nothing can separate us from God, because God, who was against us when we resisted, is for us (Rom. 8:31). This promise also makes clear that we are far from a direct relationship with God, and, furthermore, that we cannot even "be" directly in relation to ourselves. God's judgment shows what stands between God and the world, and reveals the hidden contradictions in which we exist and which oppress God's creatures.

Eschatology deals with the surprise that *we are recognized* and become transparent to ourselves in community with God. This surprise exceeds every self-recognition and understanding of the world, since every attempt to recognize oneself and others is distorted by sin. Sin causes one to become misshapen by drawing back into oneself. For that reason, although sin is so close to us, it is impossible to demonstrate what "sin" is. Only eschatology makes it possible to talk about sin as resistance to the hope that we have been granted; only through eschatology can sin be recognized as resistance.

Sin is recognized when God steps between the sinner and his sin. The sinner is no longer alone with himself and his self-restricting endeavors. The sinner becomes aware that the relationship between his actions and experiences is different from what he had previously assumed. He leaves behind an entangling web of reality which he had produced. Recognition of sin is always a liberating act, allowing for the hope of complete clarity.

Liberating and reconciling clarity is a sign that God's reality will one day render obsolete our present assumptions. Only then will perception, no longer disturbed and driven by conflict, find peace. *Who and what we are able to recognize will be completely transformed.* When Dutch theologian Oepke Noordmans (1871–1956) was lying on his deathbed, his doctor asked if the two would recognize each other again some day. Noordmans did not answer, but some days later replied, "How well do we really know each other — anyway?"

Paul says, "We walk by faith, not by sight" (2 Cor. 5:7), referring to God's judgment in which *we are revealed.* We are revealed to God and to ourselves in the way God wishes to see us; we are not naked and ashamed. That we cannot see this way during life does not mean that the hope that comes from faith is blind. If that were so, how could it help us? The vision of God perfects our status before God, and reveals how we have stood previously before God.

Eschatology speaks of *being saved, becoming whole and wholly different* — of being transformed to be one with creation. The world sighs and groans because it brings something into being out of accord with creation (Rom. 8:20–22). Activity in the world is futile to the extent that humanity desires achievement. Salvation means freedom from the urge to dominate, from all forms of egocentricity joined with alienation. But salvation does not lead to the self-dissolution in a speechless and anonymous universe. Salvation transforms the divided life and makes it whole. It does not dissolve and sublimate by separating body from soul or essence from the inessential.

The topic of eschatology is formed and re-created by God to

give salvation to the suffering. Salvation is promised to the world with all its darkness, confusion, and futility. God will bring clarity, and we will see God as God (1 John 3:2) and ourselves as we are and have been. From God persons receive hope in God. All that we have hoped for will fall away but we will still hope in *something*. Otherwise we would be blind. But it is important that we do not try to use expectation to create ourselves.

Ultimately, *God will be all in all* (1 Cor. 15:28). God rules over everything and in everything. Jesus Christ, the Coming One, will subordinate himself to God, once every enemy has surrendered, including death. God as all in all is not an all-engulfing power, but exists in everything. We can hope that God will be wholly God in every element of creation. This "fullness" is not the sum of constituent pieces. God as all in all is the *full richness* of divine community. Just as God as Father, Son, and Holy Spirit are one, without merging or being absorbed into one another, we may hope that we too will live in unity with God. Just as Jesus Christ is not absorbed into and does not come to an end in God, we will neither pass away before God nor dissolve into God. That is our hope.

Jesus Christ, true God and true man, is the Coming One who promises us community with God and who directs us toward God, the all in all. To make this statement we need an eschatology that is more than an appendix of Christology. The same applies to pneumatology, the doctrine of the Holy Spirit (see 2.5.2). The doctrine of the Holy Spirit teaches that there is something behind us which is at the same time before us, endowing time and awakening hope. Even this teaching could be misunderstood without eschatology, as if God's Spirit were an inexhaustible and unpredictable overflowing of God's inexhaustible life. Eschatology is also indispensable for the doctrine of the Trinity (3.1). If discourse concerning God is grounded in God's very own history and activity, then eschatology reminds us that the economic Trinity (God's action in the world) has its promise in God's divinity. This promise points to the immanent Trinity, to the full richness of the divine being, and to divine existence in the movement of the three persons of the Godhead toward each other. Thus, the first and last questions of theology are directed toward God's reality. That question is and remains the genuine question of hope.

3.5.2. Salvation Event + History = History of Salvation?

Oscar CULLMANN, *Christus und die Zeit: Die urchristliche Zeit- und Geschichtsauf-fassung* (Zollikon-Zurich: Evangelischer Verlag, 1946) (ET: *Christ and Time: The Primitive Christian Conception of Time and History,* trans. Floyd V. Filson [Phila-delphia: Westminster Press (1950)]); idem, *Heil als Geschichte: Heilsgeschichtliche Existenz im Neuen Testament* (Tübingen: J. C. B. Mohr, 1965) (ET: *Salvation in History,* trans. Sidney G. Sowers [New York: Harper & Row, 1967]); Karl LÖWITH, *Meaning in History* (Chicago: University of Chicago Press, 1949).

A further issue that dialectical theology's radical eschatology discarded without proper treatment was theology of history in all its forms. Bultmann and Gogarten tended to overlook history, while Tillich, Levinas, and Benjamin denied totalitarian concepts of his-tory. These thinkers raised the objection to history as a topic of theology. History must be left out as a foundation of theology be-cause God is the wholly other in opposition to all events in human activity. If we approach the question from another angle, these theologians seem to deny the existence of meaning within history, and to deny progress aimed at the perfection of human culture. These denials are tied up with an attempt to create another meaning for human existence. This was Friedrich Nietzsche's anti-Christian message, which has grown in influence since the turn of the century.

During World War II, the Jewish philosopher Karl Löwith (1897–1973) drew attention to the situation. The situation had darkened the philosophical skies of Europe, leaving the "will to power" (*Wille zur Macht*) in Nietzsche's phrase, as seemingly the only force capable of determining history. In the twentieth cen-tury, this hunger for power has been distorted and perverted to a degree which Nietzsche could not have dreamed in even his boldest prophecies. Nietzsche's revival of the doctrine of eternal recurrence[60] transforms the concept of history from a straight line moving toward a goal into a circular movement, in which things come into being and pass away. Only the mighty in history sur-vive. Because of this fact, the history of humanity is threatened with destruction.

Continuing without an ideology of progress would not be the worst possibility. Even the appeal to a historical telos has, to date, caused more harm than good. What is important is whether the

---

60. Löwith, *Meaning in History,* 214–22.

passage of time is qualified or seen only as a collection of moments. Our perception of time depends on whether as is usual we establish the present as the central point of our certainty. From the present we look forward or backward, because we consider the present to be closest. It is different when past, present, and future are allotted specific worth, because then we see ourselves within a temporal coherence in which direction is determined. When time is thus qualified, it is the middle of the span of time — the *midpoint* — that is authoritative. From the midpoint one looks both forward and back. It is not the *beginning* or the *end* that is authoritative. In contrast to the present, which we make central, the midpoint is decided by something external to us.

Christianity takes the Christ-event as midpoint. Before the Christ-event was a time of expectation or preparation, but everything afterward is influenced by the advent of Jesus of Nazareth. How this latter time is named — whether "after Christ," the age of new expectation, or perhaps the era of fulfilled expectation — is important for eschatology and must be considered. Löwith sticks with a view of history that accords with the Christian measurement of time, in which the time "after Christ," it is believed, will culminate in the end of world history. It is in the Christian idea, according to Löwith, that the roots of Western conceptions of history are to be found.

The modern belief in progress rejects such views in favor of a search for perfection that expects everything from the future. The past becomes "nontime." A powerful will selects groups to purify the world and destines other groups to destruction. This leads to the prominence of an allegedly natural will to survival, which is an enemy of history because it ignores memories and refuses to acknowledge limits. In order to ward off such terror, Löwith attempts to remind us of the foundations of concepts of history, though he does not believe such recognition can produce a new impetus for the future of Europe and the world.

Whether Western conceptions of history are really rooted in the Christian view of the "midpoint of the ages" has been much debated.[61] It is also debatable in theology whether the concept

---

61. See Walter Jaeschke, *Die Suche nach den eschatologischen Wurzeln der*

adequately expresses the relationship between the Christ-event and time.

Löwith's theological source is Oscar Cullmann (1902–99), who advocates *salvation history* (*Heilsgeschichte*) — the concept of a linear passage of time planned by God for the purpose of carrying out God's *plan of salvation* (*Heilsplan*). This concept is presented both as an alternative to radical eschatology and as a critique of consistent eschatology:

> According to the New Testament view, all the epochs which make up salvation history are oriented toward the happening of the decisive period, the cross and resurrection of Jesus Christ. The *whole* salvation history present in God's plan is latently contained in this one event. All the preceding history of salvation tends toward the occurrence of this period. The present period in the history of salvation issues from it, and the whole future of salvation history portrays it in its universal and permanent consummation.[62]

To Cullmann, the linear course of history is binding for Christian faith and hope. He emphasizes *history after Christ*. The Christ-event is developed because the salvation event is still incomplete. What happened to Christ is certain: "What is yet to come *will* come *because* the crucial event *has* occurred."[63] Jesus accomplishes what traditional apocalyptic expectation attributes to the kingdom of God by saving us from the powers opposed to God and by defeating Satan and death. But the enemies have yet to be fully conquered. Although they no longer dominate, they can still cause trouble. Only total subjugation to Christ will set the seal on God's rule.

Jesus Christ has taken on his role as ruler of the world, but his rule has yet to be established everywhere. Still, the nature of his rule means that it will one day be completed.

> The decisive battle has already been won. But the war continues until a certain, though not as yet definite, Victory Day

---

Geschichtsphilosophie: Eine historische Kritik der Säkularisierungsthese (Munich: Chr. Kaiser, 1976).

62. Cullmann, *Salvation in History,* 166.
63. Ibid., 174.

when the weapons will at last be still. The decisive battle would be Christ's death and resurrection, and Victory Day his *parousia*.[64]

In this metaphor, which Cullmann had applied already in 1945,[65] Cullmann has in mind the decisive battles of the Second World War, in which the end was repeatedly delayed by fruitless counteroffensives and rearguard actions involving heavy losses. The point of the comparison is to illustrate the eschatology of salvation history and to stress that everything that the future can bring has happened once and for all in Christ, but has not yet come to pass.

The metaphor of "Victory Day" is designed to mediate between what is "final" or conclusive, and the "end." The battle scenario can, however, easily lead to false ideas. Centuries — even millennia — could pass between the decisive battle and the final victory. The end of the world would then no longer resemble a decisive apocalyptic battle but a cleaning-up operation to dispose of remaining enemies who have not realized that the hour has struck. What a grotesque idea! What theater of war would it be if resistance could continue on large scale? What troops does a commander need to gain final victory and to end challenges of the enemy?

But it would be a misunderstanding to attribute such an extended interpretation to Cullmann, who tries to make plausible the idea that "after Christ" there can be no hope in God that does not also orient itself according to what Christ accomplished. At the same time, Cullmann's intention is to show that the christological perfect does not just permit expectation; it demands expectation. This conclusion comes from the fact that not everything ended or became perfect in Jesus' death and resurrection. The plausibility of the battle metaphor obscures the question that really must be asked: *Why is there still history,* let alone salvation history? Is it just because time goes on?

Why did time continue after Good Friday and Easter Sunday? Why did life carry on without radical change to history? Consis-

---

64. Ibid., 44.
65. Cullmann, *Christ and Time*, 84, 141.

tent eschatology asked a similar question — rather, it did not ask it, since it assumed unrestricted progress of history and averted the crisis of imminent expectation (*Naherwartung*). In radical eschatology, the question does not need to be asked at all, because the "christological perfect" leaves the modern concept of history in a state of permanent crisis. Rejecting the apparently obvious question, "Why does history go on?" is well grounded, although it sacrifices all theological concepts of coherent history within a temporal continuum.

Cullmann is not satisfied with that sacrifice. What happened to Jesus Christ is the foundation of Christian hope — he stands by that. However, this notion must accompany hope as the certain prospect of an end included in God's plans; the hope is, so to speak, preprogrammed. Further, something more must come if God's plan, proclaimed in the Christ-event, is to succeed. Cullmann's protest against consistent and radical eschatology leads to a counterreaction. Cullmann overemphasizes divine plans for the future and therefore the related right to understand world events as part of God's salvation plan, where Jesus Christ is the midpoint and crux of salvation history.

Anyone who asks why history continues must ask another question: *Is expectation perhaps more important than salvation,* if God allows history to continue for the sake of expectation? Such thinking represents a temptation, coming from a series of typical irritations within eschatology, which stem from the urge to illustrate or to draw analogies. Cullmann's battle and victory metaphor, taken from the New Testament, can lead to wondering about God's power or impotence. Kingdom of God terminology can also lead to familiar negative associations of power.

But God's victories are not designed to achieve total subjugation. They are therefore inconceivable. It would be worse to confuse the phrases "it is accomplished" with "not yet completed," so that assumptions about what it means for something to be "accomplished" lead to attempts to find out what remains to be done, and how we should be involved. Another tendency is to cultivate nostalgic ideas of the stories about Jesus and the youthful beginnings of Christianity in order to show the decadence of the church and world today and to build the hope of eliminating this state of affairs. Even the motif of "perfection" as perfect recognition (as regarded by Barth) can be deceptive, if it is stressed that full recognition of God's truth has not come since opacity and doubts remain, in which case perfection becomes a question of "wait and see."

Such perspectives and the questions from which they arise have one thing in common. "Future" is regarded as *extra nos*, external to us, in the sense that, for whatever reason, it has yet to happen. The inescapable linear understanding of time comes from this idea. We will not escape this understanding, despite well-meaning attempts (radical eschatology among them) to stress its insufficiency and that it imprisons us.

Jesus' cry from the cross, "It is accomplished," though stated in the perfect tense, is not bound to linear concepts of time, in that it must always be newly proclaimed, and therefore remains before us. Similarly hope in Christ as the Coming One does not leave us floating in a continually progressing river of time that sweeps us along as it empties into perfection. Hope in Jesus Christ confronts us with a future that is far beyond what we, given our past, would be limited to by time. Therefore, *hope based in Jesus Christ is far more the* extra nos *of our future.*

The essence of this concept in theology is *promise*. God promises God's justice, freedom, life, knowledge, and community, to mention only the most important promises in the Bible. To list such promises in detail would be a task in its own right. How God's promises fit together and how salvation arises from the promises are questions that also involve expectation.

The more the perception that God's promise qualifies time takes hold, the less conceivable it is that the mere passage of time is the ultimate in our experience. What has happened up to now has either passed away or, as the object of God's re-creating activity, remains full of life. We can look to the future as neither the mere space for possibility nor the shadowy area of uncertainty.

Christian theology has learned to investigate the relationship between salvation and history in this manner. In the early days, it had to deal with the time "before Christ" not just as a period that had been completed. It had to consider what could be said in view of Jesus Christ, not with regard to what had happened "after Christ" but in terms of what could be hoped for following his birth, death, and resurrection. Consideration had to be given to what could be said of Christ's presence. Ordering events according to the history of Jesus Christ, the Coming One, has roots in the relationship between God's ongoing activity and what we perceive of this activity and, therefore, what we can proclaim and expect.

The answer is not, even with reference to the Bible, to account for what in history has failed. Were that the case, the christological perfect would stand against a future of perfection. That would be typical of the quasi-salvation-historical viewpoint widespread within the ecumenical movement these days. According to this view, Christ has inaugurated an age which will one day reach its target, despite all obstacles and resistance. This leaves space in the world for expectations of salvation. There is room for hope which can quickly spawn "prophetic" demands, or at least the conviction that the kingdom of God is coming without delay. Christian poetry overflows with such descriptions, attempting to illustrate what is possible "after Christ" but has not yet been fully achieved. History "after Christ" is sometimes divided again into the finite and conquered dark age on one side and the current time — the "Christian century" — on the other side. This is supposedly an age of increasing insight and concern for God's intentions and for our response.

Our investigation of the relationship between salvation and history runs up against the cry from the cross, "It is accomplished!" What has happened on the cross, and how? That is the decisive question! The Father of Jesus Christ is revealed as the *hidden* God, but as one who is not absent from our time. God is unexpectedly close to God's creatures, in a way which both baffles and fulfills every previous expectation. It is God's way of being present that characterizes the history of Christ. As the Christ hymn in Colossians 1:15–20 expresses, God is present for all the world and for all ages. *God's activity is hidden in history.* That does not mean that God's activity is beyond history and therefore not to be discerned in history. Rather, *God acts in God's way, which urges us to hope and serves as an affliction (Anfechtung).* Affliction is not just caused by God's distance, but by God's proximity, which is alien.

The affliction is the result of God's hiddenness. We cannot talk our way out of what happens and what we have done by citing God's absence. The affliction of the hiddenness of God, along with the affliction that comes from human existence, is promised to us, and yet is not reconcilable with our self-perception and consciousness of time. We cannot avoid either affliction; they press together and give rise to anxiety.

The affliction chokes hope. Remaining time seems to be draining away. Does time have a direction, or does it disappear? Do we still have time to realize God's promise? If God's promise is enacted, the affliction is overcome. We are granted a period of time with direction. Since God promises that the affliction will pass, "time" is of eschatological meaning. When God is "all in all," all affliction will cease, and space will be unlimited.

It is only after these considerations that history can be seen as a unity, although, admittedly, not as a self-evident context. History can become a topic of theology, because all histories since the coming of Jesus Christ relate to affliction and hope. Are histories located in a post-Christian world "after Christ," or have they happened "with Christ" and, therefore, exist as God's activity in humanity? We all have our own histories, or stories, but only God's activity, full of promise, brings them together to form a common history.

The theology of salvation history understands *anno Domini* as the history of the church. If ecclesiology is not considered, we are in danger — even when critical of the church — of depicting the era of the church as a mere continuation of history. We have no choice but to place our stories in the time "after Christ"; that is where our faith is settled. But this place is not what God promised in Christ. It is not being in Christ (2 Cor. 5:17). It is not life with Christ in God (Col. 3:3).

Hans-Georg Hermesmann, *Zeit und Heil: Oscar Cullmanns Theologie der Heilsgeschichte* (Paderborn: Bonifatius, 1979); Geiko Müller-Fahrenholz, *Heilsgeschichte zwischen Ideologie und Prophetie: Profile und Kritik heilsgeschichtlicher Theorien in der ökumenischen Bewegung zwischen 1948 und 1968* (Freiburg: Herder, 1974); Karl-Heinz Schlaudraff, *"Heil als Geschichte"? Die Frage nach dem heilsgeschichtlichen Denken, dargestellt anhand der Konzeption Oscar Cullmanns* (Tübingen: J. C. B. Mohr, 1988).

3.5.3. Eschatology as a Theological Critique of Talk about the Future

Gerhard Sauter, *Zukunft und Verheißung: Das Problem der Zukunft in der gegen-wärtigen theologischen und philosophischen Diskussion* (Zurich: Zwingli Verlag, 1965); idem, *Erwartung und Erfahrung: Predigten, Vorträge und Aufsätze* (Munich: Chr. Kaiser, 1972); idem, *Eschatological Rationality: Theological Issues in Focus* (Grand Rapids, Mich.: Baker Book House, 1996).

How is the *extra nos* of the future to be expressed? Who are *we* who talk about the future? If all theology is affected by the fact that we are sinners and that we can only talk in broken tones concerning God, it is also the case that we humans "have" no future if we are not reconciled by God with Godself, with one another, and with ourselves.

Eschatology sketches the hope that belongs to faith. We are freed from the self-produced bondage of cyclic or linear-temporal patterns of thought. That is, we can abandon the certainty in a future already tendentially present, which only needs to unfold. *Eschatology, on the contrary, begins with God's promise* and re-calls Christ as the *eschatos* of hope given to human beings. The hope counters powers that fetter humanity's imagination and that determine humanity's hopes and fears.

Eschatology can verify the concrete aspects of Christian hope by breaking the suggestive powers of such restraining influences, without leaving humanity blind and speechless. At the same time, eschatology has to point out that Christians do not testify to hope by putting it to work and presenting it as a work, but rather by learning together to see the newly creating word of God with new eyes. Ears that hear, eyes that see, hands that do — these turn, *oblivious to ourselves and to the world,* toward the one who frees us from our origins and ends our monologues. Anyone who now speaks can do so only in repentance and conversion, by turning to this God from whom humanity still has everything to expect.

The hope that God awakens remains alien to us. But "do not be afraid" we are told, because the alien nature of hope teaches us to see.

What is surprising in God is not just that, as Creator, God remains different from creation and underivable, but that God encounters us as true God and shows us what it is to be truly human. It is not only God who is alien — we are alien to ourselves. We do not know ourselves as we really are. This ignorance has nothing to do with the ontological difference between being and reality, or, in Tillich's words, between "essence" and "existence," or because we anticipate our actual being, which we can at most follow like a shadow. To conceive such ignorance as a deficiency that, when necessary, spurs imagination and invention, would be to forget that we cannot imagine who we are even if we wanted to — and we generally do not want to. Yet, in the promise, God *has* come so close that we can no longer avoid asking who we *are* before this God. In this confrontation is a tension that must be endured. To endure it means to hope.

In this respect, eschatology deals with futurity, but in its own way. It does not limit itself to advocating that the human consciousness of time be directed forward or that "temporality" be understood on the basis of each person's end. Eschatology, in everything that it can say and proclaim, teaches us to ask what the last questions are — questions that are the beginning of thinking because they come from the perception of God's promise.

– Chapter 4 –

The God of Hope —
The Sovereignty of the Future

4.1. Outbreaks and Breakthroughs

Both consistent eschatology and radical eschatology came to grips in their own way with the theology of history that looks to the perfection of Christianity in historical progress. Theology of history attempts to bring Christian hope into harmony with the process of history. We might ask, *How far have we come, according to God's will and plan, in relation to what should happen in history? How far are we from the goal?* For Christianity, there is also a self-critical question: Has Christianity strayed from the path of God's will for history? Has it lost sight of its final goal, the kingdom of God, and should it turn back as quickly as possible? Exegetical research into Jesus' proclamation of the kingdom of God, and the consciousness of the constant presence of God developed by systematic theology, seemed to eliminate the rationale for such questions.

But the question at the root of theology of history can only be disregarded for a time. The third "eschatological storm," which broke out in the 1960s, developed in Europe and North America as a division over what should be expected from the future. The question was vital for those who were cogs in the wheels of industry and bureaucracy, objects of a technically controlled world, and for the marginalized and despised. What is their future? Is it not already planned?

Questions about what and who have a future are increasingly rooted in the tensions between impoverished and rich nations. These tensions are increasing inexorably, not just because the economic divide is growing, but also because the privileged have —

and *want* — a perspective different from the disadvantaged. That is how many theologians see the situation. They express concern for, and with, those of little hope and want to build a way to the future by changing the status quo. Intensified by the fluctuating economic, social, and political world climate, the battle for the common future has begun.

This perspective brings back ideas entertained by theology of history. *Concepts of historical perfection* are developed, *designed to clear the way for a vision of the "whole" of history.* This is how theology of history is expressed. What happens should be seen in relation to what God wills to achieve — or, put another way, in relation to what God has in mind. What God has in mind should be seen as the meaningful context of history.

This idea works on the assumption that God allows humanity to know what God has in mind. Opinions differ greatly on how humanity finds this out. Some people refer to biblical quotations that they say predict historical events. Others look to historical events in which they are convinced that God is visible, and say those events can be used to discern what else God wants to achieve. Others say that one must study the *course* of history to discover God's will. For example, in 1835 Alexis de Tocqueville (1805–59) wrote about the development of democratic equality in such terms:

> God does not Himself need to speak for us to find sure signs of His will; it is enough to observe the customary progress of nature and the continuous tendency of events. . . . If patient observation and sincere meditation have led men of the present day to recognize that both the past and the future of their history consist in the gradual and measured advance of equality, that discovery itself gives this progress the sacred character of the will of the Sovereign Master. In that case effort to halt democracy appears as a fight against God Himself, and nations have no alternative but to acquiesce in the social state imposed by Providence.[1]

These ideas are based on the conviction that God reveals or has revealed Godself in such a way that humanity can interpret what

---

1. A. de Tocqueville, *Democracy in America,* ed. J. P. Mayer, trans. George Lawrence (Garden City, N.Y.: Doubleday, 1969), 12.

happens accordingly. The idea is that humanity is in a position to read God's intentions and goals from history, and has been called to do so. The harmony between knowledge of God's will and what happens is presented interpretatively. Such interpretation can extend to God's voice being heard in certain historical situations or in the voices of people particularly affected by those situations.

Examples of both ideas of the historical future (1.2.2) show that theology of history assumes *that God is involved in history.* Some of the characteristics of this idea are listed below:

- "History" exists only in the singular — "histories" do not exist alongside or opposed to each other. There must be *one* history.

- History displays coherence that can be seen from one overall perspective, where the meaning of history shines through.

- History is a framework of events in which humans are or should be involved for the sake of God.

- God's will and human action must fit together in history.

- History — or at least history's tendencies — should be examined as a whole, so that the divinely willed direction is not overlooked.

The last idea often leads to God's attitude to history being described as an affirmation or rejection of certain events and developments. The idea is based on the conviction that we should know God's intention for the history of humanity. If God intends to steer all events rather than to intervene occasionally, this points to a telos. Therefore, theology of history leads to an eschatology that incorporates a divinely willed telos of history. This type of eschatology is, in turn, an indispensable component of theology of history. History is viewed as a coherent sequence of events.

Theology of history provides *one* answer to the question of God's involvement in history. But it follows with a further question: what stands between us and what history should achieve? How near are we to the telos?

This question is suggested by the idea that God has a plan for history, if "plan" is understood as a timetable that humans also have to honor. The passengers must not turn up late, and must be prepared to put up with unforeseeable delays. The passengers are, however, not simply passengers; they must help the train arrive at its destination. Signals must be observed, or chaos is possible.

The argument seems overstated, but is designed to draw attention to the fact that we encounter theology of history when seeking clarification of God's relationship to humanity through divine declaration. A declaration of divine will would enable us — in fact, it would command us — to measure events and happenings according to the telos of history. Such an understanding of "God's plan" indicates a facet of theology of history of which we must be aware. This plan need not to be thought of as rigid, but can also serve as the fulfillment of what is still incomplete — as the establishment of perfect justice, all-embracing peace, happiness, and perfect freedom.

Is theology of history a theologically legitimate answer to the question of whether and how God relates to history? We have come across dialectic theology's reservations concerning the theology of history that synchronizes God's revelation with cultural-historical development. If, on the contrary, every concept of "God in history" is rejected, that can give rise to the impression that God is "on the other side" of history. This will result if "history" is understood as it normally is in the modern age, as a network of causes and effects created by humanity. Such a view of history can disempower individuals and groups, entangle them in themselves, or allow them to become so arrogant that they face a big fall. Where and how is God to be found here?

God can be met in this history, but God's voice does not resound. God speaks in God's own way, which has taken form in Jesus Christ — this is what dialectic theology impresses on us. God calls humans so that they wake from their dream of supposed freedom, of self-created possibilities and perspectives. From Bultmann, Gogarten, and Rahner we hear that the point of contact between God and history is the responsibility of the historical human being and the dimension of freedom guaranteed by God. Therefore — according to this opposing stance to theology of history — the relationship of God and history has to be thought of as facilitating freedom in faith. God has not left humanity at the mercy of history,

nor history at the mercy of humanity. Rather, God frees humanity
to survive history. (Barth adds the corrective that human freedom
can only follow from confession of Jesus Christ, in whose history
the destiny of the world has already been decided.) The call to
enter the freedom of faith needs neither a world-historical perspective nor a concept of a divine plan for history, nor a concentration
on the end of history, whether seen as apocalypse or the result of
historical achievement.

Are there suitable answers to the question of God in history?
The reaction in the 1960s was negative from many sides. Both
in the 1960s and today, some critics allege that radical eschatology has no real interest in history. Others find fault because
it lacks historical coherence and its ethical challenges are faulty.
Others miss a historically verifiable foundation for Christian hope,
or at least a motivation aware of historical presuppositions and
consequences.

In this climate of opinion, there is a call for change. This change
seems to be possible only by breaking out of habitual thought patterns. *The growing interest in the historical circumstances in which
theology is "done"* constitutes such a break. Theology is not simply to be understood on its own terms or as driven by the dynamic
of its own unanswered questions; rather, it is kept alive by impulses from the surroundings. This idea of theology is increasingly
widespread.

With regard to what can be said in theology, a *change of consciousness* with particular consequences for the understanding of
eschatology has emerged. Eschatology deals with everything that
is in store for humanity. Thereby, it determines our direction and
thus our behavior and actions. Eschatology can become an almost perfect example of a theology that deals with the intellectual
and political situation of its time. It answers the challenges of the
time in a way that is progressive or, at least, not backward. The
conclusion is that theology must do so if it is to have a future.

Behind this change of consciousness lies the *discovery of the future as an open space full of unexpected possibilities.* This idea
must guide what is attempted and decided in the present. The
title of Robert Jungk's 1952 travel account of the United States
was *Tomorrow Is Already Here,* which can also be translated, *The*

Future Has Already Begun.[2] While the Old World was still busy with the consequences of war and of old ideologies, Americans set out for new technological frontiers. In seeking to pass boundaries, they remained true to a destiny that was attributed to God's providence. Venturing into space left the misery and increasingly complicated conflicts on earth behind, but the money funding the program would never have been used to ease suffering in America. The United States shows Europe the contrasting possibilities of our future. In the mid-sixties it was also announced in North America that solutions to problems caused by nature were at hand. The time had come to construct acceptable social relationships on the basis of these solutions.[3]

But despite these earlier assurances, the future looks threatening. Areas of carelessly extensive urbanization and industrialization show signs of a damaged environment that affect the entire globe and point to the increasing possibility of self-destruction. So can we live according to our hope? Or do we live against our hope? With boundaries of growth pointing to the finite nature of the world, must not human life change radically if we are to survive? This external pressure should be addressed sooner rather than later, but only when there is nothing more urgent to occupy our efforts.

Awareness of finitude can lead to a change in the inner life. Breaking away from accepted ideas demands an aesthetic revolution, in which the world is seen as a responsibility to be tackled.

This picture of outbreaks and breakthroughs in thought and behavior comes in part from reconsidering eschatology. At the beginning of the 1960s, dissatisfaction with radical eschatology had resulted in an attempt to create an equally radical new orientation. Eschatology took yet another new direction, this time of a very different character. One important motif of this new direction is theology's lack of orientation to historical futurity. This is why Karl Rahner demands:

---

2. R. Jungk, *Die Zukunft hat schon begonnen: Amerikas Allmacht und Ohnmacht* (Stuttgart: Scherz & Goverts, 1952) (ET: *Tomorrow Is Already Here,* trans. Marguerite Waldman [New York: Simon & Schuster, 1954]).

3. E.g., Herbert Marcuse, *One-Dimensional Man: Studies in the Ideology of Advanced Industrial Society* (Boston: Beacon Press, 1964).

The Christian understanding of the faith and its expression
must contain an eschatology which really bears on the *future,*
that which is still to come, in a very ordinary, empirical sense
of the word "time."[4]

Can the future really bring something new? Or does history con-
sist of the repetition of fundamental experience? History sounded
so monotonous in Rudolf Bultmann, who represented the decision
of faith, which must always be accomplished anew, like a mathe-
matical point that can repeat but that never forms a line. Bultmann
wanted to avoid, and even tried to deconstruct, attempts to "in-
habit" history. Barth wrote of the Christ-perspective, with which
one can look forward to the perfection of God's presence, even
if humanity and its theology can only approach this perfection
"asymptotically." But such hope does not seem to envision real
progress.

Is this sense of time an illusion? Beyond the objections voiced
in the sixties, the point of whether a theological sensorium for
the awaited time is lacking or underdeveloped is decisive. A sensorium for the end-time cannot be a matter of indifference for faith.
What happens in time cannot be regarded as unimportant. *Theology needs a specific sense of time, oriented toward the one who
"gives us time."* The orientation does not object to the spirit of the
age nor exist as an imaginative power that is ahead of contemporaries. It is sense for God's coming, created by God through God's
promises. The perception results from the renewal of our senses,
which ponder God's works of grace (Rom. 12:2).

In the 1950s and early 1960s, this sense of time, at least in
German Protestant theology, was intensified by internal theological
debate and by biblical-theological research.[5] It is evident that both
radical eschatology's critique of the modern concept of history and
ideas of history as a whole are insufficient in the long run. Anyone attempting to take the Old Testament seriously cannot avoid

---

4. "The Hermeneutics of Theological Assertions," in *Theological Investigations,*
trans. Kevin Smith (New York: Crossroad, 1982), 4:323–46; quotation is from
p. 326.
5. See Claus Westermann, ed., *Probleme alttestamentlicher Hermeneutik:
Aufsätze zum Verstehen des Alten Testaments* (Munich: Chr. Kaiser, 1960).

talking about history as the context of God's activity "from the creation of the world to the coming of the Son of Man."[6]

But how does this idea relate to the modern concept of history as a unified world history that embraces every human life and action? This concept and associated terminology have become more questionable. Many indicators show that there are different "histories," which on occasion overlap but are often in conflict with one another. They cannot be made into a whole, unless it were possible to forcibly unite humanity in one history. That would be organization through totalitarian compulsion.

Could theology develop a more credible concept of history and of the unity of history using the Bible? The relationship of the Old and New Testaments, explained by the theme "promise and fulfillment," gives new impulse to interest in history and eschatology. Gerhard von Rad's *Old Testament Theology*[7] takes up the term "history of salvation" without inhibition, advancing a theory of continuity between the Old and the New Testaments.

These are more than sufficient reasons for turning again to eschatology, which can be expected to clarify basic theological questions and to provide guidance for Christianity in a time full of changes and insecurities.

Carl E. BRAATEN and Robert W. JENSON, *The Futurist Option* (New York: Newman Press, 1970); Ewert H. COUSINS, ed., *Hope and the Future of Man* (London: Garnstone Press, 1973; Philadelphia: Fortress Press, 1972); Harvey COX, *On Not Leaving It to the Snake* (New York: Macmillan, 1964); Jürgen MOLTMANN et al., *The Future of Hope: Theology as Eschatology,* ed. Frederick Herzog (New York: Herder & Herder, 1970).

4.2. God in Global History:
The Answer to the Foundational Crisis of Christianity and the Western Crisis of Meaning

Wolfhart PANNENBERG, "Constructive and Critical Functions of Christian Eschatology," *Harvard Theological Review* 77 (1984): 119–39; idem, "The God of Hope," in *Basic Questions in Theology: Collected Essays,* trans. George H. Kehm

---

6. Gerhard von Rad, "Das Alte Testament ist ein Geschichtsbuch" (1952–53), in Westermann, *Probleme alttestamentlicher Hermeneutik,* 11.

7. G. von Rad, *Theologie des Alten Testaments,* 2 vols. (Munich: Chr. Kaiser, 1957–60) (ET: *Old Testament Theology,* trans. D. M. G. Stalker [New York: Harper & Row, 1962–65]).

(Philadelphia: Fortress Press, 1971), 2:234–49; idem, *Theologie und Reich Gottes* (Gütersloh: Gütersloher Verlagshaus, 1971).

As regards its content and truth all Christian doctrine depends on the future of God's own coming to consummate his rule over his creation.[8]

Wolfhart Pannenberg (b. 1928) is not simply using this principle to push the question of theological truth onto God, which could absolve humans of responsibility for finding truth within history. If Christian truth depends on the futurity of the coming of God, Pannenberg does not expect God's "coming to [us]," in his words, according to dialectical theology's definition of futurity. Pannenberg understands the coming of God in a strictly futuristic sense, as the future completion of God's rule. Is this putting off the question? Not according to Pannenberg. The meaning of God's power over creation is revealed in Jesus' resurrection. In this event the end of history is anticipated in order to demonstrate the truth of the Christian faith.

Pannenberg's project deals with the foundational crisis of Christianity as he saw it just after midcentury. According to Pannenberg, dialectical theology's strategy is flawed when it refers to faith's lack of (rational) foundation and when it states that the ground of faith can only be asserted and accepted. Another danger, according to Pannenberg, would be an escape into (moral) engagement.

Pannenberg intended to help overcome this crisis by clearing away the stumbling block of faith's origin in Easter. Establishing the historicity of the empty tomb can be the proof *per negationem* of Christ's resurrection. Easter is the turning point for the world and for the development of historical consciousness.

This reasoning presumes that the Easter event, although new, is no meteorlike strike into history. According to Pannenberg, there had been long preparation for what Jesus' resurrection reveals about the question of truth. Preparation occurs in stories of Israel in which the God of Israel announces events that God intends to bring about, or when humans refer to an event as confirmation of God's announcement. A consciousness of history gradually emerges

8. W. Pannenberg, *Systematic Theology*, trans. Geoffrey W. Bromiley (Grand Rapids, Mich.: Eerdmans; Edinburgh: T. & T. Clark, 1998), 3:531.

from the succession of announcement and confirmation. History is understood as a coherence of events rooted in God's constant activity and experienced increasingly in the destiny of the people of Israel. In Jewish apocalypticism — e.g., Daniel 2 and 7 — this concept of history extends to all the nations and includes universal history, which moved toward the kingdom of God and is thus perceivable as a whole. Hope in the resurrection from the dead at the end of all history develops at the same time. Pannenberg differentiates this concept of history from the prophetic announcement of God's intervention in history. The latter threatens the people of Israel with a historical end. The apocalyptic writers, however, speak of God as the one who steps in at the end of time. The revelation of God's power makes it known that history is moving toward this end.

According to Pannenberg, the resurrection of Jesus Christ anticipates this end "proleptically." Jesus' life history is affirmed by God and has been incorporated into divine reality. Easter is not the end of history, but in it the meaning of history is revealed. Every historical moment is brought into the fullness of God's reality, including guilty deeds. Universal history is the last judgment; it integrates everything by relativizing it according to its presuppositions and consequences.

Easter becomes the pivot, the "midpoint" of history. The end occurs "proleptically" at Easter — that is, it points to the end of the world to come. This means that the historian who comes across this singular event in the New Testament is caught up in the "power of the future." It is only the "power of the future" that can be the "object of hope and trust."[9]

Easter is God's mighty affirmation of Jesus' fate, and it is only thus that the Easter event can be understandable. Jesus' existence does not end abruptly on the cross; it is fulfilled when God takes him up into God's life. Here, the "truth that comes from the end of an event" (*Wahrheit vom Ende eines Geschehens*) is evident. This truth throws light on Jesus' life and death and makes it clear, in hindsight, that Jesus always existed in unity with God — or, put more carefully, in the hope of this unity.

---

9. Pannenberg, "The God of Hope," 243.

Since hope beyond death is characteristic of true humanity, the Easter hope does not raise Jesus of Nazareth above other humans or isolate his existence. At Easter, humanity's openness to the world and the future is discovered, but it has been there all along. In Jesus' resurrection, God does not create anything new. Rather, God encourages more thorough self-understanding.

An *anthropological foundation* corresponding to the *framework of universal history* states that every human is by nature open to the world and fulfills that nature when able to step beyond his situation. Human life is constant progress into unforeseeable openness. What Pannenberg takes from the Hebraic understanding of truth therefore also applies anthropologically. Truth is always historical; it only becomes clear at the end of a process of events. The future has "ontological priority" (*ontologischer Primat*).[10] This corresponds with the anthropological reasoning supported by a phenomenology of hope, that to be human means to be neither spiritually regressive nor overattached to what has been achieved. Openness to the world intentionally aims beyond time and moves ultimately toward God — toward the God who as the power of the future is already Lord of all time.

Pannenberg takes this belief from philosophical and medical anthropology,[11] which observes and interprets the attitudes of the dying. Pannenberg does not interpret the research according to a history of science, or, in other words, as part of an image of humanity in which the future takes priority. Pannenberg previously had placed weight on the idea that the primacy of the future with regard to truth comes from the Jewish-Christian tradition. It remains unclear whether the anthropological foundation should take credit for a conception of universal history,[12] or whether humanity's openness to the world is a cultural possession that has developed in history and that, hence, is relative. These statements give rise to the suspicion that the anthropological foundation renders the cultural development superfluous. Pannenberg sees the

---

10. Ibid., 241.
11. In particular, from Max Scheler (1874–1928) and Arnold Gehlen (1904–76).
12. As in Pannenberg's *Grundzüge der Christologie* (Gütersloh: Gütersloher Verlagshaus, 1964) (ET: *Jesus — God and Man*, trans. Lewis L. Wilkins and Duane A. Priebe [Philadelphia: Westminster Press, 1968]).

anthropological foundation as grounded in the constitution of
reality as a whole — that is, ontologically.

History is conceived inductively, possibly with surprising results,
with attention directed to what is contingent, underived, event-
ful — to what is not removed from the historical "before" and
"after." It is part of the essence of history to constantly create anew
but nevertheless to constitute a continuum. Jesus' resurrection is a
historical fact for which we are prepared through traditional expectation of the resurrection of the dead as the sign of the end of
the world. Jesus' crucifixion can momentarily distress believers and
make them waver in their hope. But Easter reinforces hope. The
death of Jesus does not bring the world to an end, since Easter allows the meaning of his death to be understood as the way to life.
As with all his words and deeds, the content of truth in Jesus' death
depends on what the future brings — and the future is resurrection.

Given this verification, the word of the cross (1 Cor. 1:18) can
exist only as a claim needing historical confirmation, not as an
offense calling to "hope against hope" (Rom. 4:18). If one follows Pannenberg, Christian hope cannot cling to the crucified one.
Rather, Christian hope is sparked to life by the resurrection, and
only then throws light on Golgotha. If, however, our hope does
cling to the crucified one and to the promise of his resurrection,
what counts is communicating Jesus' future as the one "who died
for us." But Pannenberg has in mind the historically relevant result of God's activity in Jesus. He does not perceive God's activity
as a promise which takes form in the resurrection of the crucified
one. Rather, the meaning of the resurrection is as an anticipation
of the end of the world, when God confirms everything that had
been said about Christ.

With the concept of "prolepsis," Pannenberg deals with a fundamental question in Christian theology: *What is the relationship
of "once and for all" in the history of Christ to the continuing
process of history?* Pannenberg answers that the unity of meaning
in the history of Jesus' life and work is revealed by God's affirmation. This revelation is of relevance to all living beings since it
corresponds to the traditional content of hope. Victory over death
brings the end of history into view. The end of history will disclose
universal meaning and will raise the fullness of meaning into God.

Eschatology thus discloses what is historically coherent and, finally, the universal historical fullness of meaning.

Universal history is the last judgment in the sense that the human, open to world and future, finds orientation according to the context of historical meaning. Given this statement, is a future judgment necessary? In history after Christ, God "discloses himself in that time, but not in any fundamentally new way."[13] "Thus, the end of the world will be on a cosmic scale what has already happened in Jesus."[14]

History has to continue after Easter because Jesus' fate is a microcosm of God's creation of meaning in the universe and history. Jesus' proclamation of the kingdom of God continues after his resurrection because its universal content remains unfulfilled; the kingdom of God has not yet become evident. But it is only the extent of its penetrating power that has yet to come.

> The coming of the kingdom is the basis of the message of Jesus, and without the arrival of this future it loses its basis. To be sure, the future of God's kingdom is already present by the work of Jesus among those who believe in him and his message, as is its power to change their lives on earth. It has been made manifest in the event of the resurrection of Jesus. But whether we are correctly describing what happened then depends still on something that has yet to take place: the coming of the reign of God in all its power and glory.[15]

This answers the question "why history after Christ?"— if that indeed is a legitimate question as far as Pannenberg is concerned. In Christ, nothing has really changed. The end of the world is no longer a concept, but has become visible "proleptically." The unity of world history is discerned, because the end of the world becomes plausible. Salvation seems to be connected to realization of this unity, if understood only in its integrating, healing depth. History is not yet complete — therefore it must continue.

---

13. W. Pannenberg, "Dogmatic Theses on the Doctrine of Revelation," in *Revelation as History*, trans. David Granskou (New York: Macmillan; London: Collier-Macmillan, 1968), 123–58; quotation is from p. 142.
    14. Ibid., 143f.
    15. Pannenberg, *Systematic Theology*, 3:531.

The end of history represents the completion and integration
of all moments of meaning, like completing a text. Pannenberg
considered it important not to depend on Georg Wilhelm Friedrich Hegel (1770–1831); his worry is that Hegel's philosophy of
history does not rule out totalitarian thought. Pannenberg prefers
to follow Wilhelm Dilthey's (1833–1911) hermeneutic, and applies
textual hermeneutics to an understanding of history.

Pannenberg's theological program is a large-scale attempt at integration. Because of Jesus' resurrection, we can imagine the end
of history, since it has happened "proleptically." We also know
what the end of life means, since Jesus Christ has already stepped
beyond that frontier. Both facts make it possible to bring units
of meaning together, which will in the end prove to be a universal historical coherence of meaning. Only God's advent can prove
that this coherence will come to pass. Our task is to think in that
direction.

Faith is thus brought to reason. Hope presents both faith and
reason with a sense of universal history, and at the same time limits that perspective. The openness of humanity's future would be
infinite if the end of the world had not come to pass proleptically
in the resurrection of Jesus. However, about what has happened in
the prolepsis, beyond the unity with God given to Jesus Christ that
we anticipate, we learn nothing. What we hope for remains open.

Carl E. BRAATEN, *The Future of God: The Revolutionary Dynamics of Hope*
(New York: Harper & Row, 1969); Kurt KOCH, *Der Gott der Geschichte: Theolo-
gie der Geschichte bei Wolfhart Pannenberg als Paradigma einer philosophischen
Theologie in ökumenischer Perspektive* (Mainz: Grünewald, 1988).

4.3. World-Transforming Hope as an Answer
to the Crisis of Relevancy within Christianity

Jürgen MOLTMANN, *Das Kommen Gottes: Christliche Eschatologie* (Gütersloh:
Chr. Kaiser, 1995) (ET: *The Coming of God: Christian Eschatology*, trans. Mar-
gret Kohl [Minneapolis: Fortress Press, 1996]); idem, *Theologie der Hoffnung:
Untersuchungen zur Begründung und zu den Konsequenzen einer christlichen Es-
chatologie* (Munich: Chr. Kaiser, 1964) (ET: *Theology of Hope: On the Ground and
the Implications of a Christian Eschatology*, trans. James W. Leitch [London: SCM
Press; New York: Harper & Row, 1967; Minneapolis: Fortress Press, 1993]); idem,
Die Zukunft der Schöpfung: Gesammelte Aufsätze (Munich: Chr. Kaiser, 1977)
(ET: *The Future of Creation: Collected Essays*, trans. Margret Kohl [Philadelphia:
Fortress Press, 1979]).

Pannenberg lends weight to the question of the foundation of theology, and attempts to answer it with his conception of eschatology. What is true is the whole, he states, and truth comes at the end. The meaning of this end is already indicated within history.

In a characteristically different manner, Jürgen Moltmann (b. 1926) takes up the question of foundation. He connects it to the challenge to point to the *ethical consequences* of eschatology and to deduce from these consequences the fundamental reasons for hope. The subtitle of his *Theology of Hope* is significant: *On the Ground and the Consequences*[16] *of a Christian Eschatology*. Moltmann does not wish only to enter into the challenges of the time. These challenges are more than an impetus to the rethinking of theology; theology should be a (hopefully productive) answer to such challenges.

Three issues in eschatology — framed as statements or questions — have already been raised. These are (1) "The future has already begun"; (2) "Do we live as we hope?"; and (3) "What does Christian theology say about the battle for the future?" Moltmann, in the political and intellectual heat of the beginning of the 1960s, melded these three motifs. Inspired by the mood of this time — which can be characterized as one of "outbreak" (*Aufbruchsstimmung*) — he explored these questions in *Theology of Hope*.

In this book, Moltmann works from two theological premises. First, the roots of hope are to be sought in the Old Testament, and specifically in the stories concerning the wandering fathers, understood to be documents of a nomad religion.[17] This interpretation means that to hope is to be "on the way." To settle down and stay in one place would be to betray hope. Second, hope makes a place for itself at Easter. In God's creative denial of death the ontological ground for hope is revealed.

> The future of the new existence which ends history is linked for faith with the dialectic of the negative in the historical present.[18]

---

16. The English translation *Implications* is misleading.
17. *Theology of Hope*, 96.
18. Moltmann, "The Future as a New Paradigm of Transcendence," in *The Future of Creation*, 17.

From now on, breaking through the status quo and distancing oneself from the things of yesterday are the essential characteristics of true historicity.

In this respect, Moltmann and Pannenberg think in diametrically opposite ways. Moltmann sees history stamped by contradictions, antagonisms, and clashes, which, while serving to move history further, can also drive it into the abyss. Pannenberg, on the other hand, sees history as a context which constitutes a unity, which progressively sublates, *aufhebt* in the Hegelian sense, all individual moments, all differences and opposites: they are preserved as details in the whole, provided they are not dropped as nonsense or absurdity.

Notwithstanding this difference in their understanding of history, which has primarily political consequences, both are united in thinking that eschatology must be raised from history.

> Christian eschatology does not speak of the future as such.
> It sets out from a definite reality in history and announces
> the future of that reality, its future possibilities and its power
> over the future.[19]

This also remains the dominant theme in Moltmann's most recent book, *The Coming of God*. In this work, eschatology is portrayed as an endeavor to liberate true human future from the bondage of all forces and powers countering humanity.

Moltmann's foundational historico-theological term is "promise." His understanding of the concept differs significantly from that of Pannenberg. For Moltmann, *promise is what God has held out, in the story of Christ, as a prospect in order that we attempt to realize it.* The history of the world is advancing toward the kingdom of God. Alongside the church — which should be approached as an "exodus church,"[20] formed through various awakenings and outbursts — the kingdom of God is already present in those who are pushed to the side, denied, and oppressed. More precise characteristics of the kingdom of God are justice and peace, social conditions for which God's actions are a guideline. It is only in this

---

19. Moltmann, *Theology of Hope*, 17.
20. Ibid., 304–38.

teamwork between humanity and God that the kingdom is realized. The kingdom does not realize itself. Language suggests that it is possible to "make" history through implementation of basic social concepts, which are strengthened by religion. God's promise, however, becomes real through its historical realization. Promise, then, is defined as a "real utopia."

Promise is God's contradiction of the world as it has been until now, that is, of the world as it has become in the hands of sinful humanity. A life based on God's promise means to make that contradiction one's own. Those who hope in God are sent into a world that is passing away.

> Thus the transforming mission (*Sendung*)...seeks for that which is really, objectively possible in this world, in order to grasp it and realize it in the direction of the promised future of the righteousness, the life and the kingdom of God. Hence it regards the world as an open process in which the salvation and destruction, the righteousness and annihilation of the world are at stake.[21]

> Future as mission (*Sendung*) shows the relation of today's tasks and decisions to what is really possible, points to open possibilities in the real and to tendencies that have to be grasped in the possible.[22]

These are ideas borrowed in part from neo-Marxism, the presentation of which in Ernst Bloch's *The Principle of Hope*[23] fascinated Moltmann. But contrary to Bloch (1885–1977), Moltmann does not believe that humans are born with this utopian consciousness, and that they need only look into themselves to discover the principle of hope as a lodestar. The motivation for perpetual change is rather given by the fact that God, the wholly other, has given Godself to humankind. God is to be recognized as the one who changes all things, as the motive for the *Realdialektik* of history. The necessity of change is demonstrated by those who

---

21. Ibid., 288f.
22. Ibid., 260.
23. E. Bloch, *Das Prinzip Hoffnung* (Frankfurt: Suhrkamp, 1959) (ET: *The Principle of Hope*, trans. Neville Plaice, Stephe Knight, and Paul Knight [Cambridge, Mass.: MIT Press, 1986]).

suffer: the poor and oppressed who cannot come to terms with "this world" and who cannot be consoled by a hereafter seen as "the next world." Rather, they look for a "different world." In active solidarity with sufferers, Christian hope does look to prove itself, but it is in solidarity that Christian hope finds the historical locus for the truth of Christian faith in God, who was proven at Easter to be the Living One, the dynamic, newly creating power of history. This view allows for contradiction in speaking of the "death of God," although only if the identification of God with the dying Jesus and suffering humanity is carried through completely. In this way, Moltmann seeks to give the foundation for theology. Christian hope can only be verified by the deed that changes the world in favor of those who previously had no bearable future and, therefore, no hope.

Moltmann caught the mood of many of his contemporaries. The transition to political theology created a sounding board for the foundation and consequences of his theology. Theological themes are identified through political situations and demands for social action. In this way the style of theology is altered: challenges are discovered by diagnosing the present, primarily the conflicts between those who cling to the eternal yesterday and others ready for new ideas. The latter refuse to carry on as before, and by doing so create an alternative. These challenges are given theological names, which in itself should be proof of the relevance of the Christian faith.

The systematic texture is not so easily recognizable. Moltmann understands "promise" as the announcement of "the coming of a not yet existing reality from the future of the truth."[24] It is an announcement of history; the salvation event is seen as the linking of historical events, which have a meaning beyond themselves and open up a horizon of expectation. Wolfhart Pannenberg gathers from this linkage a context of universal historical meaning, whereas Moltmann emphasizes the endowment of historical meaning created by conflict between forces pointing toward the future and the forces of inertia. Of the two forces, the former are in-

---

24. Moltmann, *Theology of Hope*, 85.

spired by God's promise of a new world, the latter by asserting the status quo.

Out of this dynamic grows the eschatologically imperative permanent opposition of theology to what is "current." Apocalyptic is also drawn into this framework. In his understanding of apocalypticism Moltmann draws close to Ernst Käsemann (see 3.2). As opposed to Pannenberg, who finds in apocalypticism the basis for a theological concept of universal history concluding with the end of the world, Moltmann emphasizes the fundamental apocalyptic opposites of "this world" and "the other world." He takes them to be synonymous with death and life, actualized in the movement of distancing oneself from the present state of affairs to intensify the dynamic of continual breaks in continuity and outbursts full of conflict. The theological theme is described as "liberation," as an exodus from oppression and alienation. Since liberation is defined as rebellion against the powerful, the oppressors and the self-seekers, it can therefore be pinned down sociohistorically.

Johann Baptist Metz (b. 1928), a Roman Catholic theologian, like Moltmann is fascinated by Ernst Bloch's *Principle of Hope,* although without working the ideas out in a detailed eschatology.[25] He shows himself particularly interested in Bloch's utopian impulses, primarily because Bloch thinks through the messianic-apocalyptic contrast between the "old" and the "new" world according to a philosophy of history, and carries it to sociopolitical actualization. Christian eschatology should lead to political theology; it contributes to political theology the "dangerous memory" of all those who have been excluded from the historiography of the mighty and the victors.[26] Bloch wanted to build this thought through a subversive hermeneutic. Texts, pri-

25. Initial stages can be found in his essay "Gott vor uns: Statt eines theologischen Arguments," in the commemorative volume *Ernst Bloch zu Ehren,* ed. Siegfried Unseld (Frankfurt: Suhrkamp, 1965), 227–41; in *Zur Theologie der Welt* (Mainz: Grünewald; Munich: Chr. Kaiser, 1968); and in *Glaube in Geschichte und Gesellschaft: Studien zu einer praktischen Fundamentaltheologie* (Mainz: Grünewald, 1977) (ET: *Faith in History and Society: Toward a Practical Fundamental Theology,* trans. David Smith [New York: Seabury Press, 1980]).

26. Johann Baptist Metz, "Erinnerung des Leidens als Kritik eines teleologisch-technologischen Zukunftsbegriffs," *Evangelische Theologie* 32 (1972): 338–52; idem, "Glaube als gefährliche Erinnerung," in Adolf Exeler, J. B. Metz, and Karl Rahner, *Hilfe zum Glauben* (Zurich: Benziger, 1971), 23–38.

marily the Bible, should be examined for traces of protest and opposition which have dug into the tradition. Even when such traces have been whitewashed by textual redaction, in order to maintain the view of the world and history favored by the mighty, it has not been possible to eradicate them completely. Metz wishes to show that this silence cannot be maintained. Jesus of Nazareth, with his suffering and death, stands against the maintenance of that silence, in solidarity with all who have been butchered and who appear to have been wiped out of memory. Jesus Christ's tomb is, so to speak, the memorial of all the unknown sufferers of history, who in his name remain immortal. This belief is grounded in the idea that all humans are gathered in the fate of Christ, the incarnate God, and constitute a universal community. This promise of the incarnation needs to be redeemed by taking responsibility, as far as humanly possible, for those who suffer today. In this act humans — not just Christians! — remain true to the creation that God, through God's saving activity, wishes to give new heart.

Wolf-Dieter MARSCH, ed., *Diskussion über die "Theologie der Hoffnung"* (Munich: Chr. Kaiser, 1967); Marko MATIĆ, *Jürgen Moltmanns Theologie in Auseinandersetzung mit Ernst Bloch* (Frankfurt: Peter Lang, 1983); Johann Baptist METZ, Jürgen MOLTMANN, and Willi OELMÜLLER, *Kirche im Prozeß der Aufklärung: Aspekte einer neuen "politischen Theologie"* (Munich: Chr. Kaiser; Mainz: Grünewald, 1970) (ET: Jürgen Moltmann et al., *Religion and Political Society,* translated and edited by The Institute of Christian Thought [New York: Harper & Row, 1974]); Christopher MORSE, *The Logic of Promise in Moltmann's Theology* (Philadelphia: Fortress Press, 1979); Richard SCHAEFFLER, *Was dürfen wir hoffen? Die katholische Theologie der Hoffnung zwischen Blochs utopischem Denken und der reformatorischen Rechtfertigungslehre* (Darmstadt: Wissenschaftliche Buchgesellschaft, 1979).

4.4. Eschatology as Religio-Political Theory of Action: Hope of Liberation for the Oppressed

Leonardo BOFF, *Vida para além da morte* (N.p.: Editora Vozes Ltda., n.d.) (German translation: *Was kommt nachher? Das Leben nach dem Tode,* trans. Horst Goldstein [Salzburg: Otto Müller, 1982]); G. Clarke CHAPMAN, Jr., "Black Theology and Theology of Hope: What Have They to Say to Each Other?" in *Black Theology: A Documentary History, 1966–1979,* ed. Gayraud S. Wilmore and James H. Cone (Maryknoll, N.Y.: Orbis Books, 1979), 193–219; James H. CONE, *A Black Theology of Liberation* (Philadelphia: Lippincott, 1970; new ed., Maryknoll, N.Y.: Orbis Books, 1990); James EVANS, *We Have Been Believers: An African-American Systematic Theology* (Minneapolis: Fortress Press, 1992); Gustavo GUTIÉRREZ, *Teología de la Liberación* (Salamanca: Ediciones Sígueme, 1972) (ET: *Theology of Liberation: History, Politics, and Salvation,* translated and edited by Sister Caridad Inda and John Eagleson [Maryknoll, N.Y.: Orbis Books, 1973]);

João B. LIBÂNIO and Maria C. Lucchetti BINGEMER, *Escatologia christã* (Petrópolis: Editora Vozes Ltda., 1985) (German translation: *Christliche Eschatologie: Die Befreiung in der Geschichte,* trans. Michael van Lay [Düsseldorf: Patmos, 1987]); Daniel L. MIGLIORE, *Faith Seeking Understanding: An Introduction to Christian Theology* (Grand Rapids, Mich.: Eerdmans, 1991), 231–51; Gayraud S. WILMORE, *Last Things First* (Philadelphia: Westminster Press, 1982).

"Eschatology is the opening up of a liberating process." The statement summarizes a series of theological constructions, developed partly according to Moltmann's sketch but also on the landscape of political theology to which Moltmann also belongs. These constructions exist at various stages of completion; some are in a state of continual reconstruction. Gayraud S. Wilmore has addressed what the approaches have in common:

> Perhaps the most important consequence of our exploration will be the discovery that what Christians believe about the "last things" may be *first* in terms of influence upon their behavior in the world.[27]

In the interests of ethics, theology has to start with eschatology, not by stepping into heaven but by tackling matters of life and death on earth.

What is sometimes reduced to the common denominator of "liberation theology" is anything but a unified phenomenon, at least as a theological concept. Advocates of liberation theology take different lines of argumentation, for the reason that they wish to think programmatically in terms of their "context" — from the situation in which they live and for the sake of that situation. This contextual relationship is designed to lend a new shape to theology. "Doing theology" is an attempt to answer those challenges which the very existence of people who are oppressed, deprived of rights, and living in misery does not allow to be denied.

Liberation is the message of hope for the sufferers and the powerless of the world, existing under different social circumstances. In order to deliver that message, it is necessary (in the opinion of liberation theologians) to gain liberation from traditional theology and its doctrine of the last things, since it is precisely that doctrine that has led to the ideology of comfort in the hereafter. It

---

27. Wilmore, *Last Things First,* 11.

is charged that the old doctrine contributed to the acceptance of an unchangeable machinery of social injustice and oppression if it did not in fact justify the system theologically. (This prejudice has taken firm root, presenting a curious misunderstanding. The truth is that idea of a future after this life offers nothing really comforting in itself. It offers no relief from the past or from what must still be done tomorrow or the next day.)

The eschatology of liberation theology can be sketched with a few strokes, with the reservation that no liberation theology as yet exists in unified form. According to liberation theology there never will be such a presentation. For now only its concepts can be placed under discussion.

Conceptually, liberation theology is indebted to the neo-Marxist theory of history. This theory pictures history as a process of change, driven by opposites in society, which brings the new into being by activating a consciousness of what has not yet been and must be realized. This revolutionary dynamic is theologically intensified by the idea that God is to be sought on the other side of all historical conditions and always anew, which ensures that the one searching always has a lead on social reality. Christian revolutionaries, however, can distance themselves from sociopolitical revolution, in order to not be swallowed up. Unreserved identification with political goals is ruled out, because all human endeavor is prisoner to sin. God is, as absolute future — according to Gustavo Gutiérrez, following Karl Rahner — beyond every moment of history and never to be identified with any state of affairs. In this way God establishes grounds for permanent revolution as the condition for all progressive history, and for our concepts of such history.

The political explanation for this historico-theological eschatology admittedly takes different forms, according to differing frameworks of sociohistorical conditions ("contexts"). For example, the Latin Americans come closer to neo-Marxist ideas than, say, African-American theologians suing for their rights in North America. That may, as Wilmore comments,[28] explain the fact that in North America the criticism of racial exclusion and social injustice can act as a sufficient lever for political change within the

---

28. Ibid., 38.

framework of the U.S. Constitution and its promise of equality and pursuit of happiness. On the other hand, countries in the southern hemisphere experience such distressing political instability and economic disorder that new frameworks have to be devised. Therefore, liberation theology in Latin America tends to equate the coming of the kingdom of heaven with the goals of the socialist revolution.

Despite these regional, cultural, and political differences, liberation theology is one in striving to win back *universality and integration* with the help of a new eschatology, which — it is claimed — Western theology has lost. The process of removing oppression and sinfully caused misery is designed to liberate the oppressors as well as the oppressed, and in doing so to establish human community. For humanity to change, new humans are needed. This liberation, therefore, cannot limit itself either to internal or external states; it must embrace both and promote both. Not only is the "thereafter" the power of the "here and now," but real changes in the here and now possess a transcendental power, capable of overstepping boundaries. The kingdom of God can be seen in such changes. In this theology, the either-or of change of consciousness and change of the world (see 2.5.1) at last seems to have been defeated. The foretaste of the coming world is experienced when hunger is stilled and solidarity achieved, when social justice can be fought for and freedom won.

Such an understanding of salvation, which understands itself to be "holistic," often shows neo-Marxist or historico-materialistic colors, but considers itself to have *sacramental* grounds. A key role is taken by the eucharist, in which Jesus Christ communicates himself as bringer of salvation to create and maintain human community in all conditions of life (see 6.5). God's incarnation in Jesus of Nazareth is seen to be repeated in the eucharist. Divine practice dovetails with human practice. Everyday life is flooded through with divine powers. Considerations of suffering and hope of victory flow into one another. The spiritual and material form a unity. The universe moves in an unforeseeable context of mutual dependence and interaction — like a mobile.

This holistic vision, although going back to elements of theological tradition such as the doctrine of incarnation and the sacraments, is raised against Western culture, stamped by European and North American thought and world mastery. It is raised against the separation of spirit and matter, the division of subject and object, humanity and nature. It is also raised against the social forms rent by class disaffection and hierarchical order, sealed and sanctioned by religion through the cleft between God and world, and immortalized by heaven and hell — the forms of which are already present in economic and social conflict.

It needs to be considered whether liberation theology's opposition to and critique of dogmatic tradition has created an enemy, at whose feet it lays guilt for the wrong direction taken by the world. This enemy only comes into being through this confrontation: it is stylized as the integrated opposite. But is it really as homogeneous as claimed?

Or are theologically important differences in the tradition, which are credible and serve hope, renounced? When Paul writes, "For the kingdom of God is not food and drink but righteousness and peace and joy in the Holy Spirit" (Rom. 14:17), it seems to be a sign of spiritualizing, thus dividing reality. But it is rather the tentative expression of a spirituality which does not withdraw into an inner world, but which hopes for justice, peace, and joy as the content of hope in everyday life. Eating and drinking are not ruled out, but they require sanctification.

Other basic theological distinctions must not be misunderstood as ontological divisions. One example occurs when the "outer" and "inner" natures (as in 2 Cor. 4:16) are distinguished — the inner nature as renewed, the outer as wasting away — and when the distinction is later applied to the difference (not dichotomy!) between spirit and flesh. Another distinction occurs between old and new in the new creation: "The old has passed away, behold, the new has come" (2 Cor. 5:17).

Such differentiations are eschatologically oriented. They express hope grounded in a final repeal from God. They stem from a power of judgment full of hope, capable of perceiving what is to come. The judgment does not deal with what happens, whether step by step or abruptly; rather, it deals with what is expected. Such differentiations do not attempt to pose a dichotomy. However, a trend today is that all differences become leveled out in favor of a process in which they disappear. With the loss of such differentiations, the eschatological perspective is also lost.

Sin and misery become, with the loss of such perspective, the result of false but correctable social circumstances. In order to get rid of sin and misery, new humans must be created — and God as absolute future is the transcendental instrument in this great cause. With this interest, liberation theology wishes to name sin empirically, in order to bring into reach eschatological gifts such as justice, peace, and joy. (The word "salvation" already seems suspicious, because — according to the criticism — Christian tradition has separated it from the general "good.") This means that the theological problem of revolution — the prejudice that says that the human is or will become good when he is consciously in control of himself and of the world — scarcely causes difficulty.[29]

Behind these interests, as has been mentioned, lies the intention to remove all forms and dimensions of division. The expressed wish to involve all humanity in the process of liberation backs up this striving — but at the same time so does the determination to preserve regional or group-specific peculiarities, that is, to remain contextual as well. The emphasis on contextual "experiences" is a protest against dogmatic tradition, as far as it is alleged to have promoted monolithic concepts. In eschatology, for example, the protest is against a doctrine of punishment, purification, and salvation in the hereafter, which apparently allows for the inferno of our world to be kept at a distance. It also apparently allows for suffering to be explained or for wounds at best to be bandaged, instead of creating circumstances that prevent suffering.

This point is a critical one for eschatology, and not because eschatology must speak in favor of an ideology of abstract universality, integrated hope, and uniform expectation. On the contrary, the history of eschatology as presented offers diverse forms for expressing the hope that comes from faith. This diversity has, however, a clear center. Its unity is the hope in Christ, and only in that hope. Jesus Christ is the one who comes for all and who saves us

---

29. See Glenn Tinder, *The Political Meaning of Christianity: An Interpretation* (Baton Rouge: Louisiana State University Press, 1989), 168–69.

from destruction. He saves us in his own way, and in doing so shows us for the first time what lack of salvation is.

Liberation theology wishes to reach universality by another path, and in so doing a different universality — namely, that of social equality. Its ideological criticism is linked with improvement for those from whom the fulfillment of basic human hopes have been withheld, those with apparently no future. Having been excluded from history, these people are destined to take over the leadership of hope in the service of the whole. But to do that, they must get to speak with a voice that cannot be mistaken. In the meanwhile, liberation theology wishes to take over that role as representative; such theology intends to be the mouthpiece of all those who previously were dumb and speechless in their suffering.

Liberation theology poses a considerable moral claim, making its arguments more or less impossible to attack. Every objection can easily be suspected of taking sides against the powerless sufferers, the oppressed, the innocent, and the outcasts. But leaving that issue aside, do representatives of liberation theology really make audible the voice of those for whom they wish to speak?

How can such an expectation be fulfilled? It would be possible — and for an elaboration of eschatology exceedingly helpful — to collect elementary statements and to reflect on them, not just concerning the hopes and motivations of the marginalized, but their future, fears, and doubts, confrontations with barriers, and external and internal opposition. If liberation theology expresses not just attitudes and intellectual activity, but a Christian spirituality, then such must come to expression in what these people pray, sing, or confess — in the connection of their confidence (or lack of) with the life of the church. One could also ask about the connection of these statements to eschatology as ecclesiastical doctrine (with or without the magisterium of the church). What Christians hope could sound distant from doctrine, because it is expressed differently — or it might have distanced itself significantly, because it no longer shares the same fundaments.

But liberation theology wants more — and something quite different. It wants to say what humans *must* believe and hope in order to be liberated. It wishes by doing so to create a right for those previously without hope — the right for their voices to be taken as theologically authoritative, in extreme cases even to be taken as the voice of God. The authorization of the voices from "below," from the depths of social powerlessness, should help indicate the content of hope, which is not dictated from "above" (from the ecclesiastical or theological establishment). In this respect, liberation theology becomes normative to an extent previously unthinkable for Christian theology — in particular for eschatology, since what Christians may hope cannot be drawn from what they know to be their needs.

Texts in liberation theology cannot be put in order very easily. But there are indications that some of its spokespersons feed on a hope which is different from that of Christian eschatology, and which therefore brings forth different fruits. For this purpose, two examples — one Catholic and one Protestant — can be mentioned.

James Evans depicts how representatives of African American theology at first called people, in the name of Christian hope, to defy the status quo. Eschatology accordingly serves revolutionary engagement, since it prompts the consciousness not to live according to the "times" — that is, not to see oneself in harmony with the powers that (still) control the present. The next step (see Wilmore) directs critical interest toward detecting the roots of one's motivation and to find those roots in the African culture. It could be asked whether this step leads toward the world of African Americans, or whether it is a construct that uses a cultural opposite as the hermeneutical key for dealing with behavior, attitudes, and motives.

Out of this comes the motto for eschatology, "the last shall be first,"[30] understood both as "the last is first in determining us" and as "the last is first in defining us." The spirit of community (in contrast to Western individualism), ties with nature (in favor of the salvation of the universe), and the refusal to deliver oneself to modern progressive thought are all taken from the African tradition. The embedding of the person in the history of the group, which includes forebears, is opposed to the linear concept of time. The sole decisive element of Christian tradition which remains is the resurrection of Christ. The power to resist threat stems from

---

30. Evans, *We Have Been Believers,* 141–54.

that element, as does the refusal to believe in an "afterlife" which
covers up the lack of hope for this life.[31]

Rosemary Radford Ruether, a feminist theologian, criticizes eschatology. No life is immortal, she claims, insofar as it comes out
of the entirety of life and returns to it. We neither can nor should
know more, but we may trust in "holy wisdom":

> It is in the hands of Holy Wisdom to forge out of our finite
> struggle truth and being for everlasting life. Our agnosticism
> about what this means is then the expression of our faith,
> our trust that Holy Wisdom will give transcendent meaning
> to our work, which is bounded by space and time.[32]

The only ones who have difficulties with this conception are men,
who are concerned about their survival in all eternity.[33]

Admittedly, Evans and Radford Ruether are extreme examples.
Liberation theology demonstrates a broad range, in which there
is also room for reading ecclesiastical dogmatic traditions anew
through critical examination of the Bible, and interpreting them
in terms of "liberation in history" (for example, Leonardo Boff,
João B. Libânio, Maria C. Lucchetti Bingemer). The use of the
Bible is inconsistent. Many theologians draw from the Bible as
from a living source, in the hope that it will speak directly to them
and inspire their everyday experiences. Sometimes, though, there is
the tendency to authorize fixed experiences, not to challenge pre-
conceived opinions and concepts. Others perceive the biblical texts
only as a historical source, or as a root, planted in different places
in differing soil conditions, which must acclimatize if it is to survive
and bear fruit.

To take up von Balthasar's dictum again, liberation theology
belongs to one of the *Wetterwinkeln* (storms) of our time. Have
these storms died or gathered strength? The theologies of history
that European authors devised in the nineteenth century appear
in comparison as a roll of thunder or, at the most, as a flash of
summer lightning. The storm that brewed and that seemed to have

---

31. Ibid., 148.
32. R. Radford Ruether, *Sexism and God-Talk: Toward a Feminist Theology*
(Boston: Beacon Press, 1983), 258.
33. Ibid., 235.

dispersed has drawn near again, and moves across the earth. What will these rains cause to grow?

4.5. History as Context of Discovery

4.5.1. Hope Growing Out of Consternation?

Liberation theology and its forerunners understand themselves to be preparing the way for political transformation and for a move beyond the previous discussion. Eschatology, in the new scheme, should belong to a theory of practice of lived hope. With this intention, a schematic developmental history is constructed in Protestant literature, which heads toward a new type of theology — a theology that is eschatologically steered, according to the motto that the last things should be the first things governing our behavior. Earlier conceptions of eschatology are registered as early stages of a political theology of the future — a theology which has the relationship between church and society in view. The church is seen as having an effect on society, and society appears open for religious questions even if they are merely seen as vital for understanding humanity. As an alternative both to orthodox objectivity and existentialist subjectivity, the new eschatology is described as turning

> to human history, to social, political, and economic realities in the process of transformation by Christian hope and action.[34]

Christian hope is said to be marked by the fact that it can no longer come to terms with the state of the world.[35] But this view neglects a crucial point: The world has always been in a process of change, not in an overall sense, but within certain relationships which confirm the world's overall cohesion and consistency. Liberation theology, however, demands radical change. For this purpose, the potential of hope is required, as well as a concept of a divinely willed telos of history (see 4.1), or at least an undoubtable sense of direction. Only with these concepts can one ask how far

---

34. Wilmore, *Last Things First*, 36.
35. Ibid., 37.

Christianity has come or how far it remains behind God's plan. Liberation theology asks if steps toward perfection in world society are restricted because Christianity remains far behind God's plan.

This fear expresses an understandable dismay with injustice, misery, suffering, and lack of hope. The consternation is increased by the sense of the abyss between the present state and God's purpose. God's justice has to become the standard for judging social injustice. God's universal justice forbids *every* kind of inequality. With this standard the tendency arises to compare the facts with what should be and with what should have happened long ago.

It is not our job to concern ourselves with the moral weight of such consternation, but rather with its relationship to eschatology as expressed in the phrase "last things first."

Within the framework of ongoing social change, there is room for various pictures of hope if they contribute to the process. In the face of irreversible cultural change, religious traditions interpret hope in different ways; these must be tested for their usefulness.

Such diversity can prosper within the religious pluralism of the United States, within which Martin E. Marty asks about the contribution of the religious traditions for dealing with the task of the future. In the United States, various concepts and patterns predominate;[36] one sometimes has the impression of jigsaw pieces or a construction set that can be put together in different ways. Religious views of the future often are sketched in terms of sociology, since the choice of ideas, visions, and programs is designed to serve society as a whole. The contribution of religions, including Christianity, must be competitive and useful. Thoughts and viewpoints are shaped toward social betterment and are examined according to promised yields. Traditional motifs are loosely described, understood as devices that can help shape a usable future. There is no place for terrifying pictures or utopian fantasies.

If eschatology is transformed into visions of a usable future, it is lost as part of the theological "context of justification" (*Begründungszusammenhang*). The theological context of justification states the foundations of Christian hope and what they are directed

---

36. M. E. Marty, *The Search for a Usable Future* (New York: Harper & Row, 1969).

toward. Instead a historical "context of discovery" (*Entdeckungs-zusammenhang*)[37] can be used to replace a theological context of justification. Through use of a theory of history, hope is to be grounded and rendered plausible. Hope grows from the insight into what history has accomplished or into what should happen.

In political theology and liberation theology, hope derives from the reactions of Christians to present challenges. What counts above all is whether the activities of Christians contribute to progress toward a common future, for which it is worthy to strive. Grounds for hope are of interest as a *background motivation*, not as a question of truth that provides certainty. Even when, for example, emphasis is placed on the resurrection of Jesus Christ — and this is almost always the case in the different versions of modern theology of history — the particulars must nevertheless be checked. Does the emphasis occur in the context of discourse about God and about God's words and actions, which become visible in the crucified Christ? Or is Easter understood as hefty plowing of the existing world, in which the power of life gains room to resist death? Such a motif would, like others, need to be measured according to its plausibility and effects.

The *question of historical circumstances* has since the 1960s gained decisive importance for ecumenism.[38] Church assemblies such as Vatican II (1962–65) and the Fourth General Meeting of the World Council of Churches in Uppsala (1968) have referred directly to social circumstances and the challenges of geopolitics.

This development has a particular effect on eschatology, especially when the *interrelation of faith and action* is to be demonstrated, and hope is expected to derive from the goals of action. Eschatology can then become the ideal tool for the theology of its

---

37. I have explained the terms "context of justification" and "context of discovery" in my essay "Eschatological Rationality," in *Eschatological Rationality: Theological Issues in Focus* (Grand Rapids, Mich.: Baker Book House, 1996), 179–86.

38. It is important to differentiate here between an undercurrent of theology of history aimed at a "better future" and the interest in a doctrine of the last things. The latter has not been developed in depth in the ecumenical movement: see Nils Egede Bloch-Hoell, *Eschatologische Texte und Aspekte im Bereich der Ökumenik: Hermeneutik eschatologischer biblischer Texte*, 21th Konferenz von Hochschultheologen der Ostseeländer 1982 (Greifswald, East Germany: Ernst-Moritz-Arndt-Universität, 1983), 79–102.

time, because "time" becomes an important element in theology's considerations.

But to what extent and how are historical circumstances analyzed? How do they affect eschatology? To confront these questions means to make a distinction. In what they say theologians are unquestionably also conditioned by their time — that is, their thought and discourse stands within a certain historical and cultural, social and political framework in which they communicate. But this fact scarcely explains what can be said theologically, because one must always be responsible before God. Only this is a credible hope; only this can keep hope awake.

If theologians pay attention to their situation, they can be all the more aware of factors contributing to their judgments. But if the sensitivity to contextual impulses becomes central, the integrity of theology is endangered.

4.5.2. Rationalizing according to Sociology of Knowledge

Through a theology of hope, political theology, and liberation theology, the idea that eschatology is ready for an outbreak of new ideas is strengthened. Moving in this direction makes eschatology an example of the influence of the sociology of knowledge on reconstructing theology.

The sociology of knowledge (*Wissenssoziologie*)[39] reconstructs worldviews on the basis of a collective attitude to the "environment." Attitudes and behavior betray whether their bearers are in a state of breaking away (flexible and open to revisions) or if they have come to terms with what is constant. (Mannheim calls the first form of social knowledge "utopia" and the second "ideology," and in doing so is already judging them.) *Hope appears as the motivating power behind action.* Eschatology and ethics blend, and in the process eschatology itself threatens to melt away.

Behind sociology of knowledge stands the assumption that hope can be derived from the confrontation between (human) sub-

---

39. See Karl Mannheim, "Historismus" and "Das Problem einer Soziologie des Wissens," in *Wissenssoziologie*, ed. Kurt H. Wolff (Berlin: Luchterhand, 1964), 246–307, 308–87; idem, *Ideologie und Utopie*, 4th ed. (Frankfurt: Schulte-Bulmke, 1965).

jects of history and their "situation." Hope would then foster the exchange.[40]

From the viewpoint of sociology of knowledge, a constant eschatological direction appears to be evidence of a Christianity that tends toward changing the world. Such Christianity gains its hope from the productive encounter between expectation of hope and the rapidly changing social environment. Such a characterization of Christianity would fit Christian theology seamlessly into the social situation of its time and place; theology would amount to showing how the one relates to the other. Eschatology then expresses a reaction to social challenges by claiming a rhetorical head start, i.e., having thought ahead.

When I plead for a critical evaluation of consistent eschatology of this type, which understands itself as an answer to the challenges of its own time (and remains in keeping with the period in its reaction to contemporary tendencies), I do not wish to deny that Christian hope can only be stated in close contact with the expectations and fears of the current day. But this is something other than a *wissenssoziologisches* self-understanding of theology, with the help of which theology wishes to declare itself productive and prove its plausibility. If theology wants thus to prove itself, it is admitting that it has no text of its own that provides the basis for its considerations. Theology renders itself speechless, and runs the danger of being explained away by sociology.

Instead of analyzing the involuntary or intended ordering in a specific, limited situation, theological thought is supposed to be drawn out of its place in the social-political "context," in the "situation," and thereby to be fully and sufficiently explained. Eschatology appears to be particularly suitable for such purposes, because (and to the extent that) its content includes a concept of time, origins, and future — and because, alongside its consideration of past, present, and future, it also takes eternity into consideration. The theme "theology of history" here becomes relevant: history in its context as reservoir of theological motifs and intentions.

---

40. See, e.g., Peter Cornehl, *Die Zukunft der Versöhnung: Eschatologie und Emanzipation in der Aufklärung bei Hegel und in der Hegelschen Schule* (Göttingen: Vandenhoeck & Ruprecht, 1971).

In presentation and evaluation, the dominating feature of a sociology-of-knowledge approach to theology has for some time been a sociological typology designed to observe how hope motivates action, and how this affects both the formation of communities and their relationship to other social groups and institutions. This is the key to explanation introduced by Ernst Troeltsch[41] and Max Weber (1864–1920),[42] and which in time has been refined and improved.

Troeltsch distinguishes between the ideal types "church" and "sect," according to how they relate to history. The church strives to guarantee its continued existence, orients itself in time, and is therefore averse to all radicality. For that reason, it avoids any firm expectation of the future. The sect, on the other hand, wishes to follow Jesus' instructions concerning action and hope, taking them as orders to realize a specific goal. A sect therefore tends to prefer short-term moral or political options, but is more vulnerable than the church because it has less institutional security. A church that wishes to survive must tame its expectations in order to avoid friction every time society changes. Such a church cannot depend for its existence on forecasts coming to pass. Religious groups with less institutional structure can, on the other hand, react more flexibly and behave more radically.

This appears to explain why intensive apocalyptic expectation is to be found primarily in fringe groups within the church or in groups on the margins of society. Often such ideas are found in conflict with church traditions and institutions. Criticism of authority appears to demand another spiritual order, which is then often found in the absolute authority of the Bible. The answer to the question of God in history is sought in earth-shattering events or in challenging situations. This order of thinking, however, demands a far more conservative and morally rigorous behavior than large religious institutions expect from their members.

41. E. Troeltsch, *Die Soziallehren der christlichen Kirchen und Gruppen* (Tübingen: J. C. B. Mohr, 1912) (ET: *The Social Teachings of the Christian Churches*, trans. Olive Wyon [Chicago: University of Chicago Press, 1981]).

42. M. Weber, *Gesammelte Aufsätze zur Religionssoziologie*, vol. 1 (Tübingen: J. C. B. Mohr, 1920) (ET: *The Sociology of Religion*, trans. Ephraim Fischoff [Boston: Beacon Press, 1993]).

Large institutions allow room to absorb conflicts and disappointed expectations.

Within this dynamic, a curious mixture of groups — particularly evident in the United States — arises, representing expectations of an end of time along with a pragmatic attitude that is not disturbed when the expected end once again fails to turn up.[43] This mixture is worthy of consideration for more than simple psychological reasons. Whether the question is one of sociology or of social psychology, what is the *theological* problem?

Theology of history turns against the doctrine of the last things and its derivation from the Bible, which contains statements that appear to be in need of explanation. Above all, theology of history opposes radical eschatology and the belief that the basis of Christian hope is "given" by God in Jesus Christ, its foundation. The objection from theology of history is that this statement only asserts the grounds of hope without introducing it plausibly into dialogue with modern time (this is Pannenberg's criticism). The appeal to God as power of change, which by definition is not to be found in history (Moltmann), is an attempt to ground theology in the Easter event and to show God's involvement in a process that breaks through and opens history so that the new can be established in place of the old. The resistance of those who hope demonstrates this appeal. Liberation theology wants to give theology a new foundation, according to what Christians expect as a better future for the world. This desire often goes with a criticism of reality, which draws its bases from utopias.

With hope represented as intensive attention to the future, "accounting for hope" changes fundamentally. The representation seems to contradict directly what 1 Peter 3:15 demands from every Christian: "...to make a defense to anyone who calls you to account for the hope that is in you." This "accounting for hope" is not a λόγον διδόναι, meant in the sense of "substantiate" (*rationem reddere*, "give reasons for"). Rather, it is demanded that Christians give account for what they have received unexpectedly and over-

---

43. Timothy P. Weber, *Living in the Shadow of the Second Coming: American Premillennialism, 1875–1982*, expanded ed. (Chicago: University of Chicago Press, 1987).

whelmingly.[44] They must speak about the hope that is *in* them in the sense that it has come *to* them. The hope "in you" is the hope that has and maintains its origins external to us in God's actions and in God's promise, which have taken form in the risen Christ. This is a hope maintained by God's faithfulness.

Jesus Christ, as the *eschatos,* is the *unsurpassed foundation of Christian hope* (2.5.1) — a reason which cannot be rendered obsolete or exceeded by any power of human hope. The church of Jesus Christ is the community of people called to such hope. In that hope they experience unity. According to this experience the church can be called to give account for this hope that forms and fulfills her.

Whoever appeals to Christ as the *foundation of unsurpassable hope* may feel the need to present his own hope to its greatest degree. That person must prove how much he or she is able to hope. If a Christian group (or church) is caught by this pressure to represent its hope, it will be tempted to repeated proofs of what that hope produces. Since such an endeavor cannot be successful in the long term, the community realizes that it has lived longer than its hope.[45]

Does a theology that consciously rejects such foundational strategies run the danger of detaching itself from its "context"? Theology can always be linked to historical context. For example, the beginnings of radical theology in dialectical theology — because of a culture-critical bent — appear in hindsight to be suited to the time. Dialectical theologians, however, were aware that they had to speak to their time theologically while refusing to be led by an analysis of the situation. They were sovereign, uninhibited, and one could also say naive about the contemporary situation and its requirements. Because they did not derive their theological insights from these observations, they were free and sensitive to questions

44. Concerning this understanding see Martin Heidegger, *Der Satz vom Grund* (Pfullingen, Germany: Günter Neske, 1957), 181: "According to Greek thinking, *lógon didónai* means to present something which is present to the comprehending perception" [Griechisch gedacht, sagt *lógon didónai:* etwas Anwesendes in seinem so und so Anwesen und Vorliegen darbieten, nämlich dem versammelnden Vernehmen].

45. This is the problem that Franz Overbeck pointed to in his criticism of church and theology (see 2.2), e.g., in his assessment of the ascetic tradition within Christianity (*Über die Christlichkeit unserer heutigen Theologie,* 2d ed. [Leipzig, 1903; reprint, Darmstadt: Wissenschaftliche Buchgesellschaft, 1963], 86–87).

and tasks which a stubborn concentration on the "spirit of the age" would have easily overlooked.

One can even attempt to explain the doctrine of the last things "contextually," although without meeting the doctrine in its deepest intention and argumentation. Is it coincidental that the doctrine — at least in its systematic form — came into being after the end of the Thirty Years War (1618–48), a time of the spiritual reorientation of Europe? The doctrine of the last things appears in that context as a rejection of "prophetic" interpretations and a taming of wildly proliferating speculations about the predictable course of events and the chances of intervention. The doctrine binds the perception of history to the theological context of the history of God with humanity.

The theologians who, in those times, were constructing an eschatology did not wish, in the situation of change and fresh starts, to convey new visions to their contemporaries, nor to portray a better world. Rather, they wished to keep the question, "What is your only comfort in life and in death?" alive, as found in the first question of the (Reformed) Heidelberg Catechism (1563). In the answer, earlier theologians had stuck firmly to the confession of hope:

> That I belong — body and soul, in life and in death — not to myself but to my faithful Savior, Jesus Christ . . .[46]

Such an answer is hardly trying to hold on to convictions whose fundaments have long since crumbled away through fierce conflict, or through an embarrassing inability to prove the world-shaping power of Christian hope.

The theologians who referenced the catechism were appealing, in their dramatic situation, to God's action in saving and judging, which conveys to humans the certainty of life from and with God. God's verdict, full of promise, forbids us to set our hope on what we are able to do, a situation that would result in despair, failure, and lasting guilt.

---

46. "The Heidelberg Catechism," in *The Constitution of the Presbyterian Church (U.S.A.),* vol. 1: *Book of Confessions* (New York: Office of the General Assembly, 1983), No. 4.001.

4.5.3. Perceptions of God in History

The question of the relationship of God to history is not an arbitrary invention, and therefore it cannot be arbitrarily left aside.
Since God does not allow Godself to be excluded from what we
call "history," we are and remain confronted with the question.

Why God cannot be excluded from human stories and therefore
from the story "with Christ" (3.5.2), was a question that Christian theology attempted to address early on with the concept of
"divine economy" (see Eph. 1:10; 3:9). Economy is the expression
of divine grace, of God's implementation of God's will, in which
God does what God promises and at the same time says what God
wills. God's word and work constitute a unity. The doctrine of the
Trinity makes clear how this economy comes into contact with humanity, and how we can perceive it: *God comes into the world
with and in Jesus Christ, and in so doing promises God's future,
God's coming. The promise "depends" on and clings to the resurrection of the crucified one.* It is Christ's life with and in God that
forms the frame of our hope. God's will is perceptible in this fact,
so that we can pray: "Thy will be done, on earth as it is in heaven"
(Matt. 6:10).

"What God wills," then, is not proclaimed so that we can seize
control of it. "Economy" is the embodiment of what God wills
for us, provided so that we may live. The economy of God's grace
is the Christ-story, which — as outlined in the Letter to the Ephesians — fills space and time (Eph. 3:18). Therefore "economy" can
scarcely be rendered by "plan of salvation." Such an interpretation leads easily to misleading questions about what God plans to
carry out.

Still, the question of God's role in what we experience as story
and in all our necessarily flawed efforts to impose order on the
story cannot be dismissed. It can, however, easily lead to error,
in that it conceals more than one trap. Expressions referring to
God's relation to us ("to have to do," "to act," "to work," "to
be obedient to God's will," etc.) are metaphorical. It is their metaphorical character that seems to introduce the problem of speaking
of God. It appears understandable, therefore, that more recent theology often avoids speech about God's activity, in order to avoid

the problem. Theology of history on the other hand — particularly liberation theology — does not shrink from the theme. Perhaps it is still sufficiently uninhibited from the wanness of doubt to wonder whether it is permissible to ask about "God in history" — a naïveté that Europe lost long ago in the face of the disasters that had also been explained by references to this "God of history."

This treatment should at least have made clear how it is *not* possible to speak of God's activity. In consideration of what must be ruled out, it is possible to sketch a framework in which responsible discourse can take place. The rule against theological identification is decisive: God's activity cannot be identified either with the course of history as a whole nor with individual moments.

One proposal is that God's activity is limited to (or at least concentrated on) what takes place between God and the individual. God's activity would then relate to the subjectivity that embraces the relationship of the human to God, to the world and to himself. In this case, the subjectivity — not to be confused with subjective concepts or viewpoints — would identify or not identify God's role in events. A reason for not wanting to discover God within space and time lies in the finite nature of the human, in that his ability to grasp reality is limited by space and time. Humans can only say something about God, the infinite and absolute, in relation to how they themselves are affected by God. So, for example, argues Rudolf Bultmann, for whom God's activity takes place in the change of human self-understanding. Christians who expect nothing from God in this godless world, except in their personal life, think similarly. In both cases, history exists as a context that humans can influence and that influences them; it exists as the framework of human action and trial. For faith, however, everything that happens in history is, in the end, a matter of indifference.

Theology of history represents the opposite position. God's activity does not correlate to the course of events, let alone a gloomy fate. God's activity comes to light in a structured context, in units of meaning which render possible integration of experiences or events. An example of such a context is the orientation toward social and economic justice, all-embracing peace, and freedom for all. This context allows for events to be interpreted — that is, to be unambiguously evaluated — according to whether they follow the accepted direction of history or resist it. Interpretation may occur with the assistance of a system of coordinates, on which lines of salvation and its opposite can be entered, and which allows history to be followed on a time line. God's intervention may also be expected in world-shattering events, perceived as marking epic change. One can and must reckon with what God's activity in history was, is, and will be. This interpretation can be limited by many reservations — by reference to the sinful nature of humanity, which allows only for broken perception, or to knowledge of the relativity of all historical phenomena (Paul Tillich) — but the ordering of "God" and "history" is given from the very beginning.

Alongside such historical examination and the sketch of its results — often only distinguishable by a hair's breadth — stands *the question of God's living will in what we experience* and of God's verdict on what happens and how it happens. The crucial point is that we *ask* about God's will, rather than assume that we know it already, and then ask how this knowledge can be brought in line with the stories we call "history."

We need to really *ask* these questions in light of contingent events, predictable developments, and supposedly manageable contexts. Such a *theology* of history (with emphasis on theology rather than history) can proceed neither descriptively nor prescriptively. It cannot prescribe God's activity, let alone predict it. Instead, it follows assertive statements grounded in the confidence of faith. God comes near to history, but not through events nor as contrary to everyday experiences, *but exactly where we do not reckon with God!*

If theology wishes to busy itself with history, it must pay attention to the saying: "For as the heavens are higher than the earth, so are my ways higher than your ways and my thoughts than your thoughts" (Isa. 55:9). The metaphor could imply that God's thoughts and ways run parallel to ours, but at great distance, until both meet in eternity. But the verse means that God's thoughts and ways do not exist at our eye level, nor can we see them when we crane our necks or crouch down. God's ways and our ways are dissimilar and cannot be compared. A judgment on the strides we make cannot be reached by comparison with God's strides. This should not prevent us from comparing strides we have made with each other, from attempting to distinguish between progress and regression. But any judgment concerning their relation to God's will is reserved for God.

In rare moments, humans may sense that God has moved across their path so that they perceive God's contingent activity. But this perception is only possible *retrospectively.* The biblical stories dealing with recognition of God always emphasize this: paradigmatically, Moses is permitted to see God's blazing "glory" only from "behind" (Exod. 33:18–23). Retrospective perception is also illustrated by the story of Jesus on the cross, and by the story of Joseph and his brothers. The latter is concerned to clarify the involvement of human intentions in God's promise of blessing. At the end, Joseph, who increasingly seems to hold all the cards, confesses: "Am I in the place of God? As for you, you meant evil against me, but God meant it for good, to bring it about that many people should be kept alive, as they are today" (Gen. 50:19–20).

Theology of history stems from an amazed cry thanking God. Its roots lie in the *prayer of thanksgiving,* which cannot analyze events. The prayer cannot and will not intrude into the unpredictable network of events that is called "history." Rather, the prayer expresses personal memory and memories of special interactions within relationships. The prayer can be a conscious refusal to understand oneself according to manageable circumstances or to calculate the influences and effects of circumstance. God is called on *to preserve the sensorium for time,* so one is able to see more clearly than is possible by trusting in a concept of history.

Attention to fragments of history instead of to *the* so-called history allows for expression of the theological conviction that God is *not* the personification of everything that happens. Different and often contrary stories cannot be brought together except in the contrived idea of *one* history, which then offers a conceptual framework for all further observations and explanations. That different histories meet and can be recognized in relation to one another, or in relation to the history of God with humanity, is a perception seldom granted. But when granted, it drives toward hope in full recognition of God and of reality. In this sense, eschatology remains concerned with theology of history.

– Chapter 5 –

ONE IN HOPE?
ECUMENICAL PERSPECTIVES

5.1. The Stunted Dialogue

Now we have reached the point at which we aimed in the introductory survey (1.3). The three characteristic types of eschatology stand alongside each other, often at loggerheads.[1] Which questions have proven indispensable? Are new storms building? Do new theological ideas render other ideas obsolete? Can Christianity unite in the light of common hope?

The new theology of history has attracted much attention, not least because it contains an ecumenical promise: an understanding of the path of Christianity as part of the historical universe. The intent is to take down barriers between the churches and to step across boundaries. Liberation theology sees this process programmatically, and has for that reason come to constitute an ecumenical movement of a particular type. In it, the divisions between different traditions belong to the burden of a divided past, which must be shaken off for the sake of a better future. Even the boundaries between church and society, according to this vision, exist only in the old world — not in the "global village" of a world society connected technologically and by all-embracing emergencies and common dangers. This community of interests bears the fate of all and must be united in concern for common survival. The "greater" hope of Christian faith, hope in God's kingdom, will prevail if it also promotes "smaller" hopes — the hope of greater prosperity, greater social and economic justice, peace among na-

---

1. In this process the doctrine of the last things is to a large extent suppressed.

tions, and freedom from exploitation and oppression — without awarding ultimate significance to such hopes.

A theology of history answers in this manner if asked if humanity is one in hope. The strategic pursuit of unity allows for the formation of coalitions among people who believe differently or who have no belief at all. The "greater" hope both allows and demands formation of alliances when pressing tasks need to be shared. Many Christians have spoken out in favor of this "operational" model, particularly when it comes into contact with socialism and socialism's projects for the future.

The "Decree on Ecumenism" of Vatican II (1964) recommends that Christians of different denominations work together in tolerance, for the sake of love and as a sign of uniting hope:

> Before the whole world let all Christians confess their faith in the triune God, one and three in the incarnate Son of God, our Redeemer and Lord. United in their efforts, and with mutual respect, let them bear witness to our common hope which does not play us false. In these days when cooperation in social matters is so widespread, all men without exception are called to work together, with much greater reason all those who believe in God, but most of all, all Christians in that they bear the name of Christ. Cooperation among Christians vividly expresses the relationship which in fact already unites them, and it sets in clearer relief the features of Christ the Servant.[2]

It is the face of the servant Christ which should shine through shared works of charity, particularly when the community of Christ's faithful has not yet become evident. Love should bring forth hope, but not as a confession of hope in Christ, the Coming One. Hope promises to be found wherever it, as inexhaustible energy in the service of love, lends endurance.

Is this then the same as *the* hope that does not "disappoint us" in the midst of all difficulties, because "God's love has been poured into our hearts through the Holy Spirit which has been given to us"

---

2. "Decree on Ecumenism," in *Vatican Council II: The Conciliar and Post-conciliar Documents,* ed. Austin Flannery, O.P., 2d ed. (Northport, N.Y.: Costello, 1980), 462.

(Rom. 5:5)? Is there no difference between the energy of hope and the hope that overcomes all challenges and completely fills those whom God loves?

Whether and how we humans can become *one in hope* depends very much on the answer to this question.

When the question of the future of the church and of theology began to be set in motion in the mid-1960s, that seemed, ecumenically speaking, to constitute a sign of hope. Even in the preceding decade, considerable argument had taken place within Protestant churches before the Second General Assembly of the World Council of Churches in Evanston, Illinois, in 1954. The assembly gathered under the theme, "Christ — The Hope of the World." To speak of Jesus Christ as the hope of the world seemed to many critics too dogmatic and too removed from tasks confronting humanity, from the increasing tensions caused by technical progress in the West, from increasing misery in the Third World, and from the menacing concentration of power in both political and economic spheres.[3] In the period that followed there were attempts to tie eschatology and ethics more closely,[4] but the consequences of such attempts for ecumenism remained limited.

That changed significantly in the sixties. The resounding echo of Jürgen Moltmann's *Theology of Hope* provides a particularly striking example. Another example can be found in the dialogue between Roman Catholic theologians, particularly Jesuits, and neo-Marxists.[5] Two volumes of *Concilium: Theology in the Age of Renewal,* which came into existence in the ecumenical climate surrounding Vatican II, seek dialogue and progressive reconciliation.[6]

---

3. See *The Ecumenical Advance: A History of the Ecumenical Movement,* ed. Harold E. Fey, vol. 2 (Geneva: World Council of Churches, 1986); Ans J. van der Bent, "WCC Assemblies," in *Dictionary of the Ecumenical Movement,* ed. Nicholas Lossky et al. (Geneva: World Council of Churches; Grand Rapids, Mich.: Eerdmans, 1991), 1091–92.

4. E.g., Heinz-Dietrich Wendland, *Die Kirche in der modernen Gesellschaft: Entscheidungsfragen für das kirchliche Handeln im Zeitalter der Massenwelt* (Hamburg: Furche, 1956).

5. See Roger Garaudy, Johann Baptist Metz, and Karl Rahner, *Der Dialog — oder: Ändert sich das Verhältnis zwischen Katholizismus und Marxismus?* (Reinbek, West Germany: Rowohlt, 1966).

6. *The Problem of Eschatology,* ed. Edward Schillebeeckx and Boniface Willems (New York: Paulist Press, 1969); *Dimensions of Spirituality,* ed. Christian Duquoc (New York: Herder & Herder, 1970).

At the same time, the Prague Spring of 1968 awoke hope of a new and more open relationship between Christianity and Marxism in Western Europe, until the intervention of Warsaw Pact countries in Czechoslovakia nipped even that bloom of hope.

But, on the other hand, the fascination with Ernst Bloch's *The Principle of Hope* remained undiminished for many theologians into the 1970s,[7] and interest in many eschatological concepts increased in the sociopolitical hothouse that was heated further by the European student revolution of 1967–69. The market value of the concept "utopia" climbed rapidly. Evidence of another type can be found in the use of the label "eschatology" in connection with intensified hopes for the future both within and outside theology. In the 1960s, the term became an insult in everyday political conversation. "Eschatologians" were counted potentially dangerous, foolish and unpredictable.

Was the interest in eschatology only one element of the changing attitudes that marked the time? Was it a symptom of the optimism that blossomed in the Western world? It is worth asking what meaning eschatology really had. The question of eschatology belonged — as we have seen — to the theological debate of the period; it reflected the new direction supposedly set in motion at the time. Whether concentration on eschatology constituted a break away from internal church problems toward taking responsibility for changing the world (Moltmann), or whether it was the logical consequence of a revision of basic theological ideas (e.g., Pannenberg), was already a matter of controversy in the mid-sixties. Such revision can lead to new ideas without really pursued strategically. Moltmann understood his concept as an answer to the "crisis of relevancy" within Christianity,[8] and the response that met his book is proof enough that many people felt the same way.

---

7. On the reception of Bloch, see the previously mentioned references to Jürgen Moltmann and Gerhard Sauter. See also Heinz Kimmerle, *Die Zukunftsbedeutung der Hoffnung: Auseinandersetzung mit Ernst Blochs "Prinzip Hoffnung" aus philosophischer und theologischer Sicht* (Bonn: Bouvier, 1966); Wolf-Dieter Marsch, *Hoffen worauf? Auseinandersetzung mit Ernst Bloch* (Hamburg: Furche, 1963); and Hermann Deuser and Peter Steinacker, eds., *Ernst Blochs Vermittlungen zur Theologie* (Munich: Chr. Kaiser; Mainz: Grünewald, 1983).

8. J. Moltmann, *The Crucified God: The Cross of Christ as the Foundation and Criticism of Christian Theology,* trans. R. A. Wilson and John Bowden (London: SCM Press; New York: Harper & Row, 1974), 7–18; idem, "Stationen und Signale:

That much that is written on eschatology is too historically conditioned to serve the task of "accounting for hope" cannot be escaped. With hindsight, the statement seems confirmed by the fact that the generation presently growing up no longer finds "future" a fascinating word. The slogan "the future has already begun" tends to give rise to fear of the future. But just as it was superficial in the past to overlook reasons pressing for a new concept of the doctrine of the last things because they had largely been excluded from theological thought, so is it fatal nowadays, because of this atmosphere, to overlook the theological grounds that lie behind the responsibility to give account for hope.

Vatican II gave new direction to self-understanding within the Roman Catholic Church, and actively encouraged a new consideration of eschatology within that framework. The Council succeeded in both when it led church dogmatics back to the theology of the Bible and at the same time attempted to understand anew the place of the church in society. The Council also helped eliminate the practice that constructed dogmatics on the basis of "tracts," and created room for stronger systematic linkage of individual dogmatic themes.

The dogmatics of Johannes Brinktrine offered one last example of the old school. Brinktrine dealt with the doctrine of the last things[9] before dealing with the doctrine of the church,[10] because in the latter case he expected new ecclesiological guidelines from the Council — in the case of eschatology he seems to have expected nothing of the sort. Both tracts are constructed along traditional lines. Individual themes in eschatology — death, judgment of the dead, purgatory, the second coming, resurrection of the body, general judgment, perfection of the world, heaven and hell — are first explained according to church doctrine, then supported by prooftexts from the Bible and tradition, and finally, if necessary, secured against contrary opinions. Only in the third part

---

Persönlicher Rückblick auf die letzten zehn Jahre," in *1845–1970: Almanach — 125 Jahre Chr. Kaiser Verlag München* (Munich: Chr. Kaiser, 1970), 84–91.

9. J. Brinktrine, *Die Lehre von den letzten Dingen* (Paderborn, West Germany: Ferdinand Schöningh, 1963).

10. J. Brinktrine, *Die Lehre von der Kirche* (Paderborn, West Germany: Ferdinand Schöningh, 1964).

of the method, if at all, do voices in Protestant theology receive the slightest attention.

What has changed since the Council can, for example, be seen in Dietrich Wiederkehr's *Perspectives of Eschatology*.[11] For Wiederkehr, eschatology forms the point of intersection for the whole of theology; eschatology is directed at the Christ-event as the pivot of both salvation history and of the relationship among God, humanity, and the world. He enters into dialogue not only with different worldviews and the arts, but also with Protestant eschatology.

Only three years later, the situation had once again changed perceptibly, with Joseph Ratzinger's treatise on eschatology.[12] Ratzinger (b. 1927) was not yet writing as the archbishop of Munich, let alone as the prefect of the Congregation of Faith and chief guardian of Catholic doctrine. But the marks of his present position are unmistakable. To Ratzinger the content of eschatology is primarily the strengthening of personal faith; eschatology serves the pastoral task of the church and one should guard against confusion with utopian activism. Protestant theologians are included only in the category of "eschatology as political theology." Questions concerning the historical future and action for that future may accompany hope in the resurrection of the dead, but may by no means be permitted to dominate the subject. Hope is connected to a new religio-philosophical interpretation of "immortality," a reflection on the invulnerability of personal relationship to God.

Ratzinger represents a countermovement dealing with the consequences of the Enlightenment; this is already clear in his study on faith and future.[13] Faith rooted in personhood is opposed to technological rationality. In place of staking confidence in predictions, recollection of and reflection on history (*Besinnung auf die Geschichte*) is recommended in order to free humanity from the chains of scientific control. These are culture-critical tones, which remind one in part of Gogarten's diagnosis (3.3).

---

11. D. Wiederkehr, *Perspektiven der Eschatologie* (Zurich: Benziger, 1974).

12. J. Ratzinger, *Eschatologie — Tod und ewiges Leben* (Regensburg: Pustet, 1977) (ET: *Eschatology, Death, and Eternal Life,* ed. Aidan Nichols, O.P., trans. Michael Waldstein [Washington, D.C.: Catholic University of America Press, 1988]).

13. J. Ratzinger, *Glaube und Zukunft* (Munich: Kösel, 1970).

Does this approach also touch on denominational differences? In his assessment, Ratzinger examines tensions within the Roman Catholic Church and its claim to the status of world church, as well as its relationship to Protestant theology. Close attention is accorded only to Protestant eschatology taken from theology of history, perhaps because Ratzinger wished to brand similar tendencies within his own church.[14] There is no longer any real search for interdenominational dialogue concerning the doctrine of the last things or concerning the radicality of eschatology. Medard Kehl[15] and Dieter Hattrup[16] continue this tendency. Certainly, the occasional trace can be found of fundamental differentiation from Protestant theology.

One point of controversy seems to be human identity as a gift inherent to the creature, which, according to the Catholic viewpoint, neither sin nor death can cancel out, because that would mean that God was renouncing God's love.[17] For modern Protestant eschatology the following statement is taken to be true: "The only identity guarantor of the creature is God and God's faithfulness to this creature."[18]

Hattrup considers that Luther, as a "person extraordinarily sensitive for any kind of claim toward God," had to destroy the identity of humans "before they can reach God and God can accomplish his work toward them." In this process, the human is thrown back on his naked existence, which at the same time is raised "to the highest blessedness."[19]

Richard Schaeffler also finds in Luther's doctrine of justification a danger to personal identity. The human sees himself released from his personal history and from the world, since according to Luther "even the blessed sinner finds his or her identity in the transition from death of judgment to life in grace not in him-

---

14. Against that he could find allies, e.g., in Gerhard Ebeling and his disciples. See for example Pierre Bühler's critique of Moltmann, *Kreuz und Eschatologie: Eine Auseinandersetzung mit der politischen Theologie, im Anschluß an Luthers theologia crucis* (Tübingen: J. C. B. Mohr, 1981).

15. M. Kehl, *Eschatologie* (Würzburg: Echter, 1986).

16. D. Hattrup, *Eschatologie* (Paderborn, West Germany: Bonifatius, 1992).

17. Kehl, *Eschatologie*, 274.

18. Ibid.

19. Hattrup, *Eschatologie*, 290.

self or herself [*in se*], for example in his essence as human being or in his personality, but only outside himself [*extra se*] in God's faithfulness."[20]

Lutheran heritage appears as an anthropologically questionable concentration on religious experience, a narrow path that has perhaps emphasized an important theological point — pure faith in the reception of grace — but that cannot bear the weight of eschatology. Anthropologically speaking, justification shrinks to a point at which it becomes loss of identity. That matches in an unfortunate way the manner in which humans are surrendered to a civilization only too ready to sacrifice personal worth on the altar of progress.

But the Reformers thought in their doctrine of justification not of the pardoned sinner and of what happens to or in him, but rather of the pardon granted to the sinner and of Jesus Christ who dwells in him. They did not think of a transformation of human qualities, but rather of new life in the power of God's righteousness. The Catholic critics that have been mentioned look to the human as responsible for his actions. Correspondingly, they wish to ascertain the possibility of coming to a reliable judgment — as opposed to radical reliance on God, in which individual human responsibility threatens to be lost.

It would be of dangerous consequence if the eschatological dimension of the doctrine of justification were reduced to a single motif: What is our part before God? Unfortunately, this shrinkage of an idea corresponds to the impression often conveyed by Protestant theology, when it still talks about justification. That God's *verdict* is delivered in God's communication of God's righteousness, in which God does *not* throw the human back on his deeds or sins, but binds him into God's own activity in him and the world, is often either omitted or overlooked. God's verdict, which both judges and saves, sets boundaries for us that are new and completely different from those apparent when we consider our finite nature and interaction with other forms of life. This truth rules out considering God's action and human action in a cause-and-effect relationship. It is not the case that God, with the verdict, only con-

---

20. R. Schaeffler, *Was dürfen wir hoffen? Die katholische Theologie der Hoffnung zwischen Blochs utopischem Denken und der reformatorischen Rechtfertigungslehre* (Darmstadt: Wissenschaftliche Buchgesellschaft, 1979), 189.

firms what we have become and have done, nor that God inspires us to another and better way of life, in order that God can in the end pass judgment on a satisfactory result.

God's creative verdict acknowledges that God sees us in God's Son, who sets himself between us and God, before whom we would otherwise perish. At the same time God confronts us with our inclination to judge ourselves according to our achievements. The Reformers set great store on these beliefs as the foundation of Christian hope. Apart from these statements, they were scarcely revolutionaries concerning eschatology. As with other doctrines, in eschatology they had no intention of breaking new ground, except that in rejecting purgatory they caused the collapse of an edifice for preaching and counsel built on the concept that the time to serve oneself does not end with death. It had been believed that the dead could expiate sins. Even more, they could receive salvation by penitence, and relatives continued to have influence on salvation by praying or by arranging a mass.

In their contradiction of the piety of the time and its doctrinal foundations, objections which led to radical change, the Reformers started with the theological context of justification (4.5.1). The doctrine of justification[21] targets the claim that human beings are able to know and judge themselves according to what they have done, or what they can and wish to do. But the doctrine is not designed to build a theory of Christian life. The two are incompatible. God's verdict cannot be used to introduce the human to his ethical situation and to render him more capable of action, nor in consideration of one's own actions can one deduce God's verdict. The radicality of the Reformers' eschatology lies here. The doctrine of justification, with regard to eschatology, focuses on God's judging and saving action. God justifies the godless, forcing the person to recognize himself as having been without God and without hope (Eph. 2:12) and granting the certainty of hope, corresponding to the origin of the church in God's word and Spirit.

Ulrich Asendorf, *Eschatologie bei Luther* (Göttingen: Vandenhoeck & Ruprecht, 1967); Friedrich Beisser, *Hoffnung und Vollendung* (Gütersloh: Gütersloher

---

21. See Gerhard Sauter, "God Creating Faith: The Doctrine of Justification from the Reformation to the Present," *Lutheran Quarterly* 11 (1997): 17–102.

Verlagshaus, 1993); Walter Ernst MEYER, *Huldrych Zwinglis Eschatologie: Reformatorische Wende, Theologie und Geschichtsbild des Zürcher Reformators im Lichte seines eschatologischen Ansatzes* (Zurich: Theologischer Verlag, 1987); Heinrich QUISTORP, *Die letzten Dinge im Zeugnis Calvins: Calvins Eschatologie* (Gütersloh: C. Bertelsmann, 1941).

5.2. The Certainty of Hope

How does this discussion of justification relate to the views of Ratzinger? His core criticism of modern eschatology — that of Protestant pedigree as well — is that it loses its character when it grants the future precedence over the present, since this degrades or even ignores that which distinguishes the human person in the light of faith. And faith, in Ratzinger's conviction, is in every case a salvific experience of the present.

Elsewhere[22] Ratzinger laments — now from an official standpoint — the translation of Hebrews 11:1 in the "ecumenical translation": "Faith means firm standing in what one hopes for, conviction of things which one does not see."[23] According to Ratzinger, this version is oriented toward Luther, while the classical and correct representation, "Faith is the substance of things hoped for,"[24] is banished to a footnote.[25]

This is by no means a mere philological dispute. Hebrews 11:1 is almost a definition of the object of faith in hope, answering the question of how faith and hope relate to each other, what constitutes the link between them, and how it can be adequately described. The author of Hebrews gets around the matter by pointing to the hope experienced by the fathers and mothers of faith. From this history, it can be gathered that God calls humanity to hope and that this call sends them on a path, which may provide

---

22. "Über die Hoffnung: Ihre spirituellen Grundlagen aus der Sicht franziskanischer Theologie," *Internationale Katholische Zeitschrift 'Communio'* 13 (1984): 293–305; see especially p. 298, n. 9.

23. The Bishops of Germany, Austria, Switzerland et al., eds., *Einheitsübersetzung der Heiligen Schrift: Die Bibel* (Stuttgart: Katholische Bibelanstalt, 1980), 1346: "Glaube aber ist: Feststehen in dem, was man erhofft, Überzeugtsein von Dingen, die man nicht sieht."

24. "Der Glaube aber ist die Grundlage dessen, was man erhofft."

25. The NRSV reads, "Now faith is the assurance of things hoped for," which is in fact nearer to the translation preferred by Ratzinger.

places for rest but knows no end. To believe means to take that path and to be ready to break camp.

On the other hand, it is not the charm of continual wandering that dominates the history of those who believe and hope. The charm lies not in a nomadic existence whose purpose is the path itself, which passes repeatedly through new experience, joyous yet unfulfilled. The path of faith into hope is marked by a junction of rest and departure — "rest" not as opposed to leaving, but as a temporary pause that does not take hold, stable but not stultifying.

The Vulgate translation, "Est autem fides sperandarum substantia rerum, argumentum non apparentium" (Faith is the substance of things to be hoped for, evidence [or proof] of invisible things), still retains traces of neo-Platonism, differentiating between the visible (interim) and invisible (heavenly) worlds. With the help of this differentiation, the writer of Hebrews probably wished to illustrate the path taken by believers to the side of the glorified Christ. What is being held ready in heaven exists above us and stands before our eyes intellectually and spiritually, able to direct us in sense and striving. To believe is to place oneself under control of this heavenly world. For this reason, the ambiguous word "hypostasis" can be treated etymologically in Hebrews 11:1 and rendered as "standing under":[26] "The faith is standing by what is hoped for and a doubtless certainty of the invisible."

In an incidental comment, written in 1510–11, on Peter Lombard's *Sentences,* and in his lecture on the Letter to the Hebrews (1517–18), Martin Luther came to grips with the neo-Platonism in the tradition without being able to free himself from it.[27] In 1546, Luther translated Hebrews 11:1 as: "Es ist aber der Glaube, eine gewisse zuversicht, des, das man hoffet, und nicht zweiveln an dem, das man nicht sihet" (The faith is steady confidence in things hoped for and not doubting things not seen).[28]

That is a particularly free rendition, and one of debatable philo-

---

26. Erich Grässer, *An die Hebräer,* vol. 3: *Hebr 10,19–13,25* (Zurich: Benziger; Neukirchen: Neukirchener Verlag, 1997), 96.

27. "Randbemerkungen Luthers," in *WA* 9, 91:13–33; see M. Luther, *Vorlesung über den Hebräerbrief,* in *WA* 57, 226:10–229:5.

28. *WA. Deutsche Bibel,* vol. 7: *Luther's Drucktexte 1522–46,* ed. G. Bebermeyer (Weimar: Böhlau, 1931), 371.

logical correctness. Luther is concentrating on the *question of certitude,* and in doing so presents a fundamental decision of the Reformers — a decision to criticize a concept of faith as inertia that, while granted by God's grace, must be preserved and proved by actions befitting such a gift. Luther tries to give hope a meaning that lends certainty.

Luther's rendition of "hypostasis" as *Zuversicht* (confidence/certainty), philologically dissatisfying as it may be, does point to the object of faith — the preceding activity of God, salvation, into which we are fitted, without having to discover within it an Archimedean point from which we may affect the world. To this extent, faith is in essence *confidence,* but not in the sense of a stronger, self-sufficient hope. Confidence looks to God; it expects God's action.

Luther answered the question of the certainty of salvation — of salvation from ruin caused by sin, death, and the associated enmity to God — by redefining it:

> And this is the reason why our theology is certain: it snatches us away from ourselves and places us outside ourselves, so that we do not depend on our own strength, conscience, experience, person, or works but depend on that which is outside ourselves, that is, on the promise and truth of God, which cannot deceive.[29]

This answer corresponds to Luther's definition of faith as reformulated in Hebrews 11:1. In my opinion, the definition remains essential if "faith" is not to be stylized as religious experience, or to be mistaken for a momentary feeling of elation, as in Friedrich Schleiermacher's statement: "in every moment to be eternal is the immortality of religion."[30] In order to avoid such misunderstand-

---

29. M. Luther, *Lectures on Galatians,* in *Luther's Works,* ed. Jaroslav Pelikan and Helmut T. Lehmann, American edition (St. Louis: Concordia; Philadelphia: Fortress Press, 1955ff.), 26:387. The commentary is on Galatians 4:6.

30. F. Schleiermacher, *On Religion: Speeches to Its Cultured Despisers,* trans. John Oman (New York: Harper & Brothers, 1958), 101: "In the midst of finitude to be one with the Infinite and in every moment to be eternal is the immortality of religion." Another English translation is *On Religion: Addresses in Response to Its Cultured Critics,* trans. Terrence N. Tice (Richmond: John Knox Press, 1969), 157: "In the midst of finitude to become one with the infinite, and to be eternal in every instant — this is the immortality of religion."

ings, insight into the nature of hope is needed. Hope is treated too briefly in Luther's work. It seems to have been disposed by the eschatological determination of faith, so that hope is no longer an independent theme.

For that reason, there is a need to elaborate on the subject. Hope is our life with God, not the life that we do not or will have, but what we *are* in Christ. The reverse of this definition runs as follows: Since this life with God *is* promised to us, we *are* people who hope, which also means that we *become* people who hope. In both explanations one finds the idea of being in becoming (*Sein im Werden*). In always being able to begin anew, we are saved in hope (Rom. 8:24).

To be clear, God's promises — of justice, peace, life, rest, and knowledge of God — must be named as the object of hope. In experience one becomes aware of hope. That is the theologically decisive relationship. Faith does not exist as religious experience of the present, containing prospects which can then count as "hopes," nor as a sketch of exciting possibilities for the future, which encourage confidence in what could come to pass.

The hope that comes from faith is not a reaching out in ecstasy toward future perfection and transportation into a better world. Rather, in hope we are torn away from ourselves and placed before God — placed before the one on whom we can rely. In God's verdict over what is and what, in the power of God's promise, will be, the form of this world passes away (1 Cor. 7:31).

To what extent does this characteristic of theology — the certainty of hope — differ from the Catholic tradition?[31]

According to Thomas Aquinas (1225–74), Christian hope — like faith and love, the other two cardinal virtues — is wholly and completely a gift of God. For that reason alone humans can be certain of this hope: not because they see occasion for positive views of the future, or because they feel a spiritual yearning within themselves that leads them to follow it. Rather, the hope granted by God forms the person that accepts hope. Hope is the "imagining"

---

31. On the following, see Michael Basse, *Certitudo Spei: Thomas von Aquins Begründung der Hoffnungsgewißheit und ihre Rezeption bis zum Konzil von Trient als ein Beitrag zur Verhältnisbestimmung von Eschatologie und Rechtfertigungslehre* (Göttingen: Vandenhoeck & Ruprecht, 1993).

of perfection as God intends it, and that transforms a person. It enters and forms him. Hope is an unconditional gift, a disposition that can be developed. It can therefore be considered a "virtue" in which a person grows and flourishes. The person who hopes becomes a being on the way (*in statu viatoris*), a person on the path toward God and toward personal perfection.[32]

Hope as a human disposition intends to do justice to the fact that God created the world with a view to its perfection. Therefore, creation has an eschatological telos, for which God alone is responsible. But God calls humanity to collaborate on this continual work. With the gifts of faith, hope, and love, God breaks through the resistance of every human caught up in sin, and calls them to repentance. The pardoned sinner assents to the divine destiny of creation, and from that point onward exists, thinks, and acts according to that direction. The supernatural, pure gift of hope then becomes a permanent task, without being relativized in the process. Whether the creature endowed with hope succeeds or fails in the task set by creation cannot harm hope. Anyone practiced in the virtue of hope can always start afresh on the path to perfection.

The creation that God intends to perfect and the virtue of hope with which God endows the human creature are therefore to be regarded as complementary. Faith and hope are balanced in such a way that the balance may not be lost.

This piece of reasoning was declared binding by the decree on justification issued by the Council of Trent (1547), and also forms the finer structure of modern Catholic eschatology. Leonardo Boff can be cited as an example. To Boff, every person is part of the cosmic process, with the target the "absolute realization" of humankind.[33] "Heaven is the final and ultimate convergence — in God — of all human longings for advancement, realization, and fulfillment."[34]

Even if one puts aside the evolutionary theory propounded by Pierre Teilhard de Chardin (1881–1955), which Boff works into

---

32. Josef Pieper, *Über die Hoffnung*, 4th ed. (Munich: Kösel, 1949) (ET: *On Hope*, trans. Sister Mary Frances McCarthy, S.N.D. [San Francisco: Ignatius Press, 1986]).

33. L. Boff, *Was kommt nachher? Das Leben nach dem Tode*, trans. Horst Goldstein (Salzburg: Otto Müller, 1982), 58.

34. Ibid.

his scheme, Boff holds fast to a view which sees the correspondence of humanity and the world. This view belongs among the affirmative elements of liberation theology, and not just in its Catholic version. Is further ecumenical agreement to be found here? Such agreement would admittedly fail to overcome early differences over the reasons for certainty of hope, but only because virtually nobody is acquainted with the differences anymore. Such would be ecumenism, but ecumenism nurtured by forgetfulness.

The disposition of both human and world to perfection undeniably has attractions, because it makes it possible to discern progress and regression. To be transferred into the presence of the risen Christ and into the expectation of the coming God on the other hand seems far less clear — it must be perceived in different ways, because it remains grounded in God's action. Even someone with little experience in faith and hope will beware of speaking of growth of faith and hope. We can only grow *in* faith and *in* hope, but once again we are not in a position to judge — only God is in a position to judge.

If one follows the Reformation doctrine of justification, whose intent is to encourage unity in hope, theological anthropology becomes a duty in a new sense. The description of hope as a virtue within the Catholic tradition does point to an ethical guideline, but must take care that it does not make hope conditional, instead of a gift of grace.

The intention is not to reopen doctrinal controversies among the churches. But in view of existing — often latent — differences, it is a good idea to remember previous theological differences that could help both sides. This is why the eschatological contours of the Reformation doctrine of justification should be emphasized.

In Reformation doctrine, the believer does not rely on himself; he lives from what God gives. The believer experiences his limitations and at the same time the sphere of his existence before God. The believer may rely on hope, because he does not have to rely on his own self. He can abandon himself and be drawn into what comes toward him, into hope in the one *who* is to come, since "*what* comes to him" will be subordinated to the Coming One, the *eschatos*. Humans are not torn out of the familiar world to discover a new point of gravity or to circle around themselves in their own destiny. God's verdict determines the standard of measurement for human awareness of space and time.

Faith and hope have the same object: God's promise. To believe means to abandon obstinacy and opposition in the face of God's promise, to say "Amen, so be it" to that promise, and not to raise one's voice against it. Hope reaches out to the promise, and uses the promise as an anchor (Heb. 6:19).

For this reason, the essence of faith and hope cannot be equated with the difference between present and future. It is misleading to associate faith only with the present, and hope with the future.

It would not be a case of favoring the present in the interest of faith to consider, for the sake of insight into both faith *and* hope, whether the present is being neglected. I refer to the present as the today, the point at which God's promise is heard: "Behold, now is the day of salvation" (2 Cor. 6:2, quoting Isa. 49:8). We run the risk of bypassing the present if it is swamped by memories or if we allow ourselves to be swept along by pleasant hopes. Thus, life appears to be fulfilled elsewhere, in the golden past or in a promising future. Blaise Pascal (1623–62) addresses this forgetfulness of the present:

> We never keep to the present. We recall the past; we antici-pate the future as if we found it too slow in coming and were trying to hurry it up, or we recall the past as if to stay its too-rapid flight. We are so unwise that we wander about in times that do not belong to us, and do not think of the only one that does; so vain that we dream of times that are not and blindly flee the only one that is. The fact is that the present usually hurts. . . .
>
> Let each of us examine his thoughts; he will find them wholly concerned with the past or the future. We almost never think of the present, and if we do think of it, it is only to see what light it throws on our plans for the future. The present is never our end. The past and the present are our means, the future alone our end. Thus we never actually live, but hope to live, and since we are always planning how to be happy, it is inevitable that we should never be so.[35]

35. B. Pascal, *Pensées,* trans. A. J. Krailsheimer (Harmondsworth, England: Penguin Books, 1966; reprint, 1981), 43 (fragment 172).

We should remember this aphorism today. It shows how eschatology and the doctrine of justification fit together. Justification, as the verdict of God, protects against intellectual escapism — escape to an idealized time — and against the tendency to anticipate that time as one of fulfillment.

Is it this concept that critics have in mind when speaking of an eschatology dedicated to the future? Ratzinger understands "future" phenomenologically, as emerging from the extension of faith. The "now" of the experience of transcendence, an experience that is still confronted with the "not yet" of fulfilled hope, is suited to faith. According to Ratzinger, it is only in this extension into the future that the human being can experience himself according to his nature — as a person of true worth, granted by the grace of God and therefore inalienable, who may approach fulfillment. On this path there are moments when we experience meaning.[36] Such moments cannot be lost, even if in them we find only temporary satisfaction; they are nevertheless preserved and cannot be destroyed even by death. For that reason, the human personality can be considered immortal. This progressive experience of meaning opens up experience of God, which is the ultimate content of immortality.

With this understanding of hope as a perspective of faith, Ratzinger is in line with a number of representatives of modern Protestantism. They interpret Luther's concept of certainty of salvation as a foundation of religious subjectivity.[37] The classic example is Schleiermacher.

---

36. Paulus Engelhardt, "Christliche Eschatologie," in *Gott — Mensch — Universum: Die Stellung des Christen in Zeit und Welt,* ed. Jacques Bivort de la Saudée and Johannes Hüttenbügel (Cologne: Styria, 1963), 795–823; Wolfhart Pannenberg, "Insight and Faith," in *Basic Questions in Theology: Collected Essays,* trans. George H. Kehn (Philadelphia: Fortress Press, 1971), 2:28–45; Wessel Stoker, *Is the Quest for Meaning the Quest for God? The Religious Ascription of Meaning in Relation to Secular Ascription of Meaning,* trans. Lucy Jansen-Hofland and Henry Jansen (Amsterdam and Atlanta: Rodopi B.V., 1996), 236–39. See my critical analysis of this religious perception of meaning in *Die Frage nach Sinn: Eine theologische und philosophische Orientierung* (Munich: Chr. Kaiser, 1982) (ET: *The Question of Meaning: A Theological and Philosophical Orientation,* translated and edited by Geoffrey W. Bromiley [Grand Rapids, Mich.: Eerdmans, 1995]).

37. See Wilfried Härle and Eilert Herms, *Rechtfertigung: Das Wirklichkeitsverständnis des christlichen Glaubens* (Göttingen: Vandenhoeck & Ruprecht, 1979), 212–21.

Religious personalism recommends itself as the protector of humanity (or at least of Christianity) against utopias and a planned future. The hereafter must not be permitted to take the form of a future designed to replace transcendence by exceeding the present or the manageable past, and in that allowing the status quo to be overridden. Future as replacement for transcendence should not be taken to imply ceaseless transcendentalizing — that would be an exhausting prospect, leading to ever increasing dissatisfaction. Therefore the advocates of religious personalism like Ratzinger deny utopias and political concepts of salvation which expect salvation only from a better future. These concepts of salvation rest on ideas not rooted in confidence in God as the creator, sustainer, and protector of personal and societal life.

Whether this diagnosis fits or not, another and more important question for eschatology lurks behind it: what is "old" and "new" in the history of God with humankind?

"New" designates the unimaginable activity of God, which we, with reason, *may expect,* but which nonetheless comes as something unhoped for. We reach out for it in affliction and hope. God presents the "old" as something that can no longer take hold of us, that is irrevocably removed from our calculations. New and old are both determined by God's activity.

Against this view, the difference between old and new is observable in a continual process of calling the past to memory and making it present. Is eschatology able to offer support through what God brought about with God's incarnation in the history of Jesus?

This either-or only becomes a clear alternative when ideologized. Theological discourse concerning the new must be set against futurism — against the intellectual position stated by, for example, neo-Marxism. Futurism gives precedence to what has never yet existed; traditions are questioned given the possibility of another situation. The new situation is then demanded. Awareness can be set free, but highly abstract schemas can be introduced which then, with hindsight, must be put in force. What started off as an unheard-of openness soon proves to be an obsession.

The same danger, however, lurks to no lesser extent in the alternative — historicism. In the attempt to deduce truth from overlooked history, the lines of development become rules, or chains. Since Christian theology primarily came to orient itself histori- cally, and to conceive solutions based on development of historical tradition, this false path has often been taken. At first the ap- proach promises familiarity, but gradually the track is lost. The approach represents traditionalism of the highest order, cultivated theoretically. It therefore seems more attractive than the crude tra- ditionalism met with in some church traditions, but is no less oppressive than those traditions.

Whether futurism or historicism has become dangerous for church and theology, or threatens to become dangerous, should be investigated. Developments in the 1960s indicated that the pendulum had swung in favor of futurism. Since then, an oppo- site movement seems to have emerged, more evident in Roman Catholicism than Protestantism. While the sixties aimed at indi- vidualistic modesty, the fear now is of a loss of personality in the flight into the future. Whether the theological core of eschatology has been touched by these dangers is a far more decisive question.

Ratzinger, as indicated, considers the prevalent eschatology — which he sees within Protestant theology — as a front of polit- ical theology. Similar hostility but in a reversed denominational direction can be found in the work of Emanuel Hirsch. In his late work concerning the essence of Christianity according to the Reformation,[38] Hirsch complains that the Christian expectation of salvation and belief in immortality — which, according to his con- viction, have their roots in rigorous religious individuality — have been dangerously stunted. "Modern theology," meaning dialectical theology and the ecumenical movement, carries part of the blame. By "propagating the external character of the expectation of the future according to the New Testament as well as its soullessly abstracted eschatological ideology derived from that expectation," modern theology blurs authoritative Reformation insights concern- ing the decisive character of faith.[39] Hirsch thinks the Reformation understood faith as moving humans to "personalities which are

---

38. E. Hirsch, *Das Wesen des reformatorischen Christentums* (Berlin: Walter de Gruyter, 1963).

39. Ibid., 182.

aligned to the Eternal."[40] Whoever believes, therefore, is already entering into life with God, and for this true life, the temporal existence cannot constitute more than a deceptively colorful frame. Lack of belief falls inevitably to decay and is from the first marked by death. Only a "sense for eternity" (*Ewigkeitssinn*) can defend against all "pressure on human self-understanding."[41] One can discern Hirsch's worry that trust in socioethical achievements, such as peace between nations, social justice, and the global redemption of human rights, may be the ruin of Christian hope, because the achievements overshadow what is prior to all human endeavors.

Ratzinger's and Hirsch's shared hostility covers over deep differences in understanding of the church. For Hirsch, the church is a spiritual community grounded in shared beliefs and values, comprised of persons aware of their irrevocable and abiding relationship to God, and who are therefore moved to individual responsibility. On the other hand, personalism has in Roman Catholic theology the function of integrating the believer in the church, so that they, in their share in the life of the church, experience their own personal worth — which is decisive in the awareness of personal immortality. We must now look into this interaction of the self-understanding of the church and eschatology.

5.3. Eschatology as the Yardstick for the Self-Understanding of the Church

For this purpose it is advisable to compare the progress of the Catholic elaboration of eschatology with internal church developments. Dietrich Wiederkehr, in his survey of Roman Catholic eschatology,[42] describes the partly disjointed theological changes alongside church attempts to deal with the destiny of the world and to make believers concerned about that destiny. If I extend his structure slightly, the following stages come to light:

---

40. Ibid., 184.
41. Ibid., 183.
42. D. Wiederkehr, "Eschatologie in der römisch-katholischen Theologie," in *Evangelisches Kirchenlexikon: Internationale theologische Enzyklopädie*, ed. Erwin Fahlbusch et al. (Göttingen: Vandenhoeck & Ruprecht, 1986), 1:1118–19 (ET: *International Encyclopedia of the Church* [Grand Rapids, Mich.: Eerdmans, forthcoming]).

1960–65: A new intellectual and sociohistorical orientation is established, given impulse by the challenges of Marxism and intensified by general hermeneutical considerations, promoted particularly by the "Dogmatic Constitution on the Life of the Church" and the " Dogmatic Constitution on Divine Revelation" of Vatican II. Also important is the Council's declaration, "The Church in the Modern World," and also the encyclical *Mater et Magistra*.[43]

1965–75: Eschatology is partially enriched by theories of evolution as Pierre Teilhard de Chardin gains in influence and partially converges with neo-Marxist thought. Similar movements are represented by the Protestant ecumenical World Conference on Church and Society (Geneva, 1966),[44] the Fourth Assembly of the World Council of Churches in Uppsala (1968),[45] and the Church and Society Conference in Bucharest (1974), titled "Science and Technology for Human Development — The Ambiguous Future and the Christian Hope."[46] The latter convenes with intent to address "integration of sciences in the responsibility of Christian faith."

1975–80: Voices warning against destruction of the environment and predicting the end of the world multiply in the church, in the face of the crisis of progress and the limits of growth. Apocalyptic is reframed as "catastrophe eschatology," for the sake of the necessary rethinking. In connection with political theology, which appears in Europe in response to the already developed Latin American liberation theology, the continued suffering of Jesus is seen in those who suffer under oppression. Emphasis on the passion replaces remembrance of the death of Jesus Christ. Parallel to these developments, the Protestant Conference on Mission and

---

43. "Christianity and Social Progress" (Pope John XXIII, May 15, 1961).
44. Lossky et al., *Dictionary of the Ecumenical Movement*, 330–31.
45. Norman Goodall, ed., *Uppsala Speaks: Section Reports of the Fourth Assembly of the World Council of Churches* (New York: Friendship Press, 1969), 5: "We ask of you, trusting in God's renewing power, to join in these anticipations [especially justice] of God's kingdom, showing now something of the newness which Christ will complete."
46. Lossky et al., *Dictionary of the Ecumenical Movement*, 332.

Evangelism in Bangkok (1972–73), with the theme of "Salvation Today,"[47] and the Fifth Assembly of the World Council of Churches in Nairobi (1975), titled "Jesus Christ Frees and Unites,"[48] should be mentioned.

1980–present: Concentration on narrow dogmatic themes (death, eternal life, salvation) can be observed. These emerge as themes of great importance for pastoral work. "Lived-out hope" is posed as an answer to questions put by secular society and its emphasis on self-discovery and fulfillment.[49]

In this context, the question of how the church as the community of those who believe and hope relates to those who do not believe becomes more of a preoccupation. Can and may Christians accept these differences? Or are there no differences? Are believers and nonbelievers united by a common perspective or action, which can determine their relationship?

One answer seems to be offered by the idea of universal reconciliation (*All-Versöhnung* or *apokatastasis*), which even in the early church constituted one of the frontiers of eschatology.

That nothing and no one, in the end, remains excluded from God's salvation has seemed to be the consequence of the universal reconciliation that Jesus Christ completed "for all." How does this notion relate to God's communication of grace in the election of people through whom God builds the church, which is to a disturbing degree seen as an example of particularity? To answer, the dialectics of universality and particularity are dissolved into a final happiness that includes all humanity in salvation. In this scenario, the church becomes more and more superfluous.

The eschatological expectation of God, who will be "all in all" (1 Cor. 15:28), is assimilated into a global religio-social theory. This theory does not express concern about those who "have no hope," as Paul wrote (1 Thess. 4:13). It is, rather, interested in the relationship between the empirical community of faith (the church)

---

47. Ibid., 332.
48. Ibid., 1094.
49. Klaus Nientiedt, "Worauf wird gehofft?" *Herder-Korrespondenz* 40 (1986): 505–7.

and those who, as far as the church is concerned, are outsiders — in other words, the relationship between believers and nonbelievers. Universal reconciliation becomes a concept to bridge this distressingly familiar breach. Such reconciliation is, for example, to be experienced in the coexistence of so-called Christians and non-Christians in common life as citizens, in social activity, and in unifying action to overcome emergencies, in which all differences are forgotten. These differences, faith included, are referred to as convictions, ideologies, conceptions of the world, or other phrases that possess practical meaning only as motivations to action.

The transformation of the doctrine of *apokatastasis* into a sociological classification of the church represents the influence of the church's own reflections on its nature and historico-theological orientation. The transformation is informative precisely because of this problematic, since the question, "What happens to the others?" which should intensify the sensorium of Christian hope[50] and protect it against false security and smugness, is turned into a sociologically manageable definition of relation.

The question of hope is made less important if the questioners see their place in the church as describing a social relationship to "outsiders," and then try to *overlook* that relationship. They overlook the difference instead of exposing themselves to a real meeting with "others," their hopes, and possible lack of hope. It is only in such a meeting that "the hope that is in you" (1 Pet. 3:15) can be brought to account.

In this example one again sees the importance of how eschatological thought is expressed. Also important are the perceptions of those who preach eschatology and those to whom they preach. The task of eschatology may well be to call others to a hope that is not simply "our" hope, precisely because it is "in us," we who have been "re-created" under its influence (see 1 Pet. 1:3). This call to hope knows no boundaries. Whether and how far this call is heard and answered is another question. The preacher is only responsible to the extent that he may not stand in the way of the message and invitation he has to communicate. Eschatology should help the

---

50. See, e.g., Hans Urs von Balthasar, *Dare We Hope "That All Men Be Saved?"* trans. David Kipp and Lothar Krauth (San Francisco: Ignatius Press, 1988).

messenger account for hope when asked, and draw attention to the circumstances in which such an account is demanded.

When the church, whether under external or internal influence, has new occasion to assume this responsibility, eschatology faces the challenge of becoming too absorbed in its own reflections. Just as dangerous, eschatology may exhaust itself by creating inflated expectations that it can meet the needs of all humanity at all times.

Roman Catholicism's contribution to eschatology in the last thirty years has moved in this area of tension. The tension has been expressed not only between the teaching arm of the church and theological research, which has gained independence in relation to the magisterium, but also with regard to the position of the church in the world today. To what extent has eschatology become a function of this social-political positioning?

While Roman Catholic (and Protestant) eschatology between 1965 and 1980 was, so to speak, dependent on global economic trends, before and after those years the internal church situation carried more weight. Internal struggles had an effect on the relationship with other churches, and theology was less able to steer against the situation.

Protestant theology also deserves self-critical appraisal. By the mid-1950s, in the course of Protestantism's own involvement in the ecumenical movement, the difficulty of maintaining a balance between eschatology and ethics had already become apparent. These difficulties have since multiplied and reached a critical point, at least in ecumenical dialogues. This balance can only be a fragile one. But it should help avoid the expectation that Jesus Christ merely guide the church in challenges around the world. In other words, the fragile balance between eschatology and ethics argues against accounting for hope only in emergency situations.

The question "What dare we hope?" has increasingly been adapted to address such tensions. In Roman Catholic eschatology, pastoral interest has constituted a strong counterbalance. At times the question has retreated into the background, but has never been driven out completely. It is worth bearing this fact in mind, for it shows the rootedness of eschatology in the life of the church. This rootedness is not a symptom of stunted perceptions of hope, but, on the contrary, is both a sign of hope and a witness to society.

Chapter 6

HOPE IN THE LIFE
OF THE CHURCHES

Until now, we have examined the consequences of eschatology for church praxis and attempted to apply ideas coming from eschatology to the experience of faith — to give hope a "concrete" form. Now it is the intention to approach eschatology from the opposite angle and to take *church practice* as the starting point.

Deep-rooted changes, crises, and new approaches often show themselves more lastingly in church activity than in programmatic concepts or in developing thought patterns. "Accounting for hope" is particularly necessary these days when dealing with sensitive areas of church activity. The aim is to make clear, despite superficial similarities in ecumenical movements, differences in thought and expression, why these differences exist, and if they must continue to exist.

Starting points of eschatology in the life and activity of the church cannot be portrayed directly in ecclesiological doctrine. Differing approaches to the subject have developed in churches and denominations, contributing to different understandings of what the church is. But other developments within eschatology — shifts in emphasis and course corrections — have proven significant.

6.1. Accounting for Hope as Intellectual Pastoral Care

EVANGELISCHE KIRCHE DER UNION, *Die Bedeutung der Reich-Gottes-Erwartung für das Zeugnis der christlichen Gemeinde: Votum des Theologischen Ausschusses der Evangelischen Kirchen der Union* (Neukirchen: Neukirchener Verlag, 1986); L. BERTSCH et al., eds., "Unsere Hoffnung: Ein Bekenntnis zum Glauben in dieser Zeit," in *Gemeinsame Synode der Bistümer in der Bundesrepublik Deutschland* (Freiburg: Herder, 1976), 1:84–111; PRESBYTERIAN CHURCH IN THE U.S., GENERAL ASSEMBLY, "Confession of the Presbyterian Church," in *The Proposed Book of Confessions of the Presbyterian Church in the United States* (Atlanta: Office of the General Assembly, 1974).

The 1967 confession of the United Presbyterian Church (USA) may be cited as a document reflecting an eschatological deficit in the church's self-understanding. It is clearly influenced by the spirit of socioethical awakening seen in the social conflicts of the 1960s. After an opening summary of the reconciling work of God, the central section encourages the church to reconciling action in the world. The concluding section, in which one would expect an eschatological statement, is brief and of little substance. It emphasizes that God's work of reconciliation embraces the whole of human life and its environment, and is directed toward completion under Christ's rule. Eschatological visions and images serve to encourage social involvement for the sake of a better world and to prepare the world for the last judgment and salvation. "Judgment" and "salvation" remain no more than key thematic terms. One is left with the impression that the church committee responsible for the declaration ran out of breath once the socioethical impetus had been exhausted.

In 1975, the German Catholic Bishops' Conference published "Unsere Hoffnung" (Our hope), with considerable contribution from Johann Baptist Metz. Despite its minimal influence, the text is informative about the way in which hope is nowadays accounted for. It is not a world-shattering document, but is pastoral in the best sense of the word. Its intent is to assist intellectual orientation and to clarify the challenges of Christian existence. It addresses questions contentious for Catholic Christians and others, and attempts to broaden and deepen perspectives. Unlike most texts devoted to pastoral care, it deals with the subject of "hope." Even hope for closer ecumenism, a "living unity of Christians," is addressed.[1] Three quotations convey the tenor of the whole:

> The world needs no doubling through religion of its hope-lessness. It needs and seeks (if at all) the counterforce, the explosive power of a lived-out hope. What we [Christians]

---

1. "Unsere Hoffnung," 108.

owe the world is to compensate for the deficit of vividly lived-out hope.

The message of hope concerning the resurrection of the dead, which is grounded in the Easter event, proclaims a future for all, the living and the dead. And just because it proclaims a future for the dead, that they, the long-forgotten, are not forgotten in the memory of the living God and live in him always, therefore this message of hope tells about a truly human future. . . .

The hope in the resurrection of the dead, the belief in the complete breakthrough of the barrier of death, liberates us to a life directed against a mere self-assertion whose essence is death. . . . [2]

Ten years later, the theological committee of the German Evangelische Kirche der Union (EKU), under the chairmanship of Eberhard Jüngel, published "Die Bedeutung der Reich-Gottes-Erwartung für das Zeugnis der christlichen Gemeinde" (The significance of the expectation of the kingdom of God for the witness of the Christian community). Like the Bishops' Conference document, it brings into focus the Christian consciousness of time. Pastors have criticized the document as being correct, but deadly dull. However, it should be kept in mind that documents written by a committee are rarely more than a formula for consensus, here expressing a mood of hope, while stressing certain aspects of the subject and suggesting what needs to be clarified.

The EKU document speaks of a balance between expectations of the future and faith in the present. In line with Karl Rahner's principles (3.5.1), the hoped-for future can be spoken of as that which remains temporally outstanding. Rahner is one of the theological authorities quoted in the EKU document, which includes clauses from theological traditions dating to the early church — an indication of ecumenical foundation.

The critical intensity of the EKU document comes from a carefully formulated warning against confusing the kingdom of God

---

2. Ibid., 101, 91, 92.

with an improved world. But, at the same time, it emphasizes responsibility for the world, without any claim that hope is fulfilled
in action. That is the dilemma that has accompanied eschatology
for over a century, at least as far as German Protestant theology is
concerned.

These two texts, the EKU document and the resolution of the
German Catholic Bishops' Conference, show many convergences.
Perhaps this is because, while both have their church contexts
clearly in view, they scarcely touch on the delicate points of church
activity at which the expression of hope has entered a crisis. Both
documents subordinate all issues to the crisis concerning the orientation of Christians in the world today. But the differences between
Roman Catholic and Protestant approaches should be clarified,
and a determination made whether the differences must remain.

In the Roman Catholic perspective — particularly in the theology of the magisterium, the teaching office of the church —
the content of eschatology serves above all to strengthen personal
faith. Eschatology serves the pastoral task of the church, whose
purposes differ fundamentally from shaping a vision of the future.[3]
An internal Roman Catholic debate — furious at times — regarding
a new philosophical-theological understanding of "immortality"[4]
scarcely found an echo in Protestant theology, probably because
such topics were considered outdated. In any case, these topics do
not seem necessary for theology, and appear to favor a private religion that lacks hope.[5] No wonder that mutual interest in theology
is still mainly expressed in broad conceptual frameworks. Otherwise, Protestant and Roman Catholic theologians would tend, also
in the case of eschatology, to take different paths.

---

3. J. Ratzinger, *Eschatology, Death, and Eternal Life,* ed. Aidan Nichols, O.P.,
trans. Michael Waldstein (Washington, D.C.: Catholic University of America Press,
1988), 48–52.

4. See Ulrich Ruh, "Perspektiven der Eschatologie," *Herder-Korrespondenz* 33
(1979): 249–53; Augustin Schmied, "Rückkehr zur Übersetzung 'Auferstehung des
Fleisches' und die Frage der Auferstehung im Tode,'" *Theologie der Gegenwart*
29 (1986): 238–46; idem, "Fragen um die Auferstehung Jesu: Zu beachtenswerten
Veröffentlichungen," *Theologie der Gegenwart* 30 (1987): 58–64.

5. Only in most recent times has there been a change in this tendency. For
example, see the articles of Joachim Ringleben and Theodor Mahlmann in *Die Zukunft der Erlösung: Zur neueren Diskussion um die Eschatologie,* ed. Konrad Stock
(Gütersloh: Gütersloher Verlagshaus, 1994), 49–87 and 108–31.

6.2. Hope beyond Death: "Immortality of the Soul" or "Resurrection of the Dead"?

The first example in this section deals with Protestant pastoral care for the dying. There is a tendency to see this help as a final integrating aid to life. Assuming that social relationships should be preserved for as long as possible, even if the dying person is gradually taking leave of them, pastors encourage people to look back on their lives and to put them in order. The dying are prepared for dying, not for death. This procedure corresponds to anticipation of a catastrophic end to the world, which prompts enriched possibilities of decision to help one cope better with the present. Looking to death, it is believed, should help one find the way back to life. Once the illusion passes, and one has unrestricted time at one's disposal, realism returns. False hope must not destroy individual catharsis. For this reason, every hope is said to be dangerous if it does not introduce action that will outlive the individual.

A further symptom of this trend in Protestantism is that, in many areas, petitionary prayers no longer remember the dead. For dogmatic reasons that merit closer examination, prayer for the fate of the dead has not taken place in a long time. There is a considerable difference between a community that remembers and commends its dead before God, who has called them to God's self, and one that prays for those close to the deceased, but not those who have passed away. The conviction seems to be that "the dead are dead. Let us concern ourselves with the living, their mourning, and their future." Many funeral services make this assumption, and serve essentially to help those left behind.[6] The idea is to close gaps in the net of social reality, which are brought about by death or brought to consciousness by death, as quickly as possible.

In the background lies the battle against the concept of immortality that has dominated German Protestant theology for the last half-century. The contrast is to English or North American theology as characterized by philosophy of religion.[7] This dispute has

---

6. See Manfred Josuttis, "Zwischen den Lebenden und den Toten: Pastoraltheologische Überlegungen zum Leben-Tod-Übergangsfeld," *Evangelische Theologie* 41 (1981): 29–45; for an expanded form, see idem, *Der Pfarrer ist anders: Aspekte einer zeitgenössischen Pastoraltheologie* (Munich: Chr. Kaiser, 1982), 107–27.
7. See H. D. Lewis, *The Self and Immortality* (London: Macmillan, 1973); idem,

continued within the church, although it should be asked how and
to what extent theology has accepted changes in contemporary
thought. Three themes should be considered:

1. The connection of the doctrine of immortality to the legacy of
   Greek philosophy and its distinction between soul and body.

2. Reference to the continued existence of identity, understood
   as the constitutive element of human beings, as a level of
   existence that cannot be lost, and as a foundation of hope
   beyond death.

3. The disappearance of hope in immortality for most "people
   of today."

The first theme is foreign to the biblical understanding of humanity. Biblical discourse concerning the resurrection of the dead
does not speak of a continuing existence of the human self, but
of God's new creation. Since hope is in God the Creator, who does
not allow God's creatures to perish, this expectation of continuance
includes humanity in all its fullness (see 1 Cor. 15:35–50).

It is precisely here, however, that careful distinctions are necessary. Since our creaturely nature is indivisible, the whole may not
be reduced to mere "bodiliness" and hence to "worldliness." The
entire creature is constituted by the unity of God's action in him,
not by the death that closes life in every sense. Death is the last
enemy that must be conquered, so that we can die in the hope of
living with Christ.

This approach has nothing to do with anthropological monism,
that is, with an understanding of human beings as the meeting point for external events and the internal processing of those
events. That is a closed process, which comes to a natural end

Persons and Life after Death (London: Macmillan, 1978); John Hick, *Death and
Eternal Life* (New York: Harper & Row; London: Collins, 1976); Paul Badham
and Linda Badham, *Immortality or Extinction?* 2d ed. (London: SPCK, 1984);
Paul Badham, *Christian Beliefs about Life after Death* (London: Macmillan, 1976);
Stephen T. Davis, ed., *Death and Afterlife* (Basingstoke, England: Macmillan,
1989); and John W. Cooper, *Body, Soul, and Life Everlasting: Biblical Anthro-
pology and the Monism-Dualism Debate* (Grand Rapids, Mich.: Eerdmans, 1989).
For the point of view of Eastern Orthodox theology, see Georges Florovsky, "The
'Immortality' of the Soul," in *Collected Works* (Belmont, Mass.: Nordland, 1976),
3:213–40 and 315–16.

in death. Monism of this sort not only accords with the criticism that materialism aims at idealistic dualism, but also with the notion that the "soul" is only a secretion of the brain. Anyone who considers the biblical image of humanity, particularly the image found in the Old Testament, must guard against applauding materialistic monism. The often-invoked Old Testament insistence on the "here and now" has as little to do with such monistic ideas as the hope in resurrection found in the New Testament has to do with the idea of immortality.[8] The difference, however, is sometimes blurred. Dietrich Bonhoeffer (1906–45), for example, in his criticism of religion that disposed of the concepts of "hereafter," appealed to the Old Testament:

> In my opinion it is not Christian to want to take our thoughts and feelings too quickly and too directly from the New Testament.[9]

The second point of controversy concerns human identity. The expectation of God's action in persons who have died cannot appeal to identity, an inalienable part of the human condition that can be asserted even against extreme threats. For this reason, Paul says that the wonder of the New Creation is similar to the wonder of the seed, in that it represents continuity within discontinuity (1 Cor. 15:37f.). But even in the case of such discontinuity, not every connection between "old" and "new" is lost. God regards those God has created with creative steadfastness; death does not wipe the slate clean. Rather, our attention is directed to the fact that God is Lord over life *and* death.[10] Even while alive we experience moments of death, in which we do not perish (thanks be to God!). The lesson should not be that we escaped, but that we are

---

8. See Oscar Cullmann, *Immortality of the Soul or Resurrection of the Dead? The Witness of the New Testament* (New York: Macmillan, 1958, 1964).

9. "Wer zu schnell und zu direkt neutestamentlich sein und empfinden will, ist m. E. kein Christ" (D. Bonhoeffer, *Letters and Papers from Prison,* translated by Reginald Fuller et al. with additional material translated by John Bowden, enlarged ed. [London: SCM Press, 1971], 103–4).

10. See Raymond Sherman Anderson, *Theology, Death, and Dying* (Oxford: Basil Blackwell, 1986; reprint, Fuller Theological Seminary, 1992); Nicholas Wolterstorff, *Lament for a Son* (Grand Rapids, Mich.: Eerdmans, 1987).

"as dying, and behold, we live!" (2 Cor. 6:9).[11] It can also be said that death is not a transition, but the irrevocable end. Yet death brings us to face the presence of the Spirit of God, which represents God in us and us before God. It is the pledge of a future life, fully transformed (Rom. 8:23). We will not destroy what is created in the power of the Spirit, which we experience as God's action, and which, as such, we can never control.

The gradual habituation to a world in which death has the last word — this mark of Western civilization — is indeed difficult. Is it possible to convey the message of resurrection from the dead, to find a response, and to understand hope in relation to resurrection?

Roman Catholic writer Reinhold Schneider (1903–58) described the gradual trend in our time toward speechlessness on the subject of immortality.

> The faith in resurrection presupposes the longing for resurrection — or the fear of the nothingness. But neither this wish nor the anguish is self-evident.[12]

For Schneider, there was another, personal matter in question. From his youth he suffered from melancholy, and he was himself unable to see beyond death, or to be afraid. All that he hoped for from death was peace and an end to suffering — and that was precisely the difficulty. It seemed to him that to ask both for eternal peace and eternal life was an indissoluble contradiction. Only endless sleep could promise healing, but yearning for endless sleep cannot reach into eternity.

Schneider believes in the resurrection of Christ, but lacks — and who knows if it is a lack! — the yearning for personal survival. But is faith necessarily coupled to such a yearning, or even dependent on it? Perhaps hope in the resurrection of the dead can only grow when this yearning no longer drives life and thought "beyond death." Schneider did not ask such questions, perhaps because he thought he would have to ask for some kind of continuation of life in order to be able to hope.

---

11. For more on the subject, see G. Sauter, "Leben in der Einheit von Leben und Tod," *Evangelische Theologie* 41 (1981): 46–57.
12. R. Schneider, *Winter in Wien* (Freiburg: Herder, 1962), 67.

Otherwise, he certainly hit on a sensitive spot. The question of
immortality cannot be pushed to the end of life or incorporated
within a world-changing hope in better times. Rather, the question should remind us that hope in the resurrection of the dead can
never be separated from the proclamation of God's judgment. The
harbinger of judgment, of the last judgment at the end of all days,
is the recognition of trespasses and the forgiveness of sins. Forgiveness allows for hope in a new beginning, in God's re-forming of a
past that brings death and destruction into new life in community
with God, and with all others included in the promise of God's living Spirit. Precisely in the promise of God's Spirit rests the hope
for the dead.

The promise does not rest in the relationship of human existence, by nature temporary, to God as the hereafter. The objection
can be raised to Karl Barth, who understands death, conquered
once and for all by Jesus Christ, as the enforcement of temporal
finiteness. He makes the assertion according to the thesis that the
human being dies completely, and only then is given over to God;
being eternally with God is interpreted as

> the "eternalizing" of this ending life . . . the unveiling and glo-
> rifying of the life which in his time man has already in
> Christ.[13]

Eberhard Jüngel follows Barth on this point.[14] Both touch on
Karl Rahner's understanding of "total, whole, entire death" (*Ganztod*),[15] in which the accomplished life completes itself.[16]

---

13. Barth, *CD* III/2: 624. It can be assumed that Barth would have taken this
explanation, articulated within the framework of anthropology, further in eschatology. But is it not the case that the sequence of life and death should be treated in
theological anthropology, especially when — as in the case of Barth — it is to be
christologically grounded?

Pannenberg cites Barth incompletely when he writes, "Barth speaks of the 'eter-
nalizing' of the earthly life story of human beings" ("Tod und Auferstehung
in der Sicht christlicher Dogmatik," in *Grundfragen systematischer Theologie:
Gesammelte Aufsätze* [Göttingen: Vandenhoeck & Ruprecht, 1980], 2:156).

14. E. Jüngel, *Tod* (Stuttgart: Kreuz Verlag, 1971).

15. *Ganztod* refers to the holistic concept of death — the conception that both
body and soul are involved in death.

16. K. Rahner, *Zur Theologie des Todes* (Freiburg: Herder, 1958) (ET: *On the
Theology of Death*, trans. C. H. Henkey, 2d ed. [New York: Herder & Herder,
1967]).

If God is spoken of in such a way, the finite nature of human-kind seems sealed. The boundary of death can become the place of encounter with God, or a wall at which all ways come to an end, at which every human being is cast back on those relation-ships in which he continues to exist. Death, which cuts through all these relationships by releasing the human existence into full lack of relationship (*Verhältnislosigkeit*, in E. Jüngel's terms), warns us to form these relationships in a way worthy of life. Death balances out life, and in this sense it is the fulfillment of life. But is death not rather the enemy we fight, without being able to defeat? "But thanks be to God, who gives us the victory through our Lord Jesus Christ" (1 Cor. 15:57).

The return from death to worthwhile life is supposed to be enough, according to the ethical train of thought that has caught eschatology in its spell.

> My death, which I think of, is always a fictive death, a death anticipated in thought. The death of others is terribly concrete.

> Only thinking of death liberates life, liberates it from the chains of repressed fear of death. In that perspective death becomes the necessary condition of freedom, equality, and detachment (*Gelassenheit*).

> To know the death of others — and not to wish for it — helps overcome the private, egoistic yearning for life. Such knowl-edge concerning death opens the positive rule "immediately to become committed for the happiness of others."[17]

The distinction between death and life is leveled out in order to set "the self" in right relationship to "the other." As long as the self lives, it is privileged in comparison with those who have to die. The self has only to meditate its own necessary death.

Such expressions may be armor against criticism that has been around since Ludwig Feuerbach (1804–72) and Karl Marx (1818–83) — that Christianity is eager to withdraw from the world; that

---

17. Henning Luther, "Tod und religiöse Praxis: Die Toten als Herausforderung kirchlichen Handelns. Eine Rede," *Zeitschrift für Theologie und Kirche* 88 (1991): 407–26; quotations are from pp. 422, 415, 426.

it is guilty of prevarication in talk of the hereafter; that it has fallen prey to "escapism." But at what price is this sublime reconciliation of death and fulfilled life in "natural death" achieved? Some of the practical theological side effects have been mentioned above. Psychiatrist Joachim Ernst Meyer has observed a further problem. He observes, principally among Protestant clients, an increased fear of death, and a fear that the self will be annihilated in death. This he traces to a deficit in theological doctrine and to the impression that death erases everything that has been experienced.[18] Just as "ecclesiogenic" neuroses were diagnosed a few years ago, found primarily in functionaries with unhealthy relationships with church institutions, one can nowadays speak of widespread "eschatologenic" neuroses, with roots in eschatologies that seem neurotic.

In spite of pastoral efforts to be honest and to avoid awakening any unreasonable expectations, many roots of accounting for faith are cut. The way of life in which accounting for hope can prosper has been stunted.

On the Catholic side, the situation does not look so dramatic. At least not at first glance. Even the visionary constructions of political theology are based on sacraments that know no abrupt boundaries between life and death. Boundaries remain unclear even when death is characterized as the final moment of decision. The eucharist counts as nourishment on the way to death. The sacrament of the sick should help overcome threats to life. Even the dead belong to the church and are accompanied by the petitionary prayers of the faithful. Their fate has not been decided.[19] These practices complement an extended theological debate on hope in eternal life and the possibilities of expressing such hope adequately. New impetus came from Joseph Ratzinger between 1975 and 1985.[20]

18. J. E. Meyer, *Todesangst und das Todesbewußtsein der Gegenwart* (Berlin: Springer Verlag, 1979), 18–23; idem, "Psychotherapeutische Fragen an die Theologie," *Evangelische Theologie* 41 (1981): 57–65, with reference to Eberhard Jüngel.
19. Klemens Richter, ed., *Der Umgang mit den Toten: Tod und Bestattung in der christlichen Gemeinde* (Freiburg: Herder, 1990).
20. See n. 4 above and Gisbert Greshake and Jacob Kremer, *Resurrectio mortuorum: Zum theologischen Verständnis der leiblichen Auferstehung* (Darmstadt:

It would be a fallacy simply to trace this theological interest to church requirements, although church practices do constitute the breeding ground in which "accounting for hope" grows. This is even more the case in Eastern Orthodox churches, since the liturgy embraces the entirety of salvation history and is directed toward heavenly perfection. That so-called individual eschatology and "social" or "historical" eschatology have been separated in Western theology — and that they often appear to be competing — surely stems in part from church practice, in which care for the dying was cut off from concerns about the future of humanity.[21] When dogmatics began to appear less as a coherent ordering of systematic statements and more as a collection of themes in loose sequence to be rearranged, problems arose.

One of the most recent examples of Roman Catholic eschatology may be found in a document issued by the Congregation for the Doctrine of the Faith.[22] The document is shaped according to "individual eschatology" and emphasizes the resurrection of the whole human being. Such teachings help prevent theology from avoiding questions of pastoral significance.

Wissenschaftliche Buchgesellschaft, 1986); Gisbert Greshake and Gerhard Lohfink, *Naherwartung — Auferstehung — Unsterblichkeit,* 5th ed. (Freiburg: Herder, 1986); Wilhelm Breuning, ed., *Seele — Problembegriff christlicher Eschatologie* (Freiburg: Herder, 1986).

For surveys see *Hoffnung über den Tod hinaus: Antworten auf Fragen der Eschatologie,* ed. Josef Pfammatter and Eduard Christen (Zurich: Benziger, 1990); Albert Gerhards, ed., *Die größere Hoffnung der Christen: Eschatologische Vorstellungen im Wandel* (Freiburg: Herder, 1990); Franz-Josef Nocke, *Eschatologie,* 3d ed. (Düsseldorf: Patmos, 1988); Herbert Vorgrimler, *Hoffnung auf Vollendung: Aufriß der Eschatologie,* 2d ed. (Freiburg: Herder, 1984); John R. Sachs, *The Christian Vision of Humanity: Basic Christian Anthropology* (Collegeville, Minn.: Liturgical Press, 1991), 83–91.

For treatments by contemporary Roman Catholic philosophy of religion, see Georg Scherer, *Das Problem des Todes in der Philosophie,* 2d ed. (Darmstadt: Wissenschaftliche Buchgesellschaft, 1988); idem, *Sinnerfahrung und Unsterblichkeit* (Darmstadt: Wissenschaftliche Buchgesellschaft, 1985); Josef Seifert, *Das Leib-Seele-Problem und die gegenwärtige philosophische Diskussion: Eine systematisch-kritische Analyse,* 2d ed. (Darmstadt: Wissenschaftliche Buchgesellschaft, 1989), esp. pt. 10: "Tod und die Frage nach Unsterblichkeit: Philosophische Kritik der Ganztodthese."

21. This trend is already present in Bonaventura (ca. 1217–74): see Hinrich Stoevesandt, *Die letzten Dinge in der Theologie Bonaventuras* (Zurich: EVZ-Verlag, 1969).

22. Vatican Doctrinal Congregation, "The Reality of Life after Death," *Origins,* August 2, 1979, 131–33.

What is expected at death, according to the confession of faith, is the new constitution of humanity (*carnis resurrectio*). This formulation from the Apostles' Creed, which agrees with older forms, is designed to ward off false expectations and to nullify incorrect interpretations of hope. But the literal translation of the phrase, "resurrection of the body," has often led to misunderstandings. Every translation is an act of interpretation designed to confirm Christian confidence, not just in relation to the future of the believers but also to the future of humanity; the Creed has a universal horizon because Jesus Christ is the universal judge.

When expectation of the "resurrection of the *dead*" is now pronounced in church services, the revised translation refers to the New Testament (1 Cor. 15:21, 42; Heb. 6:2) and the creeds of Nicaea and Constantinople (325/381).[23] Thus, the formula *resurrectio mortuorum* occurs in the one creed that is accepted by all Christian churches, in the one text that is truly "ecumenical." At the same time, the phrase takes into account a personal understanding which these days seems to be the only suitable understanding. The antispiritualist "resurrection of the body" sounds far too materialist, if not incomprehensible. But the translation still requires interpretation. Taken in itself it can leave room for very different understandings: existence beyond the threshold of death, for example, or resurrection from some kind of sleep. Any attempt to address this lack of clarity means instruction in the hope that comes from faith. This touches on the task of elementary practice in Christianity, necessary for every account of hope — yet another example of the demands placed on eschatology today.

Without our interest in understanding the Creed, eschatology would be left to academic discussions concerning the postmortem state of human beings, or, worse, delivered to dreams of the hereafter, as encouraged by those who allegedly have suffered near-death experiences. The feelings described presume a neurophysical state that has not been destroyed. For that very reason, no hope can be placed in this account of life beyond death. But when such reports — or even reports concerning stages of death and psycho-

---

23. "The Constantinopolitan Creed," in *Creeds of the Churches: A Reader in Christian Doctrine from the Bible to the Present,* ed. John H. Leith, 3d ed. (Louisville: John Knox Press, 1982), 33.

logical approaches to coping with the stages — take priority in Christian discussions of the last things, that should signal alarm for both church and theology.

6.3. The Promise of the Coming One

Statements related to a time beyond death have something to say for us here and now. Statements in eschatology intend to intensify awareness, to encourage, to shake up, to admonish, to disturb, to comfort, and to give fresh heart. Only in this way can eschatology address questions such as: "What dare we hope for in death?" "What comes afterward?" "Where will we be, and how?" How these questions are phrased, and with what intent, is important. Are they designed to address the destiny of humankind to the end, and to say how human existence is fulfilled? Or should such questions express the postulate that we are not simply caught up in a process of existence and decay, since the ultimate reason for our being breaks through the barrier of finitude?

An eschatology that looks to Jesus Christ as the ultimate, as judge and Savior (Rom. 1:4), will pursue neither of these directions. Rather, it will ask about the relationship that exists between us and the resurrected one, who is "the same yesterday and today and forever" (Heb. 13:8). Jesus Christ *fulfills everything* that God intends for the world. In this sentence, Christology and eschatology merge. In Christ, what God and humankind in relationship to God have wished for and have performed reaches God's goal. This goal, however, is not a conclusion in the sense of a final reckoning. Rather, it signifies a fusion or fullness that does not simply fill all things, leaving no room, but that shines through all that remains.

This fulfillment is at the same time the revelation that completes. God steps into view, establishing God's divinity. End and completion are one and the same in the coming of Jesus Christ. He is known as the Coming One because he brings God's fullness. Every experience of salvation transports us into the confidence of the *parousia*, the presence of Jesus Christ we await. Each experience points to the fullness of Christ. The object of our hope — our expectation of Jesus Christ — is the fulfillment and perfection of our faith, which grants us a share in the life of Christ. Since "faith" also means to subordinate oneself to Christ (*unter Christus stehen*), it is exposed to the fire of judgment which consumes everything not founded in Christ. Hope means confidence in awaiting this judgment, since nothing can perish if it is grounded in Christ.

The cosmic and individual aspects of eschatology merge in the christological perspective. The unity of human beings and the world they live in can only be expressed eschatologically when we discard two ideas: that human creatures are merely part of the world and that the world is merely the space for human activity. In the first case, hope of perfection would be linked to outcomes in history; the second point of view would place too much emphasis on individuals. The expectation of Christ's *parousia,* on the other hand, includes the idea that Jesus Christ, the crucified and resurrected one, brings about the consummation of the world. In the process, he is present, yet hidden beyond the circle of those who commemorate him. In their actions worshipers are, instead, dependent on his fulfilling presence, and directed toward the time when that presence will be revealed in all its fullness. For this reason, the content of expectation is the standard both for Christians' concepts of end and perfection, and for the perception of the unity of humanity.

The universal expectation of Christ explains why time factors seem relatively unimportant in New Testament discourse concerning death and the dead. The dead are removed from our reckoning of time, not because they have disappeared from the scene, but because they find their purpose in Christ alone. And yet, since we cannot perceive them as God does, we find it difficult, if we bear them in mind at all, to think about them outside our own awareness of time. They are thought of as sleeping because they are no longer present in our realm of conscious action. The question of the fate of the dead only emerges with the expectation of the coming Christ, which is connected to the question of how long we, the living, have yet to wait. Both questions prove to be wrongly framed as soon as the relationship of Christ to the living and to the dead becomes decisive.

Paul himself had to deal with such questions. His answers

concentrate on the coming of Christ, directing attention toward the oppositions that threaten the Christian community from both without and within (cf. 1 Thess. 5:1–11; 2 Thess. 2:1–12). This opposition — not distance in time to the coming of Christ — is what places pressure on the community. Paul insists that death is the final enemy to be conquered, but that we cannot conquer it. It attacks us, and we are lost if we are not torn from its power. But the outcome of the struggle is not decided at our death, which is far from being a moment of deliverance.

6.4. "Purification" as Therapy?

The perspective changes when death is considered as the end of life. Then the question about the destiny of men and women, their fulfillment, perfection, and continuing life, arises from this perspective. The question also finds expression in images of postmortem condition, in which what was neglected in life may be redeemed. This idea forms the core of the doctrine of purgatory, whose intent is both to address the state that exists between death and last judgment, and to oppose the view that resurrection already has taken place in death. Both viewpoints persist today.[24]

The doctrine of purgatory, hotly debated among the denominations, is another touchstone for the question whether the churches are one in hope.

In his *Eschatologie,* Medard Kehl addresses the Roman Catholic doctrine of purgatory. Purification, Kehl writes, after death at last removes the opposition of the will in self-assertion (*Widerspruch des Selbstbehauptungswillens*), as we experience such opposition in our lives when we try to follow the will of God.

---

24. The idea of "resurrection in death" can be traced to Gisbert Greshake. The neo-Platonic doctrine of *anima separata* stands in the background as a foil, together with the motif that traces the (apocalyptic) concept of resurrection of the dead "at the end of time" to an individual death. See G. Greshake, *Auferstehung der Toten* (Essen, West Germany: Ludgerus Verlag, 1969); idem, *Stärker als der Tod,* 8th ed. (Mainz: Grünewald, 1984); idem, " 'Seele' in der Geschichte der christlichen Eschatologie: Ein Durchblick," in Breuning, *Seele,* 107–58. Karl Rahner accepted the concept of resurrection in death after some hesitation. See "The Intermediate State," in *Theological Investigations,* trans. Margret Kohl (New York: Crossroad, 1981), 17:114–24.

Such conversion is always something like swimming against the stream of the inclination toward evil; it needs to overcome personal and corporate opposition against this conversion, often linked with a painful process of separation and purification. In death, where the whole of one's life should be joined in relation to Christ, such conversion takes an integrated shape.[25]

Death exposes a person's confrontation with him- or herself. In serving as a balance to achievements of life, death moves men and women to God and brings them into the perfection of a relationship with God. Redemption is seen as a process of integration.

If this is the content of the doctrine of purgatory — rather than purgatory as a continuation of personal efforts to put right after death what went wrong in life — then there are considerable parallels, if not convergences, in Protestant theology. That the entirety of life appears in death and so perfects life in death, is also, for example, the opinion of Eberhard Jüngel. For that reason the prospect of death leads the way back to responsible living. "Being toward death" (*Sein zum Tode*) bears fruit in cleansing life from everything that threatens to lessen its value. Moments in life can be won, as Jüngel indicates,[26] that death cannot wipe away. The therapeutic overtone is unmistakable.

The Reformers argued against the image of purgatory, initially in view of the scandal surrounding indulgences, in which the idea was that one could work to influence one's fate, or others' fate in the hereafter.[27] The idea was purification through extreme exertion in an attempt to achieve salvation, which God held out like a prospect but does not accomplish. Against this view, the Reformers advanced the idea of justification by faith alone. The doctrine speaks of God's judgment as one in which human beings receive and preserve their identity before God. This judgment maintains a

---

25. M. Kehl, *Eschatologie* (Würzburg: Echter, 1986), 286.

26. E. Jüngel, "Leben nach dem Tod? Gegen das theologische Schweigen vom ewigen Leben," *Evangelische Kommentare* 22 (1989): 31–32.

27. In an exhibition, "Himmel — Hölle — Fegefeuer: Das Jenseits im Mittelalter" (Heaven, hell, and purgatory: The hereafter in the middle ages), in Cologne (1994), a collection of paintings from the time of the Reformation was entitled "Unter den Reformatoren erlischt das Fegefeuer" (The fires of purgatory are stamped out by Reformers).

view to Jesus Christ, who takes our place and speaks for us. Our life, being in Christ, "survives" in the light of Christ's advocacy; we are promised the presence of Christ in our own time and space. For this reason, Christ is our hope — not an umbilical cord linking us to transcendence, nor the perpetuation of a life well-lived. To be justified and redeemed means to experience God's action in the presence of Christ, to "let it happen." What we experience in this manner will not pass away, because it is existence with God. Eternal life is the finalizing of *this* present. Its extent, fullness, and perfection will be revealed in the *parousia* of Christ.

One could interpret justification by faith so that nothing remains of the human being (see 5.1). Only the fact that God speaks to him can give the individual confidence. Although true, false consequences can be drawn. A view of humanity can develop in which men and women cannot step beyond the boundary of death — a critical self-understanding with an agnostic, possibly nihilistic, taste. This is the charge leveled at Protestant theology's account of eschatology. But its advocates can accuse Roman Catholic doctrine of making it both possible and necessary to *earn* eternal life.

One misses in this confrontation the subtle harmonies in both Protestant and Catholic discourse. Common to both is the capitulation to therapeutic instructions for a fulfilled life. Key words and phrases such as "integration," "perfection," "fullness," and "totality of meaning" (Pannenberg) indicate a process of unification and maturation. Paul speaks another language when he describes God's judgment. God's fire seizes hold of our works, which are built on the foundation of Jesus Christ, and tests their quality (1 Cor. 3:10–15).[28] Paul has the teachers of the church in mind in this section, but not exclusively. The trial by fire tests what is of lasting quality, and in the process may reverse our ideas of what constitutes quality. Yet we do not perish because of work that does not withstand the test, even if we are, so to speak, singed by the flames. What is essential is that God's Spirit, "which dwells in [us]" (1 Cor. 3:16), is not destroyed.

---

28. See Wolfgang Schrage, *Der erste Brief an die Korinther* (Zurich: Benziger; Neukirchen: Neukirchener Verlag, 1991), 298–310.

6.5. The Lord's Supper:
Proclamation of the Coming Christ

The phrase "community with Christ" leads us to one constituent
element of this community, the Lord's Supper. Most of the strands
mentioned above come together in this topic.

The eschatological character of the presence of Christ in the
Lord's Supper was emphasized as early as in the *Arnoldshainer
Thesen* of 1958.[29] This document of consensus among the German
Protestant churches offered a theological understanding of communion that helped to overcome divisions within these churches.
Those who drafted it did not intend simply to direct attention from
the past — table fellowship with Jesus and arguments about the
presence of Jesus in this — toward an eschatological future. The
expectation of the coming Christ is more than a prospect for the
future. It places all those who commemorate him in the promise
of his presence, which is the sole foundation of the community of
faith and therefore of the unity of the church. Community with
Christ excludes division in the church — and vice versa. The statement can only be made by those who are confronted with the
coming Christ and who find their unity in him. Otherwise the
Lord's Supper exists as an event for religious groups, and is based
on what the group has in common — one aspect of which may be
remembrance of the founder of the community.

It would be an exaggeration to claim that the eschatological
foundation of table fellowship has become decisive in the church's
search for unity and consensus, at first within German and European Protestantism, and then in the wider ecumenical framework.[30]
Had the instruction "for as often as you eat this bread and drink
the cup, you proclaim the Lord's death until he comes" (1 Cor.
11:26) stood at the center of the debate, it would have been considered more carefully that Jesus Christ, in his death, is fully broken,

---

29. *Zur Lehre vom Heiligen Abendmahl: Bericht über das Abendmahlsgespräch
der Evangelischen Kirche in Deutschland 1947–1957 und Erläuterung seines Ergeb-
nisses*, 2d ed. (Munich: Chr. Kaiser, 1958), theses 3 and 4.
30. See Max Thurian and Geoffrey Wainwright, eds., *Baptism and Eucharist:
Ecumenical Convergence in Celebration*, Faith and Order Paper 117 (Geneva:
World Council of Churches, 1983).

and only in God comes into being as living unity. Therein lies our hope. When the community gathers around the Lord's Table, it does not commemorate a unity that already exists. In the commemoration, the community is prepared for the power of God, in which the crucified Christ lives. Receiving the bread and wine, the elements of the Lord's Supper, indicates that the community shares in a unity that transcends its circle. In the Lord's Supper, men and women are incorporated into the body of Christ, which embraces the full promised presence of Christ. For that reason, commemorating Christ leads on to the call of expectation, *marána tha!* (*Didache* 10:6; cf. 1 Cor. 16:22). In that cry, the proclamation of the death of Christ reaches its intended purpose.

This means that the church — the individual community as well as the church as a whole — is the community of justified sinners. It exists as community only because every member is saved within it by the forgiveness of sins in hope. As community the Christian congregation is open to all who have need of community with Christ. The congregation receives the hidden presence of Christ as his body and blood.

The Lord's Supper thus relates to the parables of the kingdom that speak of a heavenly banquet, and to the stories of the miraculous feeding of Jesus' audience and of his table fellowship with "tax collectors and sinners." (The last meal with the traitor Judas amidst the disciples also belongs to the latter category.) This connection has been treated adequately only occasionally in traditional theological teaching. Exegetical studies, new liturgical formulas, and attempts to reform the structure of the celebration have enriched the theology of the Lord's Supper considerably. Themes are often torn out of their theological context in the process, leaving them disconnected until they grow together in another way.

The first advance toward an eschatological concept of the Lord's Supper was undertaken by Methodist theologian Geoffrey Wainwright (b. 1936) in his *Eucharist and Eschatology.* Citing New Testament texts that deal with table fellowship, he describes the eucharist as an anticipation of the heavenly feast of joy, open to all who have need.

For eschatology that means, "The last is like a feast" (*Das*

Letzte ist wie ein Fest).[31] Images of God's judgment dominate the conceptual world of many Christians with various modifications, such as the end of time as a divine death sentence over sinful humanity, or the idea that the judgment already has taken place. The theme is nevertheless of marginal importance compared with the parables of the heavenly feast, to which God invites us. The parable of the royal wedding (Matt. 22:1–14) ends with the turning away of a guest whose clothing is not worthy of the celebration. But who can consider themselves worthy? Who does not need to be clothed by God (2 Cor. 5:2–3)? The joy of the feast can come only from God's grace. *Chara* and *charis* overlap: God is present in both at the same time. The judge's dealings with humanity are intended to be completed in community with them.

Inclusion in the community of those who have heard God's promise and who exist in the hope of being justified is admittedly not the central feature of more recent variants on the Lord's Supper. Rather, what stands in the foreground is the meal as symbol of participation, as a community-building element. In the Roman Catholic Church, the eucharist is increasingly understood as a community event rather than as the sacramental consummation of Christ's sacrifice. This change reflects a dramatically altered attitude to the institution of the church and to the administration of the sacraments. Communicants experience a sense of belonging to one another as a social body; the presence of Christ is experienced principally as one that endows community. The encounter with Christ and the sharing in his gifts takes place through the community. Table fellowship becomes the dominant motif as the source of solidarity, of mutual responsibility, of caring and sharing in the fullness of life.

The idea of sharing is emphasized by the motif of the joyous eschatological feast, brought down to earth from heaven and at the same time anticipated — the future come to the present. This idea is emphasized particularly in liberation theology. It comes to light in a celebratory meal, as a sign of the fullness of wealth that has been withheld from the participants. That each person receives ex-

---

31. Georg Kugler, "Ermunterung zum Fest," *Pastoralblätter* 114 (1974): 660–67; quotation is from p. 666.

actly the same share in communion anticipates the equality of all in the kingdom of God. Put more directly, the meal is realized eschatology in the socialism of communion. The commemoration of Jesus' meals with tax collectors and sinners, now principally understood as an enacted symbol of his solidarity with the rejected and marginalized members of society, encourages action on behalf of the poor, the oppressed, and the exploited. Social roles are canceled out in communion. In 1900, the French Protestant Wilfred Monod (1867–1943) said in one of his sermons:

> The more one thinks about it, the more one perceives in the community at the eucharistic table a total transformation of the established order, an interruption, which the social revolution could never accomplish; one recognizes an image of the "new earth, where righteousness is at home" [2 Pet. 3:13].[32]

I wish to demonstrate a tendency, and perhaps in order to show it clearly I have slightly exaggerated the situation. Roman Catholic doctrine of the sacraments holds to the concept that the eucharist must be understood in light of the doctrine of grace. Christ is central, having been sacrificed for the sins of the world. Nonetheless, one must ask — especially in view of changes that have taken place in the rite — whether the table fellowship, with the inclusion of Jesus Christ as the ultimate source of community, is what really dominates the scene. This is the impression given by many parishioners, across denominations, when asked about their experience of the eucharist. What is taught dogmatically and preserved in the forms of the liturgy is a different matter. This is not to be taken as criticism of dogmatics and liturgy, but to draw attention to a separate liturgical dynamic. Liturgy develops a "theology" of its own, based on experiences that proceed from independent actions. Actions whose theological impetus is no longer clear develop their own meanings, especially as symbols of solidarity. If the Lord's Supper primarily takes the form of a community feast, Jesus Christ is only present as a means linking the members together.

---

32. W. Monod, *L'Évangile du Royaume: Recueil de sermons,* 2d ed. (Paris, 1903), 333; cited by Karl Barth, *Predigten 1913,* ed. Nelly Barth and Gerhard Sauter, 2d ed. (Zurich: Theologischer Verlag, 1994), 113.

This changed understanding of the eucharist among Roman Catholics is paralleled by Protestant tendencies, not to mention the denominational overlap in liberation theology, in which the eucharist has won a central role.[33] This blurring of denominational contours is not, in my opinion, a sign of shared hope, but rather a symptom of the necessity in many places of using similar methods to come to grips with the challenges of social change and social emergencies. The mass poverty in Central and South America and the anonymity of conurbations everywhere in the world have motivated people to seek new forms of Christian community. A newer and more closed context of symbols and meaning has emerged from these pressures, and has altered the coordinates of eschatology. The problem becomes clearer when we observe what may *no longer* be said or expected in the new context, or said only in revised form. The forgiveness of sins, directly tied to the faithful hope in the resurrection of the dead and eternal life, no longer exists as the hallmark of the church. This sequence in the Creed appears to have been superseded by an all-pervading ecstatic experience of the integrated, liberating, tangible presence of salvation. At the same time, sin is no longer recognized as having roots in the plea for forgiveness. Since sin is apprehended as a mere social phenomenon, it is more important to resist and conquer it in acts of reconciliation.

It would be wrong to dismiss this trend as secularization and to lament the loss of transcendental hope. Rather, what is evident is an attempt to sanctify everyday social life with the help of intensified sacramentalism (that is, with acts that cooperate with God's action and make God's action evident). This attempt feeds on a piety in which the "hereafter" and the "here and now" are mingled in Christ, the incarnate God. In this way, the theology of incarnation absorbs eschatology, even if individual eschatological motifs continue to exist, perhaps with more significance than previously.

In the process of liturgical reform eschatological aspects are

---

33. See Nicholas Lash, *His Presence in the World: A Study in Eucharistic Worship and Theology* (London: Sheed and Ward, 1969); Tissa Balasuriya, *The Eucharist and Human Liberation* (Maryknoll, N.Y.: Orbis Books, 1979); Frederick Herzog, *God-Walk: Liberation Shaping Dogmatics* (Maryknoll, N.Y.: Orbis Books, 1988); James L. Empereur and Christopher G. Kiesling, *The Liturgy That Does Justice* (Collegeville, Minn.: Liturgical Press, 1990); and Monika Hellwig, *The Eucharist and the Hunger of the World* (New York: Paulist Press, 1976).

coming to be expressed more strongly than before,[34] but this does not mean that the emphasis is noticeable. The expectation of the coming Christ is now more often pronounced, which avoids the concentration of attention on what happened for us in Jesus' death, and on that alone. The Lord's Supper is not simply a service of remembrance. If the attempt is now made, within the liturgy, to bring to the foreground the joy in the continuing presence of Christ, and to emphasize this joy with the prospect of his coming, then this is a necessary correction. For too long an almost foreboding seriousness has accompanied the service of the Lord's Supper in Protestant churches. But in the process of this liturgical change, the promise of the forgiveness of sins threatens to be accidentally lost. In any case, the promise takes less of a role in liturgical formulations. It has been abandoned, as one can see when referring to the Apostles' Creed:

> I believe in the Holy Spirit, the holy catholic church, the communion of saints, the forgiveness of sins, the resurrection of the dead and life everlasting.

In this sequence, the forgiveness of sins is the work of the life-giving Spirit, who represents God before us and us before God. The Spirit *places us before God* and tears us away from all our relationships, considerations, and prospects with which we form our own lives, whether high-handedly, self-consciously, or powerlessly. This change through God's Spirit in no way leads to isolation and retreat into private life. This must be said repeatedly, with theological justification. This change must be revealed in actions in which we confess the faith in the Spirit. To take part in such actions means to pause from other activities, to step away from them for a time. Human beings are placed before God, and their community (not just their common fate) is constituted by that. To stand before God

---

34. An example is the *anaphora* of Orthodox liturgy in the tradition of John Chrysostom. The fourth eucharistic prayer in the Roman Missal of 1970 follows it closely. The four new eucharistic prayers of the Church of England (*The Alternative Service Book*, 1980) demonstrate just as much of an eschatological viewpoint as the *Lutherische Abendmahls-Agende* (1955, with revisions in 1976 and 1977); the "Great Thanksgiving" of the United Church of Christ (1969) and the United Methodist Church (1980); the *British Methodist Service Book* (1975, alternative rite); the *Book of Service* of the United Reformed Church in England (Edinburgh, 1980); and the communion liturgy of the French Reformed Church (1982).

means that one is prepared for God's verdict and confident in God's grace.

It is difficult these days to express the metaphor "standing before God." It is probably easier for a writer of fiction to capture the mood that prevails in mass society:

All naturally were frightened of the future. Not death. Not that future. Another future in which the full soul concentrated on eternal being.[35]

This mood gives rise to fear, a sense of the soul being cast back on itself. That the soul does not remain caught, but is called out of imprisonment, is the sense of the action in which the metaphor "standing before God" gains form. These actions include the proclamation of the death of Jesus until he comes, baptism as dying with Christ, and pastoral care as preparation for death. That God enacts one's "standing" is the hope of Christians — and this hope binds the churches together, and the churches together with everyone whose expectations they hope to represent.[36]

---

35. Saul Bellow, *Mr. Sammler's Planet* (New York: Viking Press, 1969), 89.

36. For more about the eucharist, see Geoffrey Wainwright, *Eucharist and Eschatology,* 2d ed. (London: Epworth Press, 1978); Alister I. C. Heron, *Table and Tradition* (Philadelphia: Fortress Press, 1983); and Horton Davies, *Bread of Life and Cup of Joy: Newer Ecumenical Perspectives on the Eucharist* (Grand Rapids, Mich.: Eerdmans, 1993).

– Chapter 7 –

BASIC QUESTIONS
OF ESCHATOLOGY

7.1. Conceptual Sources of Friction

To give an account of hope in the life of the church leads to rehabil-
itation of the rather disdained doctrine of the last things. Pastoral
counseling as a preparation for death, for instance, cannot avoid
the question of what the end of life means for the "I," namely, for
an "I" who has learned to say "the life I now live is not my life, but
the life which Christ lives in me" (Gal. 2:20).[1] Can we, at death,
speak of a continuing life for the same "I"? I do not think so, for
whoever speaks in such a way has already experienced the end of
his or her "I" — the "I" that wants to construct himself by his acts.
This "I" insists without ceasing: "I vouch for myself. I understand
myself as absolutely responsible, and as such I will live by whatever
form my acts take." However, one who says "Christ lives in me"
will not rely on self-reference, but on the promise of Christ. His
speech will remain linked to the living presence of Jesus Christ, for
this is where the "I" of that speech is located. With the expectation of the revelation of God's action in our living and dying, the
"I" as the subject of speaking is not excluded — the "I" that is supposed to receive and to respond to the fulfillment. One may or may
not call this notion "personal identity"; it all depends on how the
word "person" is understood. But from the outset one must use
the framework of eschatology, which speaks of God's unsurpassed
calling everything out of nothingness into being and into unending
community with him.

---

1. NRSV: "And it is no longer I who live, but it is Christ who lives in me."

We may also look at the eucharist as the proclamation of Jesus' death until he comes. As a self-communication of Jesus Christ, the eucharist communicates what life from God is and will be. Those who receive the body and the blood of Christ — a form which was destroyed but raised by God to a new unity and to a different form — accept God's judgment on the one who was crucified. Thereby, they experience God's verdict on the sin of the world — not its full extent, but to an extent that the final judgment does not remain a remote idea. This caveat explains why Christians are admonished not to receive the body and blood of Christ as a verdict on themselves, i.e., as a death sentence (1 Cor. 11:29–32). The verdict is not a gloomy threat which causes scrupulous soul searching to distinguish between those who belong to the Lord's Table and others who may not be allowed access. The self-analysis involved may be highly instructive, but can anybody ever see themselves as worthy? Rather, it is essential not to distort the gift of Christ, not to turn it into a means of self-assertion, for example, by using it to show what human beings can do.

The proclamation of Christ's death until he comes accords with the dialectic of Galatians 2:20: "The life I now live is not my life, but the life which Christ lives in me; and my present bodily life is lived by faith in the Son of God, who loved me and sacrificed himself for me." Christ is not a power that is at work inside of us, but steps in for the "I" that is disposed to say "I live." He steps in for us without erasing the one who says "I live." "The life I now live is not my life — my life is lived by faith." This statement points to the living Christ, the Coming One. Thus, the "my life" of Galatians 2:20 has a different meaning than the self-asserting expression, "I am (still) alive."

Pastoral counseling and the eucharist are only two examples that remind us of the importance of eschatology. It is clear that eschatology must not be pushed aside into a collection of curious objects addressed by the history of theology. What makes it so important is that it helps to direct hope to life in communion with God.

Eschatology does not derive its meaning from the repertoire of topics under its dictionary heading: death, judgment day, deliverance to heaven or hell. The unfortunate location of this doctrine at the end of dogmatics contributed much to the poor image of these "last things." On the one hand, they were seen as belonging outside of, and unrelated to, human existence. But on the other hand, they were also viewed in terms of human existence, namely, as a conceivable prolongation of it.

This is the price theology seems obliged to pay, if not willing to admit that the question, "What dare we hope?" can no longer be answered. However, once theology drops this question, it comes to see that, for the sake of proclaiming the Coming One in preaching, sacrament, and pastoral counseling, it is not allowed to remain silent.

Against such an arrangement of time and eternity we have to consider the objections of radical eschatology. This strand believes that God puts an irrevocable end to the course of time and to human beings who understand themselves within the sequence of the past, the present, and the future. God, the wholly other, does so by addressing them and by qualifying history through a decision-laden moment. In this manner time is, so to speak, torn open for eternity. The break that puts an end to everything cannot be understood in terms of an event that "comes last," but it is the new beginning that will never pass. This is why we are not allowed to speak of the eschaton as the concluding link in the chain of time, as if there was some "last but one" that the last event simply follows. This would legitimate distinguishing a preliminary event from the definite and essential, a legitimation we do not have.

Radical eschatology, by introducing "eschatological" as a radical boundary marker (*Grenzbegriff*), pressures us to give an account of what we consider to be "last questions." Do these questions relate to death, which everybody must face? Are the questions concerned with the finitude that belongs to everyone? Or do "last questions" head toward a fulfillment in which everything imperfect can finally be left behind? Radical eschatology rejects this alternative — and thereby intends to direct hope exclusively toward God alone. Are we not thereby illegitimately deprived of our last questions, whatever they may be? Not at all, is the reply. From radical eschatology's perspective, the future in the naive sense of things still to happen — including those things that have never been — cannot be considered theologically irrelevant. The future tense, on the contrary, is of extremely great, even final, importance. For God has given everything a goal, which must be achieved; i.e., it does not simply come by itself. Accordingly, in order to discover what still needs to be done, one has to measure everything that has happened, as well as everything that has been left undone, against the measure of perfection.

Personality, according to radical eschatology, which is attuned to a theology of history, is always embedded in contexts of life and action. There is no such thing as an isolated case of "standing before God"; therefore, one cannot speak of a discrete moment of decision. Neither is there a new beginning for faith and hope without the chance of progress and the danger of regression. God is never just the "beyond" of human finiteness, neither in the moment of death nor in any other experience of finitude. God is rather to be understood as the one who calls human beings to transcend their situation. Therefore, humans ought to deal with their history and ask if the direction of one's history should be continued. A change of direction may result from asking such a question. The goals of one's action may have to change.

The problems, however, that we discover in the course of this approach concern the knowledge of history. How do we know what ought to happen? The expectation of things that will happen in history quite frequently turns into a set of demands. The "becoming" confronts claims of the "ought to be." What ought to be done, in order for it to become? A corollary question also arises: What could happen, if we do not do what we ought to do?

These questions provoke another question familiar to radical eschatology: Can the readiness to become different be identified with a renewal of thinking, the metamorphosis that directs us to the will of God, in which we may discern "what is good and acceptable and perfect" (Rom. 12:2)? Does the world really change depending on human actions, which at present seem earthshaking but from a distance turn out to be superficial and harmless? Is humanity not generally disposed to point to human action as a means of evading our own end? Are we able to carry on by ourselves and to move toward an unforeseeably open future? If we seek ourselves in what can be changed and through which we may finally find fulfillment — what if these things end?

The various types of eschatology balance each other, and this is for the good. They all have a tendency to overemphasize statements while ignoring disturbing questions which, in the long run, cannot be left aside.

The three characteristic types of eschatology differ significantly in how they speak of the things to come. In this respect they cannot easily be combined.

According to the *doctrine of the last things*, the final events are seen in order, and one needs only to follow this order. Therefore, it also seems possible to turn the story into a succession of images in which observers can place themselves. Observers may wonder whether they will move on or fall into an abyss.

If *radical eschatology* could be visualized, the focus would be on the expressionistic moment in which the individual is struck by eternity, as if by lightning. All else is covered in darkness. Familiar contexts of living and acting, while not extinguished, cannot shed light on the individual. However, radical eschatology does not conjure up the crucial moment. All it can do is to prepare for it by making others familiar with God's immediate calling and by pointing to the ways in which God has already spoken and acted, and how human actions and speech have simply broken down. Human speech, as a result of God's call, would no longer be fluid, but would be marked with breaks and new beginnings.

The variety of eschatology conceived by *theology of history* provides overviews of historical trends that are in tension. Sometimes advocates of this perspective give the impression that all essential lines in history meet in the end and that, therefore, one must keep all of history in view. More often, however, the observer is asked to see world history as judgment of the world. We must ask if we belong to those with a future, or if we stand with the dead who bury their dead (Matt. 8:22; Luke 9:60). The "becoming" of the world is presented as an "ought to be," and the proclamation of things to come is transformed into a set of demands. Everything is at stake. The rhetoric of theology of history pressures listeners to sharpen contrasts, in order to break through the gray areas in which most people slumber.

These eschatological types seem to resist attempts to combine them. Can they be conceived as complementary? How do the types of eschatology touch at points of friction? The interplay often helps to clarify differences, but at other times supports the impression that eschatology as a theological doctrine is outdated and has long since been replaced by a plurality of "eschatologies."

7.2. Controlling Questions

In this reconsideration of eschatology I have tried to work toward questions that have come up in the past hundred years of theological debate. Most of these questions have been analyzed in systematic theology, and central points of contact have been discovered. The points of contact emerge from enduring — not temporary — questions, which need to be asked over and over again. The questions give coherence to eschatology, and only through these questions is it possible to write an introduction to eschatology.

A simple application of these questions does not offer a summary of eschatology. They only assist us in being aware of eschatology's crucial points, and in not overlooking its important aspects. The interrelationship of the questions is essential. The following list presents these questions systematically, and the section numbers where the questions are addressed are given parenthetically.

1. What does it mean that Jesus Christ is called "the last one"? What does it mean for our understanding of the last things, the last questions and for an understanding of the term "eschatology"? (2.4; 3.5.1; 4.1)

2. In what identity and role do we expect Jesus Christ, the Coming One? What is the possible meaning of "end" and "perfection" regarding Christ? We cannot know *what* comes last, but we do know *who* comes last. What does the change from *what* to *who* mean? (2.5; 3.5; 6.3; 6.5)

3. What has changed due to the coming of Jesus Christ, and how? (2.3–2.5; 3.5.1; 4.2–4.4; 5.2)

4. What dare we hope, for ourselves, for others, for "the world"? What can we *say* about our hope when we live in

the expectation of God's presence, i.e., when we do not expect anything but God? Does a hope that itself is to be hoped for, different, but not separated from, a desired future, define the confession of hope? (3.5; 6.2–6.4)

5. How is hope as both "subject" and "act" constituted? Is hope merely an expectation of the future? (4.5)

6. How do faith and hope relate? How does hope affect the perception of things that happen? What is "the knowledge of hope"? (3.5.1; 5.1–5.2)

7. How do hope and action relate? (4.1; 4.3–4.5; 5.3; 6.1)

None of the types of eschatology can claim to answer all of these questions. None of the types can consider all the questions to their full extent. No single answer to any of the questions will be sufficient, especially if given in isolation from other questions and answers. This presentation of eschatology has shown that eschatology is not a multiple choice test, with only one right answer per question.

It might help us answer these questions by finding a common denominator, which this book has attempted to do. Possible common denominators include:

• the consummation of creation, or, more precisely, God's desire to make perfect what was begun with the work of creation (4.2);

• the fulfillment of God's promises (3.5.2) when God universally establishes God's kingdom and when opposition is overcome (see 4.3–4.4);

• the constitution of new human beings and their transformation into eternal life (see 5.2).

Even though each of the common denominators is basic, each alone is insufficient to develop eschatology solely from it. Considering the common denominators by themselves blurs the differences in insights into unavoidable problems, divergent beginning points, and countervailing ideas, out of which together the greatly different tone colors of eschatology come into being.

To use a musical metaphor: Eschatology's rich and varied tone qualities develop when one brings together the differences in insight, the unavoidable problems, the divergent beginning points, and the countervailing ideas offered by the different common denominators. Considering one common denominator in isolation impoverishes the sound. On the other hand, the themes cannot merely complement each other, or they lose their specific sound. They best serve as leitmotifs in the score "Eschatology." Each theme returns to emphasize features of each eschatological type, interacting with the others and moving to the background as another leitmotif is developed. Being leitmotifs, they are interwoven and modulated, but do not determine the tone of the whole.

One cannot speak of creation without considering that creation is discovered and seen through God's promises and that, thereby, both the history and the future of creation can be perceived. On the other hand, promises do not float above the world; neither are they predictions of future events. They pronounce God's action, which addresses human beings and draws them into that which God wills. Thereby, human beings become oriented to the whole of God's creation, surmounting the resistance of their own experiences.

These leitmotifs cannot summarize eschatology; rather they awaken interest in the score and demonstrate its fragmentary nature. This nature remains even when one becomes more familiar with the score and goes deeper into it. We will now look at the overall construction of the score.

7.3. Where Do We Look When We Answer?

1. Eschatology — at least Christian eschatology, if not Christian theology in general — starts with *amazement about the fact that human beings are allowed to hope*. In the face of Jesus Christ the crucified, human beings see that up until the time that they encounter Christ in spite of their sometimes highly raised expectations, they lacked hope and were "without God in the world" (Eph. 2:12). One purpose of eschatology is to serve as a reminder of this hope and how it originated. Those who hold on to a hope given as a surprise are to live with their first amazement.

This is how eschatology and the doctrine of justification are related. Both acknowledge that the "hope which is within us" was a gift, although we neither deserved nor asked for it. We have not always been disposed to have this hope. It is not a hope anybody would want, or would be able to advertise with a sign saying, "This is my hope!"

God gives hope as well as future. Therefore, people cannot find hope within their souls, nor can they express it as a common good. The hope does not represent universal intentionality, which everyone shares in a step-by-step development. The genuine verbal expression of this hope is the confession in 2 Peter 3:13: "In accordance with [God's] promise, we wait for. . . . " This "we" emerges from the expectation caused by "[God's] promise." Eschatology as a theological discipline consists of intellectual experiences with the confession of hope.

Our expectations — the expectations of those who join the "we" — are nailed to the cross of Jesus Christ, and only in this way can they be raised to hope. What human beings hope for or desire in attempts to help others and themselves — to compensate for imperfections, to achieve improvements, and to open themselves to necessary changes — is all reoriented by God's judgment. The desires are not simply erased, but need God's justification and sanctification, which do not leave these expectations unchanged. The expectations from now on belong to the hope of Christ who is the Coming One.

Christ is called the Coming One because he comes from God, and he will come as the victor over everything hostile toward God and, therefore, toward us. He is called the Coming One not in the sense that he will remain alone, but in that he will submit everything, including himself, to God, so that God's fullness may penetrate everything in the universe.

Why does the Christian church in worship pray: "*Marána tha* — Our Lord, come!" (1 Cor. 16:22)? Does he have to return because he forgot to say or do something? Because he had not been able to accomplish something decisive which would now be possible? Questions like these may sound trivial, but they cannot be suppressed when we speak about Jesus Christ as the Coming One. It is not merely an intellectual challenge with the goal of saying that Jesus had to come in order to return. This explanation may have led to the theological idiom of the first and second comings of Christ, which by the time of Justin (died ca. 165) had entered the church's discourse. The question, rather, is basic to Christian life and to theological thinking in particular: Are you he who is to come? Or do we expect someone besides Jesus, in light of what he said and did, as one who suffered, died, and rose from the dead. The confession of faith always implies hope. While we cannot know exactly what Jesus' exclamation on the cross, "It is accomplished!" (John 19:30) means, we do know that we cannot say the opposite. We can say neither, "It is accomplished," nor, "It has not been accomplished."

To "hold fast to the confession of our hope" (Heb. 10:23) does not mean only that we pronounce what we expect as salvation, but also that we express how deliverance is experienced as a foretaste of salvation. This deliverance is the act of a hidden God who acts in a way that may at times contradict our ideas of salvation. We are delivered for the hope of the Coming One.

We must hold on to the confession of this "deliverance in hope." We must give an account of it in the face of existing expectations and fears, including those expectations to which human beings cling when they are worried by their conclusion that "it has not yet been accomplished." These expectations can be high and may have been raised by biblical descriptions of life in the fullness of God's blessings, or caused by remembrance of conditions in paradise, or nurtured by the story of Jesus and its interpretations.

The history of Christian eschatology shows that problems result from a process of clarification, from painful self-examination, and from comparing Jewish and Christian traditions of expectation with the unsatisfying and depressing condition of the world. Furthermore, people's imaginations, without which no expectation can exist, have to undergo a transformation. Imaginations may at times even be destroyed, especially when circumstances develop which, in the face of the world situation and personal experience, lead to resignation and faithlessness. Not by accident are there passages in the New Testament in which the congregation is admonished to remain watchful and sober — especially when they are instructed about hope (1 Thess. 5:6; 1 Pet. 1:13), and told that they should not become intoxicated with expectations. The point is not simply to reduce exaggerated expectations in order to set hearers on a more reasonable course. The crucial point is that hope not lose itself to illusions. Yet this is much easier said than done!

2. The more an account of hope is required, the more clearly and intensively this account needs to hold on to God's promises, both to the things God promises and to the manner in which God has made the promises. *Promise* is the basic category of eschatology (3.5.2–3.5.3), *the category for perceiving God's faithfulness in God's sayings and doings.*

In Ephesians 2:12 it is said that "we," the heathen, have been given access to God's promises through Jesus' death — access to things God had promised Israel as a blessing for all nations. What does it mean to participate in these promises?

This is one of the topics which needs further explanation. To participate in the heritage that was granted and promised to Israel does not mean to inherit it. It would be theologically misleading to reduce God's promises to elements of the history of tradition which began with Judaism, and was continued, though altered, in Christianity. Paul characterizes the relationship between Christian hope and God's promises in terms of Jesus Christ, who is the "yes" pronounced to God's promises: "For in him every one of God's promises is a 'Yes' " (2 Cor. 1:20). Christ incarnates God's blessing for the whole world. God wills justice, complete peace, a new home, life in communion with God, and clear knowledge of God's truth — all gathered in Jesus Christ and seen in a new way. In individual cases in the history of Israel people had been able to name what God promised. Yet, in the death and resurrection of Christ, "promise" appears as God's pledge that overcomes borders, even the one over which death watches. In Jesus Christ and in everything which happened to, with, and through him as the Coming One, God's promises are confirmed. Jesus Christ reveals God as the God who promises faithfulness.

In Jesus Christ, God acted in a promising way. This event does not lie behind us, but ahead of us. It is God's prevenient and involving initiative (*zuvorkommendes Handeln*). God's promise calls us to do God's will for the world. In paying attention to God's will we become more attentive to the way in which God acts, and become open to God's future and God's coming. Space is thereby marked out for account "of the hope which is within you."

A conversation among the types of eschatology is again necessary. There is an agreement among the types that "promise" does not mean prediction of future events. For the doctrine of last things, "promise" means God's announcement of the Coming One, not prediction. In the eschatology of history, promise is understood not as an arbitrary announcement, but as a statement of God's *initiative*, with which God announces what God wants and entrusts the future to human beings. It is not an initiative in which God works unilaterally to achieve God's wants. If one takes this view to its extreme, God is seen only as a commentator and critic of world history, and "eschatology" is reduced to world leaders' statements in the daily news. Not what we may hope for, but what we must do in order to create the preconditions for hope or to make hope credible — this is now what the label "eschatology" means.

Radical eschatology — at least to the extent that it was described in 3.1–3.3 — understands "promise" as God's affirmation. It thereby contradicts the eschatology of history, which declares the contents of God's promises — peace, God's kingdom, life, justice — as programs for action. Promise as God's affirmation, however, effectively communicates what has, once and for all, happened in Jesus Christ. God's peace, justice, and salvation are proclaimed, and freedom in God is thereby granted.

Promise, however, without excluding any of the described meanings, is God's *pledge* to be with us, the pledge of God's faithfulness and sovereignty. God pledges even to include us in this process which gives us a history. We learn to perceive God's promise in God's justice, peace, life, and truth as they are revealed in the coming of Jesus Christ and as they affect our lives. Together these acts outline God's faithfulness as it surprises, involves, and overtakes us, and gives us a future. Promise is the object of hope — and at the same time it is the category of perception for how human beings are encountered by God. Accordingly, the eschatological category of "perception" changes the mood of theology as a whole. A familiar subject will be heard in an entirely new way.

3. In the course of this book we encountered time and again a choice between notions of the type of change caused by Jesus

of Nazareth: whether Jesus enacted changes in personal attitudes or changes to the world. Radical eschatology tried to break
through this fatal either-or. Bultmann's expression "change of self-
understanding," which is created by God's coming in the message
of the cross (3.2), does not make sufficiently clear that faith in God
does not exhaust itself in the correction of self-understanding — as
crucial as such a correction may be. Our self-understanding may,
in the confrontation with God who promises, be given reason and
occasion to change. But the emphasis should be on the one who
confronts and who cannot be confined to our self-understanding.

Therefore, a renewal of thinking (see Rom. 12:2) that does not
allow us to remain who we have made ourselves to be is required.
This metamorphosis is caused by the earthshaking disruption in
which we are transfigured; and our part is to let this happen.
This is how human beings grow when God's hope takes hold of
us. Whereas the old human being dies in the decaying world (see
2 Cor. 4:16–18), the new human being grows in being renewed
and confirmed in hope day by day.

Part of this growth is an overall sensitivity to Christ as the Coming One, which is necessary for eschatology to be relevant. This
is not just a readiness for the so-called Second Coming of Christ,
because the Christ may be present in many particular events that
are of great relevance for faith, but those who haven't developed a
sensitivity for the Coming One may miss Christ's presence. God's
promise points us to the events in which we may sense Christ's
presence (see Matt. 25:31–46).

The pattern of time that can be organized in terms of past,
present, and future has been broken. But the broken pieces are still
there and hurt us. The question that troubles us most concerns the
future: What is it? Is it an open space of unconceived possibilities
(4.1) or the field of imprecise perceptions?

"We never actually live, but hope to live," said Pascal (5.2). We
see new light shed on these ambiguous words. Whoever hurries
into the future with hopes of finding himself, whoever misses the
present and suspends life, will become exhausted and lost.

Pascal also writes, "We never keep to the present," and sounds
puzzled. If we were in the present and not simultaneously considering prolonging the present, we would see our poverty much more

realistically. For we would have excuses neither in our strangely
lost past nor in our future, for which the slightest sign of a change
seems to guarantee improvement. But attention to the present,
which does not come naturally, is possible because God's promise addresses us "here and now" from outside ourselves. Nothing
makes this clearer than the time between "past" and "future." The
present is more than just a time — the present is what we are.
The present is the time in which we "have ourselves" in a way
we do not want. We keep our distance from what we are, and
thereby avoid the real foundation of our existence which was, is,
and always will be in Jesus Christ.

We hope to live with Christ because we have died with him.
Through his death, the seemingly natural sequence of life and death
has been broken. Death is no longer primarily the future ending of
life, and therefore it no longer dictates our final questions. We have
died with Christ and hope to live with him (Rom. 6:2–11). This
hope can no longer be destroyed by death, and thereby our expectations get a new orientation. Life and death become metaphors
and no longer have a natural function in human beings' sense of
direction in time. The way in which human beings locate themselves has changed. It is now possible for them to live intensively
and to experience time while hoping to be accepted by God and
held by God's promises.

In confrontation with God, who does not avoid history, we
are sometimes called "into" or "out of" our own experience.
Since we experience neither history nor God's word to us as
"final," we experience the possibilities and impossibilities of our
actions, decisions, and expectations as affliction (*Anfechtung*). Precisely in the confrontation with the Final One, the Promising One,
who acted once and for all in Jesus Christ, the material for our
self-searching slips through our hands. All human attempts at self-
aggrandizement, self-affirmation, and self-justification before God
and humanity fail. These attempts fail when we seek such things
in intimate encounter with God, where immanence and transcendence touch, so absorbing and fulfilling the person so that there
is no room for, or need for, hope. They fail as well when we
seek such things in community with other people by moralistically
pushing others to act in ways that make us appear righteous. We

are never able to put ourselves into the position of righteousness or perfection, of being the last, because God always confronts us by Godself's (and not ourselves') being the Last. There is a need for eschatology, because we cannot merely address God in Jesus Christ, the Promising One, as the Last, and, in such action distinguish between the First and the Last. We are not able to make this distinction.

Questions challenge our hope. Some questions concern our acts and others concern internal disappointment and affliction. These questions are often beyond the level of theological introduction and lead to a different language (4.1; 4.5).

A crucial element of the account of hope is the acknowledgment that this hope does not depend on one's experience with hope. We must hold on to this acknowledgment. The account of hope may be formulated differently, according to the biographical context of the one who gives the account. The account, nevertheless, will always be directed toward the hope being hoped, and one's ability to hope with different intensities and expressions will become clear within the wider context of hope.

The answers to the questions listed in 7.2 cannot be found by searching, but are received as questions. Individuals are asked for the foundation of hope within them, precisely because it is not in their power to construct hope. That is why hope can grow, and why its foundation cannot be described any other way.

Ludwig van Beethoven (1770–1827), in setting the Creed to music in his *Missa Solemnis* (originally performed in 1824),[2] dedicated almost as much time to the three words *vitam venturi saeculi* — the expectation of the life of the world to come — as to the rest of the Creed. Those three words take up almost half of Beethoven's composition. Perhaps this hope is better set to music than to words. Words will not be able to express anything different than, "We believe in the hope of the coming life." Yet definition and clarification are necessary to stay attentive for God's promise. Making readers attentive has been the task of this reconsideration of eschatology.

---

2. See "The Constantinopolitan Creed," in *Creeds of the Churches: A Reader in Christian Doctrine from the Bible to the Present*, ed. John H. Leith, 3d ed. (Louisville: John Knox Press, 1982), 33.

INDEX OF SCRIPTURAL REFERENCES

OLD TESTAMENT

Genesis
15:1–6	*20*
50:19–20	*159*

Exodus
20:4	*100*
33:18–23	*159*

Psalms
5:12	*91*

Isaiah
49:8	*175*
55:9	*158*

Ezekiel
38:1–39:26	*16*

Daniel
2	*16*
7	*16*

NEW TESTAMENT

Matthew
5:12	*42*
6:10	*156*
8:22	*213*
10:22	*42*
10:23	*34*
11:3	*49*
12:25	*62*
16:28	*51*
21:8–10	*49*
22:1–14	*204*
24:43	*59*
25:31–46	*221*
27:51–54	*58*

Mark
13:30	*51*
13:32	*104*
15:39	*58*

Luke
7:19–20	*49*
7:23	*49*
9:60	*213*
17:20	*62*
24:21	*46*
24:26	*46*
24:27	*46*
24:32	*46*

John
1:29	*43*
3:3	*7*
5:24	*82*
5:28–29	*83*
14:3	*50*
14:26	*56*
16:8–11	*56*
16:13	*56*
16:13–15	*57*
16:14	*57*
19:30	*46, 76, 218*
20:28	*45*
21:22	*50*
21:23	*50*

Romans
1:4	*197*
4:17	*xiv, 21, 42*
4:18	*xiv, 21, 48*
5:5	*162*
6:2–11	*222*
6:8	*21*
8:20–22	*107*
8:22–23	*60, 90*
8:23	*58, 191*
8:23–24	*71*

Romans (continued)
8:24   *83, 172*
8:31   *106*
10:4   *86*
12:2   *221*
12:12   *12, 71*
13:11–12   *59*
14:17   *142*

1 Corinthians
3:10–15   *201*
3:16   *201*
7:31   *45, 65, 87, 172*
11:26   *47, 202*
11:29–32   *210*
15   *44*
15:16–19   *43*
15:19   *43*
15:21   *196*
15:28   *48, 108, 181*
15:35–50   *189*
15:57   *193*
16:22   *xv, 203, 217*

2 Corinthians
1:20   *42, 219*
1:22   *58*
4:16   *142*
4:16–18   *221*
5:2–3   *204*
5:5   *58*
5:7   *107*
5:16   *45*
5:17   *47, 60, 116, 142*
6:2   *82, 175*
6:9   *191*

Galatians
2:20   *209–210*

Ephesians
1:10   *156*
2:12   *7, 21, 168, 219*
3:9   *156*
3:18   *156*
4:4   *xv*

Colossians
1:15–20   *115*
3:3   *116*

1 Thessalonians
4:13   *181*
5:1–11   *199*
5:2   *59*
5:6   *218*

2 Thessalonians
2:1–12   *199*

2 Timothy
2:18   *55*
3:1–5   *55*

Hebrews
2:4–18   *105*
4:4–16   *105*
6:18–19   *56*
6:19   *175*
9:15   *58*
9:26   *57*
9:28   *58*
10:23   *218*
10:37   *58*
11:1   *169–71*
12:2–3   *49*
13:8   *197*
13:20   *49*

1 Peter
1:3   *5, 7, 20, 44, 58, 182*
1:13   *218*
3:15   *xi, xv, 7, 60, 153,*
                     182

2 Peter
3:4   *55*
3:10   *59*
3:13   *53, 205, 217*

1 John
3:2   *108*

Revelation
1:8   *48*
1:17–18   *48*
16:16–21   *16*
20:2   *16*
20:4   *16*
20:4–6   *x*
20:6   *16*

Index of Names

Allison, Dale C., 58
Althaus, Paul, 4, 11
Anderson, Raymond Sherman, 190
Asendorf, Ulrich, 168

Badham, Linda, 189
Badham, Paul, 189
Baker, Charles F., 16
Balasuriya, Tissa, 206
Balthasar, Hans Urs von, 25, 27, 33, 68, 146, 182
Barth, Karl, 68–80, 93, 98, 103, 105, 124, 192, 205
Bass, Clarence, 15
Basse, Michael, 172
Beethoven, Ludwig van, 223
Beisser, Friedrich, 168
Beker, J. Christiaan, 87
Bellow, Saul, 208
Benjamin, Walter, 101–2, 109
Benz, Ernst, 17
Bingemer, Maria C. Lucchetti, 139, 146
Bloch, Ernst, xiii, 135, 137, 163
Bloch-Hoell, Nils Egede, 149
Boff, Leonardo, 52, 138, 146, 173–74
Bonaventura, 195
Bonhoeffer, Dietrich, 190
Boyer, Paul S., 16
Braaten, Carl E., 126, 132
Brinktrine, Johannes, 164
Brunner, Emil, 68
Bühler, Pierre, 166
Bultmann, Rudolf, 5, 37, 68, 78, 80–90, 93, 96, 98, 100, 103, 106, 109, 122, 124, 157, 221

Calvin, John, xiv
Carlson, Carole C., 16

Celan, Paul, 99–100
Chapman, G. Clarke Jr., 138
Cone, James H., 138
Cooper, John W., 189
Cornehl, Peter, 151
Cousins, Ewert H., 126
Cox, Harvey, 126
Crossan, John Dominic, 67
Cullmann, Oscar, 109, 111–13, 190

Daley, Brian, 2
Darby, John Nelson, 16
Davies, Horton, 208
Davies, William David, 66
Denzinger, Henry, 5–6
Dilthey, Wilhelm, 132
Dodd, Charles Harold, 63–66

Ebeling, Gerhard, 102, 166
Edwards, Jonathan, x
Efird, James M., 16
Empereur, James L., 206
Engelhardt, Paulus, 176
Erickson, Milard J., 26
Escribano-Alberca, Ignacio, 2
Evang, Martin, 84
Evans, James, 138, 145–46

Faulkner, William, 6–7
Feuerbach, Ludwig, 193
Feuillet, André, 32
Florovsky, Georgij (Georges), 66, 86, 189
Ford, David, 75
Frisch, Max, 91

Garaudy, Roger, 162
Gehlen, Arnold, 129
Geisser, Hans Friedrich, 26

227

Gogarten, Friedrich, 68, 78, 90–
   93, 98, 100, 103, 106, 109, 122,
   165
Grässer, Erich, 170
Greshake, Gisbert, 194–95, 199
Gutiérrez, Gustavo, 138, 140

Haenchen, Ernst, 64
Hafstad, Kjetil, 80
Härle, Wilfried, 176
Harnack, Adolf von, 27–28, 54
Hattrup, Dieter, 166
Hayes, Zachery, 62
Hegel, Georg Wilhelm Friedrich,
   xiii, 100, 132, 134
Heidegger, Martin, 88, 90, 99, 154
Hellwig, Monika, 206
Heppe, Heinrich, 4
Hermesmann, Hans-Georg, 116
Herms, Eilert, 24, 176
Heron, Alister I.C., 208
Herzog, Frederick, 206
Hick, John, 189
Hirsch, Emanuel, 95–96, 178–79
Hjelde, Sigurd, 3
Hoekema, Anthony A., 62

Jaeschke, Walter, 110
Jenson, Robert W., xi, 75, 126
Jeremias, Joachim, 64
John Chrysostum, 207
Josuttis, Manfred, 188
Jüngel, Eberhard, 186, 192–93,
   200
Jungk, Robert, 123–24
Justin, 218

Kabisch, Richard, 37
Kähler, Martin, 72
Käsemann, Ernst, 87–89, 137
Kehl, Medard, 102, 166, 199–200
Kennedy, John F., 14
Kiesling, Christopher G., 206
Kimmerle, Heinz, 163
Klappert, Bertold, 105
Klein, Günter, 60
Koch, Kurt Emil Karl, 132
König, Adrio, 68

Körner, Johannes, 90
Kraus, Norman C., 16
Kremer, Jacob, 194
Kugler, Georg, 204
Kümmel, Werner Georg, 52
Kunz, Erhard, 2
Kutter, Hermann, 70

Lannert, Berthold, 36
Lash, Nicholas, 206
Lévinas, Emmanuel, 100–101, 109
Lewis, H.D., 188
Libânio, João B., 139, 146
Lindsey, Hal, 16
Lohfink, Gerhard, 195
Loisy, Alfred, 36
Lona, Horacio E., 2
Löwith, Karl, 109, 111
Luther, Henning, 193
Luther, Martin, xiv, 91–92, 166,
   169–71, 176

Mahlmann, Theodor, 187
Mannheim, Karl, 150
Marcuse, Herbert, 124
Marquardt, Friedrich-Wilhelm, 53
Marsch, Wolf-Dieter, 163
Marsden, George M., 16
Marty, Martin E., 148
Marx, Karl, 193
Metz, Johann Baptist, 102, 137,
   138, 162, 185
Meyer, Joachim Ernst, 194
Meyer, Walter Ernst, 169
Migliore, Daniel L., 139
Mojtabai, A.G., xi
Moltmann, Jürgen, xii–xiii, 126,
   132–39, 153, 162–63, 166
Monod, Wilfred, 205
Montgomery, William, 32
Moorhead, James H., 13
Morse, Christopher, 138
Mozart, Wolfgang Amadeus, 79
Müller-Fahrenholz, Geiko, 116

Niebuhr, Reinhold, 4, 13, 97
Nientiedt, Klaus, 181
Nietzsche, Friedrich, 109

Nocke, Franz-Josef, 195
Noordmans, Oepke, 107

Oblau, Gotthard, 80
Oelmüller, Willi, 138
Oepke, Albrecht, 54
Origen, 1
Ott, Heinrich, 5
Ott, Ludwig, 2
Overbeck, Franz, 35, 154

Pannenberg, Wolfhart, xii–xiii, 126–34, 136–37, 153, 163, 176, 192, 201
Pascal, Blaise, 175, 221
Peter Lombard, 170
Peterson, Erik, 36
Pieper, Josef, 173
Pokorny, Petr, 62

Quistorp, Heinrich, 169

Rad, Gerhard von, 126
Ragaz, Leonhard, 70
Rahner, Karl, 97–98, 103–5, 122, 124, 140, 162, 186, 192, 199
Ratzinger, Joseph, 165–66, 169, 176–79, 187, 194
Reagan, Ronald, 15
Rich, Arthur, 66
Ringleben, Joachim, 187
Ritschl, Albrecht, 27, 38
Rowden, Harold H., 16
Ruether, Rosemary Radford, 146
Ruh, Ulrich, 187

Sachs, John R., 195
Samse, Ulrich, 97
Sandeen, Ernest, 15
Sauter, Gerhard, ix, 2, 54, 117, 163, 168, 191
Schaeffler, Richard, 138, 166–67
Schäfer, Philipp, 2
Schäfer, Rolf, 36
Scheler, Max, 129
Scherer, Georg, 195

Schierse, Franz Josef, 32
Schlaudraff, Karl-Heinz, 116
Schleiermacher, Friedrich Daniel Ernst, 23, 79, 171, 176
Schmied, Augustin, 187
Schneider, Reinhold, 191
Schneider-Flume, Gunda, 95
Schrage, Wolfgang, 201
Schreiner, Josef, 2
Schwab, Gustav, 54
Schweitzer, Albert, xiii, 32–41, 44, 51, 54, 70, 89
Seifert, Josef, 195
Shorrosh, Anis A., 16
Stadtland, Tjarko, 80
Stoevesandt, Hinrich, 77, 195

Teilhard de Chardin, Pierre, 30, 173, 180
Thomas Aquinas, 172
Thurneysen, Eduard, 78
Tillich, Paul, 68, 93–98, 106, 109, 118, 158
Tinder, Glenn, 143
Tocqueville, Alexis de, 120
Troeltsch, Ernst, 24, 27–30, 33, 38, 70–71, 90, 152

Vorgrimler, Herbert, 195

Wainwright, Geoffrey, 203, 208
Walvoord, John E., 16
Walvoord, John F., 16
Weber, Max, 152
Weber, Timothy P., 16, 153
Weder, Hans, 66
Weiss, Johannes, 32–33, 35, 37–39, 62–63, 66, 70
Wendland, Heinz-Dietrich, 162
Werner, Martin, 36
Wiederkehr, Dietrich, 165, 179
Wilmore, Gayraud S., 139, 140, 145, 147
Witherington III, Ben, 62
Wohlmuth, Josef, 102
Wolterstorff, Nicholas, 190

Index of Subjects

apocalyptic, 15–16, 101, 180
apocalypticism, ix, 83, 87–88, 104, 137
   Jewish, 128

christological perfect, 105, 112, 115
church, 16, 23, 36, 134, 144, 152, 181–83, 184, 203, 209

death, 2, 3, 7, 11, 188–96, 199–200, 209

Easter, xiii, 127–29, 131, 133
eschatology ix–xvi, 2–25, 48–50, 71–80, 83–90, 98–99, 103–7, 117–18, 123, 163–65, 168, 216
   consistent, xiii, 25, 27, 31–41, 50–55, 59, 65, 72, 111–13, 119, 151
   Jewish, 37, 92
   in perfect tense, 102
   radical, xiii, 18–20, 24, 80–85, 97–119, 123–25, 153, 211–13, 220–21
   realized, 63–64, 66
   task of, xiv
eschaton, 65, 78, 93
eternal life, 2, 3, 54, 74
eternity, 8, 19, 29, 64–65, 72–73, 81, 93, 211

faith, 3, 6–8, 81–87, 90–92, 107, 117, 132, 165, 169–75, 198
fundamentalism, 14–15
future, 11, 28–31, 56, 64, 81–84, 91–92, 101, 119–33, 148, 176–77, 186, 217
   anticipation of the, 104
   as *extra nos*, 114, 117
futurism, 177–78

God, 12, 20–21, 42, 48, 57–67, 74–78, 91–92, 99, 106–8, 122–23, 168, 217
   action/activity of, 6, 20, 56, 59–60, 66–69, 75, 105, 115, 134, 154–58
   advent of, 71, 89, 132
   coming of, xiii, 125
   the Coming One, 74
   grace of, 156, 171
   eternity of, 74–75
   hiddenness of, 116
   judgment of, 21, 34, 60–66, 74–83, 95, 106–7, 192, 200–201, 210, 217
   promise(s) of, xiv, 18, 116, 117–18, 125, 134–35, 154, 172, 175, 204, 217–22
   revelation of, 99
   transcendence of, 78, 98, 101, 103
   truth of, 77, 114
   will of, 158–59
   word of, 84, 222

history, x, 9–17, 28–31, 37–41, 75, 85–115, 122–26, 130, 134, 156–59
   of Christendom, 69
   of the church, 103
   the end of, 132
   philosophy of, xiii, 12, 18, 90, 93, 99, 137
   teleology of, 11–12, 18, 38
   theology of, xiii–xiv, 9–18, 24–25, 93–96, 102, 109, 119–22, 146, 151–59, 212–13, 220
   universal, 129, 131
historicism, 177–78

Holy Spirit, 56–60, 69, 72, 75–76, 105, 108

hope, ix, xiv, 3–9, 20–22, 55–60, 71, 79, 90–92, 103–8, 113–18, 130–36, 147–54, 169–76, 197–99, 217–23
    account of the, xi–xii, 7, 60, 209, 219, 223
    certainty of, 172, 174
    of Jesus Christ, 40–45, 48, 54

imminent expectation (*Naher-wartung*), xiii, 34, 60, 113

immortality, 5, 29, 165, 176, 178, 192

Jesus Christ, 5–6, 60, 75–79, 81, 105, 113–14, 123, 141–43, 156, 196, 222
    advent of, 88
    the Coming One, 48–50, 73, 88, 102–3, 108, 115, 174, 197–202, 210–11, 217–21
    the cross of, 41, 43, 82, 86, 217
    death of, 21, 32, 38, 41–48, 56–61, 67, 82, 112, 130, 219
    as the *eschatos*, 48, 117, 154, 174
    resurrection of, 43–44, 47–48, 56–58, 67, 76, 112, 127–32
Jesus of Nazareth (historical Jesus), 31–41, 43, 50–53, 57, 63–67, 105, 138, 220–21

justification, xiv, 66, 77, 176, 201, 217
    doctrine of, 7, 166–68, 174, 176, 200–201, 216

kairos, 93–94

kingdom of God, xi, xiii, 13–14, 27, 44, 54, 62, 69, 96, 113, 134–35, 141
    Jesus' proclamation of the, 25, 31–38, 42, 53, 131

last judgment, 128, 131, 185

last things, doctrine of the, 2–9, 18–22, 39, 72, 73, 83, 98, 103–4, 139, 153, 209, 213, 220

life, 72, 82

Lord's Supper, 202–8, 210

messianic, 13, 101

messianism, 12, 53, 101–2

parousia, 34–36, 56, 59, 76, 198, 201
    delay of (*Parusieverzögerung*), 36

present, 19, 56, 73, 82–84

reconciliation, 78, 185
    universal (*All-Versöhnung/apokatastasis*), 181–82

redemption, 7, 8, 200

resurrection, 3, 53, 55, 74, 186, 189

salvation, 24, 53, 59–66, 73–83, 101, 107–8, 126, 177–78, 181, 185
    all-embracing, 8
    event, 136
    history, 111–13
    plan of, 111

theology, 77–78, 87, 103, 106, 114, 123, 125, 139

time, 2, 8, 56, 64–66, 72–75, 81–82, 93–94, 110–11, 114, 116, 125, 211

utopia, 94, 135, 177